SMART YARD

SMART YARD

60-Minute Lawn Care

Jeff Ball and Liz Ball

FULCRUM PUBLISHING
GOLDEN, COLORADO

ISBN 1-55591-138-2

Printed in the United States of America

This book is dedicated to our very own turf expert, Bob Scanzaroli. His advice and effort on behalf of our lawn and this book were indispensable.

Table of Contents

Acknowledgments

Although the authors get their names on the front of books, there are usually lots of people who contribute to them in critically important ways. This book was no exception.

We are particularly indebted to Jim Brooks at the Lawn Institute and Bill Knoop at Texas A&M University for keeping us up to date on the latest research and answering our questions. Jane Arimoto kept us smiling with her whimsical interpretations of our sketches and never complained about having to rework or polish a drawing. Bob Scanzaroli was an ever-present source of practical information and insight about lawns.

The lion's share of thanks goes to Jay Staten and the crew at Fulcrum who put up with major inconvenience and delays so that Jeff could teach himself how to do graphics on his beloved computer.

$\mathcal{I}$ntroduction to Lawn Care

For some homeowners, caring for their lawn is a pleasure and something of a hobby. However, for most of us, taking care of the lawn is basically a duty. We dream of having a lawn that is beautifully green and healthy, whatever its size. While we are at it, we also dream that it takes very little time and effort to care for it. We also would prefer to avoid using lots of fertilizers and pesticides.

The reality is that lawn care involves considerable time and work. We put in the effort because we want the grass to look good and contribute to the beauty and value of our homes. The frustrating thing is that it often seems as though our efforts are not rewarded. All the time, energy and money we devote to our grass often do not result in a truly lovely lawn.

Our own experience, as well as the recent research we have consulted, suggests that many of the traditional lawn care techniques American homeowners have been using are, in fact, counterproductive to a healthy, attractive lawn. We are, paradoxically, creating more problems than we are solving with our intensive efforts, and we are spending more time than necessary on lawn care.

We have discovered that it is possible to wean ourselves and our lawn from the constant attention that traditional practices—which are essentially high-maintenance ones—require and end up with a healthy, vigorous but low-maintenance lawn. This process requires significant effort in the first year or two, but down the road the grass will be better able to thrive with a minimum of effort on our part.

This book will give you some practical help in making the dream of a low-maintenance lawn come true. We have written it specifically for ordinary homeowners, whom we call "yardeners." Yardeners willingly take responsibility for the care of the grass, trees, shrubs and other plants on their property, but they prefer to devote most of their free time to golf, tennis, church, grandchildren or whatever. So the emphasis is on saving time. Recognizing that most of us are not—and do not want to be—gardeners and yard care experts, the information here is basic, practical and nontechnical.

We hope that this book will help yardeners, over time, to realize the dream of a lovely, low-maintenance lawn. It is equally useful whether the work is to be done by a professional service or by yardeners themselves.

For the North

We have limited the discussion in this book to lawns of "northern" or "cool weather" grasses. The map shows the parts of the country where these grasses are appropriately grown. Northern grasses include Kentucky bluegrass, turf-type tall fescue, perennial ryegrass and various fine fescues. We also include zoysia grass, orginally a southern grass, since it grows in the North fairly successfully. We do not deal with the care of southern grasses such as Bermuda grass, St. Augustine grass and centipede grass.

Making Choices

Most of us learned to care for our lawns from our parents. Upon reading this book you will discover that your parents may have been doing it all wrong. Most American lawns are overwatered, overfertilized, mowed too often and cut too short. Those cultural mistakes are responsible for most of the weed, insect and disease problems that American lawns suffer. To help you avoid these problems, we will explain alternative approaches to watering, feeding, mowing and pest control to enable you to make informed choices about how you care for your own lawn.

LOW- VERSUS HIGH-MAINTENANCE LAWN CARE

If you are dissatisfied with your lawn, you are not alone. Surveys indicate that over half the yardeners in this country are unhappy about the general condition and appearance of their lawns. They are disappointed that all their time and effort have not resulted in an attractive, healthy turf.

The true test for yardeners is, how does the lawn look? Tests conducted in Maryland by the Smithsonian Institution showed that a high-maintenance lawn (given frequent feeding, watering and pesticide treatments and regularly mowed 1 1/2 inches high) was almost indistinguishable from one given what is considered low-maintenance care and mowed 2 inches high. So we figure it makes all kinds of good sense to save time and money by using "low-maintenance" lawn care practices. It's better for the environment too.

So, our focus will be on "low-maintenance" lawn care. Because of the hectic pace of life these days, we yardeners do not want to spend one more hour than is absolutely necessary working in the yard. We will discuss how to move away from the "high-maintenance" lawn care techniques, largely adapted from golf course managers and other commercial turf professionals who have time and money—scarce commodities for most of us. We will help you move toward low-maintenance techniques that make more sense for homeowners.

A "high-maintenance" lawn in our view is one that requires three or four applications of fertilizer a year to keep it looking nice and green. In summer it needs watering once or twice each week. Each year it usually needs a crabgrass preventer in the early spring, a herbicide for broad-leaved weeds in the late spring and a general-purpose insecticide to keep it looking good. It needs mowing quite frequently, especially in the spring and early summer. Because the clippings clump up on its surface, they must be collected and disposed of almost every time the lawn is mowed. This kind of lawn requires constant service, so we consider it a "high-maintenance" lawn. We believe that most of the lawns in America are "high-maintenance" lawns.

Having a "low-maintenance" lawn does not mean settling for an inferior lawn. On the contrary, it means enjoying a superior one. A low-maintenance lawn, by our definition, is a self-reliant one. With very little help from us, it is uniformly green all season long. It has no more than 10–15 percent weeds, which are virtually unnoticeable. It needs less-frequent mowing and seldom needs watering. It gets fertilized once, or maybe twice, a year and, while it may receive some "snacks" and "vitamins" occasionally, it does not require them. Its soil drains well, retains water for a long time and has lots of earthworms and a very active population of microorganisms. It rarely suffers pest problems, so pesticides are rarely used on it.

In short, a low-maintenance lawn is one that can pretty much take care of itself. That is what we mean when we use the term "low-maintenance" throughout this book. How to transform your present lawn into one that can take care of itself is what this book is all about. It's possible to start the transition immediately by simply changing how you care for your present lawn. You may prefer to go further and rehabilitate it by adding new grass seed or go all the way by starting a whole new lawn.

We have experimented with all of the techniques we are suggesting to you on our own suburban lawn. Our neighbors have gotten used to the idea that periodically Jeff kills our entire front lawn with herbicide and replants the grass to test a new type of seed. They see Liz out mowing the lawn at different lengths, often using different mowers. Gradually won over, they now borrow our aerator and enjoy the results on their own lawns.

The four chapters in the first section of this book describe basic low-maintenance techniques for caring for the lawn. While some of them are familiar tasks—mowing, fertilizing and watering—there are tips for how to do them more efficiently and effectively. Other tasks may be new for you—aerating and topdressing the turf with organic matter. The extra effort invested in adding these new activities to your maintenance routine every year or two will pay off in much more self-reliant grass year in and year out.

How far you want to go toward a low-maintenance lawn is up to you. We present the choices and what the stakes are for each choice. In our experience, even a modest change in mowing height makes a difference. Collectively, all of these care techniques make a profound difference. We spend less time on our lawn than our neighbors do and it is basically weed free, lush and green, even in August.

Choose the approach to mowing, feeding and watering that seems good for you. You will find that the appearance of your lawn can be greatly improved simply by changing the way you take care of it each week.

Lawn Condition Controls Amount of Work

Whether you have a lawn that is already in great condition or it needs some improvement, there are some things you must do every year— they are mowing, fertilizing and maybe some watering. The frequency of the other maintenance tasks will be determined by the condition of your lawn. We are referring here to tasks such as aerating, adding organic matter to the soil, spreading lime and overseeding. If your lawn is in poor shape, then these additional tasks should be done every year for a few years. When

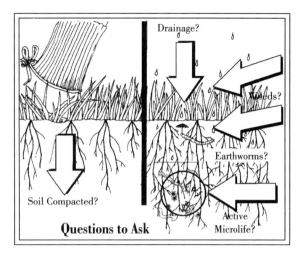

the lawn becomes lush and healthy, these tasks are only necessary once every three or four years.

What About Organic?

Many yardeners are interested in having what is called an "organic" lawn. Based on the definition of "organic" developed by the food industry, having an organic lawn means trying to grow grass using only "natural" fertilizers. It means controlling insects, disease and weeds with only "natural" products—no synthetic chemical products. The question is, does this approach produce a beautiful lawn?

Our answer is "maybe." It is impossible to have an attractive, healthy, dense turf with few weeds if you try to shift from traditional lawn care practice to "organic" practice in just one season. Just as it takes farmers three to five years to shift from chemical-dependent farming techniques to organic techniques, it will take a homeowner at least two, maybe three, years to shift to what is considered a truly "organic" lawn. Once that transition takes place, an organic lawn can be as healthy and as good-looking as any lawn in the community.

Our approach in this book is best described as "environmentally responsible, low-maintenance" lawn care practice. We try to help yardeners move toward lawn care techniques that come very close to satisfying the definitions of organic. However, we feel in some cases that the use of some products that are not "organic" is justified on the basis of efficacy, convenience and safety.

We feel readers should have choices.

Hiring Lawn Care Service

Many yardeners have neither the time nor the inclination to care for the lawn themselves. The question is, can a lawn care service or the high school kid down the street provide the

kind of care for your lawn that sustains its low-maintenance character? The answer is yes, but you have to select the caretaker carefully.

Generally speaking, people who make a living cutting and otherwise caring for lawns use high-maintenance techniques. Often, like us, they learned from parents or turf pros and are not familiar with modern, low-maintenance practices on a residential scale. Also, economic reality favors traditional, high-maintenance practices which require many visits to your property by the small businessmen who do this work. The more visits, the more money they make. Frequent fertilizings, cuttings or sprayings (whether needed or not) justify many visits.

To get low-maintenance care from a professional service, you must find one that is willing to respond to your instructions. Then you must insist that they adopt the practices recommended in this book. For instance, require that the grass be cut at 2 inches, that it be dry when cut, that the clippings be left, that the fertilizer be granular with slow-release nitrogen and that the lawn be aerated periodically.

Tell them they are not to use any insecticide without showing you what the problem is and that you must OK the product that they use. You may end up paying more, or at least paying the same for fewer visits, but it will be worth it.

Annual Lawn Care Cycle

Important Jobs versus Optional Jobs—How much time we spend caring for the lawn varies with the calendar. Lawns require some attention each season, but we do have some choice in what we do and when we do it. For instance, fertilizer can be spread at several different times. The overview of the annual lawn care cycle below will help you decide on the lawn care strategy that works best for you.

SPRING LAWN CARE

Odd Jobs, but Not Major—Grass starts to grow in the spring because of rising soil temperatures and increased sunlight. As it shakes off dormancy it grows vigorously; its fresh green blades stretch toward the sun they need to convert the nutrients in the soil into energy. Everyone's lawn seems to look great during this period of renewal and regrowth. The trick is to maintain that healthy look throughout the growing season.

While this might seem like the time to get out into the yard and start performing all kinds of springly tasks, reconsider. Some jobs, such as seeding and fertilizing, might better be done in the fall. Also, most homeowners get out on the lawn much too early in the season as far

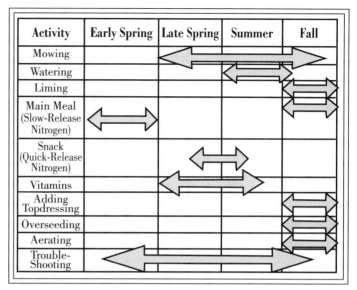

Activity	Early Spring	Late Spring	Summer	Fall
Mowing		←		→
Watering			←→	
Liming				←→
Main Meal (Slow-Release Nitrogen)	←→			
Snack (Quick-Release Nitrogen)		←→		
Vitamins		←	→	
Adding Topdressing				←→
Overseeding				←→
Aerating				←→
Trouble-Shooting	←			→

as the soil is concerned. If the soil is still very wet from the winter rains and snows, then any walking on it will cause much more serious compaction than when the soil has had a chance to dry out.

Granular, slow-release nitrogen fertilizer applied during the fall promotes good root development for the following spring and fosters some grass green-up in the spring. Consequently, fertilizing in the spring is not as essential as many might think. Some slow release nitrogen in the spring will definitely help the grass grow even greener, so we consider it an optional task. Liz decides whether it is necessary on a year-to-year basis. The general condition of the lawn and her schedule influence the decision.

If you do fertilize in the spring, do it late in the season rather than early. Early spring fertilizer will encourage the grass to grow faster, which means you have to mow more often, investing even more time and energy than normal in lawn care during the spring. You may choose the low-maintenance option of fertilizing in the fall only, especially after a year or two when you have rehabilitated your soil so that it can take over most of the responsibility for providing nutrition for your grass.

Generally, once it is on a low-maintenance regimen, a lawn needs very little attention during the spring except mowing. If the lawn isn't yet quite in perfect condition, a dose of slow-release fertilizer and some other measures to build long-term health, such as aerating, may be in order.

SUMMER LAWN CARE

Fight the Heat and the Bugs—The main enemy of grass in the summer is heat. Northern grasses suffer in the heat and react to the stress by shutting down. They don't die, they just turn brown and go dormant. One technique to ease this source of stress is to raise the lawn mower so the mower blade cuts higher. Longer grass shades the soil and the grass roots, cooling them. By reducing the heat stress we help keep the grass green.

Traditionally, watering the grass has been utilized as a method to reduce heat stress. However, this takes time and uses a scarce resource. You may agree with us that adopting alternate ways to keep grass cool, such as mowing tall and leaving the clippings, is easier on you and the environment. In any case, when you do feel you need to water, it is important to water properly to avoid causing bug and disease problems. Summer is the season for pest problems, so it might also be necessary to take some measures against these problems during this season if they appear in your lawn.

FALL LAWN CARE

This Is the Major Time for Major Work—Late summer through early fall is the period of the year when the major lawn care maintenance duties are most effectively done. A busy time, it is also the best time for rehabilitating the lawn. Intensive effort now results in a healthier lawn and less work for next season.

Fall is the best time to routinely fertilize and deal with any broadleaf weeds that have invaded. To upgrade and maintain soil health you will want to incorporate aerating and adding a layer of humus, or organic matter, to the lawn soil into your fall regimen. This topdressing can be easily accomplished by leaving a layer of chopped leaves. You may even wish to overseed your existing lawn with some high-quality grass seed that is more disease and insect resistant. Fall is also the best time to add lime to your lawn soil. In short, there is a fair amount of work to do on the lawn in the fall. Eventually, though, you will mow less, you will water less and you'll have fewer weeds and bugs to worry about during ensuing growing seasons. You'll even have less to do in the fall.

WINTER LAWN CARE

Not Much, but Important—Most yardeners regard winter as time off from yard care. Certainly, after that fall schedule we deserve a break. Nevertheless, there are two things that will improve the appearance and condition of your lawn in the future.

Cut the grass back a bit from the summer length of 2 or 3 inches to 1 1/2–2 inches, no higher. This removes the older parts of the blades made up of frost-sensitive cells. New, hardy "tillers" or grass blades keep growing, but slowly. Closer mowing helps grass resist winter browning and matting in soggy winter weather. Grass may keep growing a bit throughout the winter whenever conditions are favorable, but resist the urge to cut grass any shorter than 1 1/2 inches for winter, or you will harm it.

Try to avoid walking on the grass during the winter. It took us awhile to train the family and the mailman to stick to the sidewalk, but it is worth it. Turf that is wet, possibly even frosty, is easily damaged by foot traffic. The ice crystals that form inside cell membranes of grass plants in freezing weather damage the tissues when they are compressed by any weight on the lawn.

Tips to Avoid Winter Lawn Damage

Avoid walking on your lawn during the winter, especially if it has no snow cover and the soil is frozen. Definitely do not walk on wet, frozen grass. Any activity that compacts the snow may promote the build-up of an ice layer on the turf. This becomes a problem in the spring because compacted snow insulates the grass, keeping it cold even as the soil begins its natural warming. The grass can be smothered. If you've had no snow or little rain all winter, then it is wise (no matter what the neighbors think) to water your lawn at least once each month that has had no natural rain or snow fall. The plants may be dormant, but they are still transpiring, or losing moisture.

How to Use This Book

Because we believe that a picture really is worth about a thousand words, we have put the emphasis on graphics in this book. It seemed to us that if it is to be really clear, practical and easy to use, then the information has to be immediately available.

So, this book is for easy reference. Use it to find the information you need when you need it, rather than feel obligated to read it from cover to cover. We have divided it into sections to make it easier to find the information you need. Section I describes general lawn care maintenance tasks for those readers whose lawns are in fairly decent shape. Section II covers the major remedial tasks necessary to rescue seriously suffering lawns. Refer to Section III for the particulars on turf problems. Take a few minutes now and flip through the chapters to get aquainted with the general format and to get a feel for the charts and drawings. The index will then get you back to the right page for the topic of your choice when you need it.

SECTION I

MAINTAINING YOUR LAWN

Chapter One

Soil Comes First

Why Is Soil First?

If this is a book about lawn care, why is the first chapter about dirt? Simple: The condition of the soil under your grass is more important to the overall health of your lawn than any other variable you deal with. While in the next three chapters we'll deal with routine maintenance of the grass in your lawn, we want to impress you with the importance of the steps you take to care for the soil first. Routine care for the soil can do as much toward achieving

a truly low-maintenance lawn as all the cultural tricks related to caring for the grass itself combined. Soil maintenance is not a major project every single year, but it needs to be included in your routine every few years.

Making the Case for Your Soil

We know that very few American lawns are growing in healthy soil. These days soil takes a real beating when homes are under construction. Builders skim the topsoil from the property

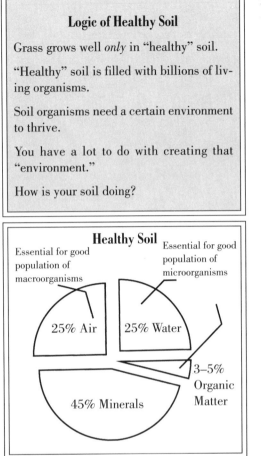

Healthy soil is half soil solids and half space, filled equally with air and water.

first thing, and then bring in heavy construction equipment which invariably compacts the soil. If, when the house is finished, they replace the topsoil at all, it is a skimpy layer which just barely obscures the "fill" of construction debris left behind. By the time the owner takes possession, the yard amounts to not much more than sterile, compacted "dirt." It certainly is not a healthy medium in which to grow grass plants.

What is soil in the first place? What constitutes "healthy" soil? Almost half of the volume of a healthy soil is taken up by mineral particles (from pulverized rocks) and flecks of organic material. The other half of the volume is taken up by space between these particles. This space is taken up half by air and half by water in the form of a film over the solid particles. The organic particles in soil are typically concentrated in its top 12 inches. Ideally, they represent from 3 percent to 5 percent of the volume of that top layer, or topsoil. These particles are bits of humus and other organic material that host microbial life which break them down into plant nutrients as they go about their life cycles. When soil has sufficient air, water, minerals and organic material, we call it "healthy" because it supports life—lots of microbial activity.

Typically, the layer nearest the soil surface (about 2 or 3 inches down) of a healthy soil is richest in organic material, so it teams with microbiotic life and is the part of the soil that is alive, or fertile. If you have soil with lots of microbes and other creatures generating nutrients for plant roots, you are almost assured of having a healthy, low-maintenance lawn.

WHY SOIL CREATURES ARE IMPORTANT

There is more life concentrated in the 3 inches below the soil surface (assuming a "healthy" soil) than anywhere in the world above the soil! The macroorganisms (bigger

guys) like earthworms, springtails and mites move through the air spaces in soil, while the microorganisms (very little guys) like bacteria and fungi live in the water film.

These microbes perform an enormous amount of work for you and your lawn. They break down minerals from the rock particles to make them available to plants. Along with the macroorganisms, these little guys recycle through decomposition enormous amounts of organic matter, again producing valuable nutrients for plants. Soil microlife also prevents lots of problems by attacking potentially problematic fungal spores and dangerous bacteria and viruses.

The more active the microbiotic life in your soil, the more likely that you will be able to reduce your use of fertilizers and pesticides, saving you time and money. There will then be reduced risk of problems from inadvertent excessive use of fertilizers and pesticides. If you do have to resort to the use of pesticides, a healthy population of soil microorganisms will help break down those chemicals more quickly before they cause long-term problems.

How Many Microorganisms?		
Organism	Number of Organisms in 1 Pound of Soil	Pounds of Organisms per 1,000 Sq. Ft.
Bacteria	910 Billion	12
Fungi	450 Million	35
Actinomyces	20 Billion	17
Protozoa	670 Million	8
Total	931+ Billion	72*

*Those 72 pounds of microorganisms will contain close to 7 pounds of nitrogen and several pounds of phosphorus and potassium, a perfect composition to be taken up by grass plants.

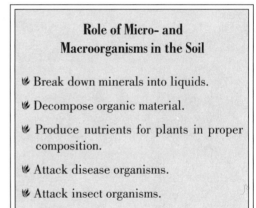

Role of Micro- and Macroorganisms in the Soil

❧ Break down minerals into liquids.

❧ Decompose organic material.

❧ Produce nutrients for plants in proper composition.

❧ Attack disease organisms.

❧ Attack insect organisms.

The bigger creatures in the soil, the macroorganisms, make important contributions as well. Creatures like nematodes, which are less than a millimeter in length, and the comparatively giant earthworms, which are 3 to 5 inches long, have jobs to do. Also included in this crew are a number of different insects including millipedes, sowbugs, springtails, ants and mites, just to name a few. Under favorable conditions, there can be almost two million macroorganisms in 1,000 square feet of soil around plant roots in your yard. Virtually all these insects will be killed by an application of any broad-spectrum insecticide on your lawn.

Lots of earthworms are desirable because they aerate the soil, improve soil drainage, aid decomposition of organic matter and provide fertilizer for plants. Don't worry if you have not seen an earthworm in years. As soon as you aerate, add some organic material and make sure the pH of the soil is adjusted, you'll start seeing earthworms. Earthworm egg casings can lay dormant as deep as 20 inches in the soil for as long as twenty years. All they need is some encouragement to hatch and thrive. They are everywhere, everywhere!!! However, one application of a granular or liquid, quick-acting nitrogen fertilizer over your lawn will chase these good guys away for at least a month.

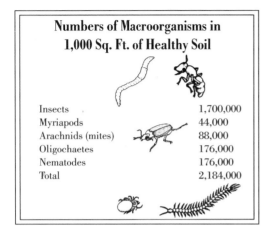

Numbers of Macroorganisms in 1,000 Sq. Ft. of Healthy Soil	
Insects	1,700,000
Myriapods	44,000
Arachnids (mites)	88,000
Oligochaetes	176,000
Nematodes	176,000
Total	2,184,000

As for the other macropals, they contribute to healthy soil too. The mites and springtails promote decomposition of organic material, producing nutrients for plants. The tiny nematodes produce nutrients for plants, control pathogens in the soil and even control pest insects in larval and egg stages.

So What Does This Soil Stuff Have to Do with You?

Probably because most of us never really included the soil in our list of things in our landscape to take care of, we have been inadvertently harming it month after month. By walking behind a lawn mower we promote compaction; our weight squeezes the air from between the soil particles. With its oxygen content reduced, the soil cannot support its population of microorganisms.

Also, we often overfertilize and use lots of chemical pesticides, which makes the chemical environment in the soil hostile to earthworms and microorganisms. We often overwater, which floods soil air spaces, reducing their volume of oxygen and driving away the earthworms and killing more microorganisms. About the only plants happy in this suffering soil are weeds.

In short, we are not taking very good care of the soil that we expect to nurture our lawn. If it is not healthy enough to maintain grass plants itself, then we have to take on the responsibility. This means more work for us. We must substitute extra fertilizer for the nutrients normally provided by microbial life in the soil. We must resort to pesticides to control pests normally controlled by soil organisms. We seed more often since the existing grass, struggling in a poor soil, dies more readily. We water more frequently to compensate for the inability of compacted soil to hold and drain water properly.

The bottom line? Lots of work all season year after year. To maintain an attractive lawn in poor soil an enormous amount of labor (not to mention time and money) is required. Lawns growing in unhealthy soil are "high-maintenance" lawns. The way to get off the high-maintenance treadmill is to rehabilitate the soil under your turf. By restoring it to good health, you restore its ability to do most of the work of maintaining an attractive lawn. Then you will have a low-maintenance lawn.

So our approach to soil care should now be pretty clear. First, do everything you can to avoid harming the existing populations of soil organisms in your soil. Second, do everything you can to create an environment conducive to their multiplying naturally.

Maintaining and Encouraging Microlife in Your Lawn Soil	
DON'T:	DO:
❧ Use quick-acting fertilizer.	❧ Use slow-acting nitrogen fertilizer.
❧ Routinely apply pesticides.	❧ Use pesticides for spot treatment only.
❧ Ignore compacted soil.	❧ Aerate or spike compacted soil.
❧ Ignore drainage problems.	❧ Add humus to soil periodically.
❧ Collect grass clippings.	❧ Mow high and leave clippings.

So What Should You Do?

We are assuming here that you have already determined that you have pretty healthy soil with a decent amount of organic material supporting earthworms and microorganisms. If you think your soil needs serious attention, then consult Chapters Five and Six where we talk about major soil renovation. The rest of this chapter deals with normal soil maintenance for lawns with moderate to good soil conditions.

AERATE YOUR SOIL

No matter how much we'd like to avoid the problem, the soil under our lawn is subjected to compaction every year. We tromp over it twenty to thirty times walking behind our mowers. Scientists can measure the pressure of one single footstep of a 150-pound person down as deep as 15 inches (walking on tiptoes makes no difference!). Those of us riding a mower cause even more pressure on that soil. Every time it rains, especially if the turf is not real thick, the raindrops compact the soil just a little bit. Kids often use the lawn for their games—one reason why we have a lawn—compacting the soil as they play.

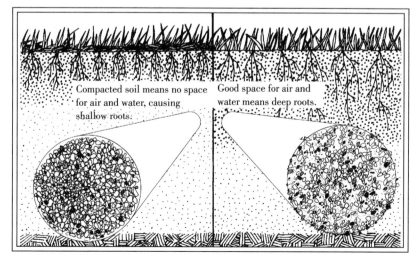

Compacted soil means no space for air and water, causing shallow roots.

Good space for air and water means deep roots.

Why is compacted soil bad for lawns? Grass roots need easy access to water, air and nutrients in the soil to be able to metabolize energy and grow vigorously. Compaction of soil destroys the tiny pockets in the structure of the soil where air is held available to plant roots and an active microbial population. Lack of air spaces also causes soil to drain poorly. Because the roots have trouble moving through soil that has had most of the air compressed out of it, they become stunted. The resulting shallow root systems are hard put to support the grass plants, so they are under stress all the time.

Compacted soil also hinders the circulation of earthworms and the lack of air discourages the activity of microorganisms which enrich the soil. Compacted soil promotes the buildup of thatch as grass roots accumulate near the surface of the soil, matting and obstructing the rapid decomposition of clippings. Obviously, by routinely addressing this one problem yardeners can make an enormous step in keeping their lawns looking wonderful.

There are several ways to deal with soil compaction, but the most effective is by core aerating the turf periodically.

Core Aeration

The best way to dramatically reduce the normal compaction of the soil your grass grows in is to mechanically punch holes in the turf to introduce oxygen below the soil surface. This is accomplished with either a power-driven core-aerating machine or a hand core-aerating tool. These devices have hollow tines which penetrate 2 or 3 inches below the soil surface. When they are withdrawn, they pull out a core of soil about 1/2 inch in diameter and from 2 to 3 inches long, which they deposit on the lawn surface. They leave a hole in the turf at each spot.

A properly aerated lawn has thousands of these aerating holes and thousands of little soil cores sitting on the surface. In fact, a properly aerated lawn will have from twelve to sixteen

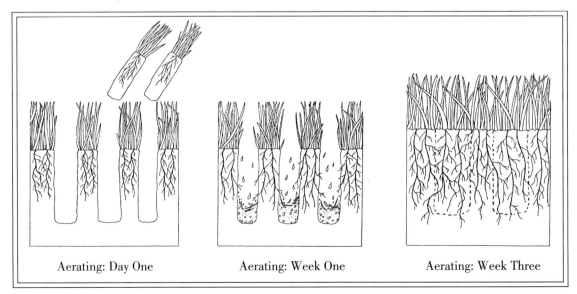

| Aerating: Day One | Aerating: Week One | Aerating: Week Three |

cores covering every square foot of the lawn! While it initially looks as if a thousand Canada geese just walked across your lawn leaving their droppings, don't worry, this is only temporary. The little soil cores rapidly decompose in the weather and, in about two or three weeks, the lawn looks better than it ever did.

The oxygen that enters the soil through the aerating holes reverses any decline of soil health almost immediately. It stimulates the activity of soil microorganisms which busy themselves with reproduction and feeding, which brings the soil alive. Earthworms move more freely through the soil, leaving their castings that provide nutrition to grass roots. Better able to find and take up soil nutrients, grass roots now begin to grow vigorously and vertically, finding it much easier to penetrate the soil.

Core-Aerating Machine

Not only are they no longer forced to grow near the soil surface, but those roots that have spread laterally and cause thatch problems near the soil surface are broken down by aeration. As the little cores of soil left on the turf begin to disintegrate, the microorganisms in them stimulate decomposition of the accumulated thatch to a layer that is an acceptable 1/4 inch or less. Normally, thatch buildup occurs in three- to five-year cycles, so aerating the lawn every two or three years controls thatch and prevents it from accumulating.

AERATING TOOLS

Power-driven core-aerating machines, which can be rented for about $50 a day or purchased ($800–$1,200), are the best tool for a lawn that is over 5,000 square feet. You can cover a lot of ground fairly rapidly, with time left over for your neighbor to use the machine too. The first time we aerated, Jeff was a bit cautious. He made one pass over the entire turf area.

Aerating Cores

An experienced neighbor insisted that he repeat the process several times, in a different direction each time. When Liz came out to check his progress, she was sure the lawn was destroyed. After a tense few weeks, the treatment paid off. The lawn looked wonderful.

There are hand aeration tools on the market ($15–$25) that also do the job, albeit somewhat more slowly. Because the person doing the job gets as much aerobic benefit as the lawn,

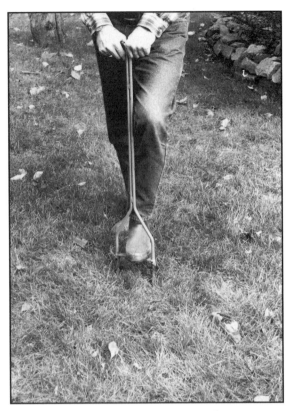

Manual Core-Aerating Tool

we recommend using hand aerators for smaller lawns and narrow areas near walks, drives and patios. Always aerate around trees with a hand aerator.

How Often to Aerate

If your lawn and soil are in pretty good condition, it is not necessary to aerate the entire lawn every year. Some homeowners with poor lawns aerate annually for two or three years because their soil is so badly compacted (see Chapter Six for more details about dealing with serious compaction). Once soil compaction is somewhat reduced, core aeration once every two to three years—perhaps more frequently in high-traffic areas—is sufficient to maintain the level of improvement. Remember, thatch buildup tends to occur in three- to five-year cycles, so routinely aerating the lawn at those intervals will probably control most thatch buildup too.

Fall is the best time to aerate, because the grass is shifting its attention from blade growth to root growth. Providing oxygen and loosening the soil at this time really stimulates root development. If the fall is inconvenient, spring is the next-best time to aerate. Wait until the soil has dried out from spring rains, though. Do not aerate in the summer. Grass plants are at peak growth, possibly coping with heat and reduced moisture as well, so they will be badly stressed by aeration.

Spiking the Lawn

Another mechanical way to introduce oxygen into compressed soil and loosen it is by spiking. While not as beneficial as core aerating, spiking can mitigate compaction problems, even as they develop. Professional golf course maintenance supervisors know this. They spike the most heavily trod parts of the golf course regularly, often weekly. This prevents bare spots from developing in areas where grass gives up from too much punishment from foot traffic.

Spiking tools do not take a core out of the soil. Their 3- or 4-inch pointed metal spikes simply make lots of small punctures instead. (The spikes on golf shoes are not long enough to do the job.) Often a little spiking is enough to keep the soil from getting too compacted where the mailman cuts across the yard, where kids take a shortcut to the neighbor's house or where you walk to put the trash out. While there are power spiking machines, probably a hand spiking tool makes the most sense for residential yards. They are portable and handy, so it is easy to duck out and routinely spike the problem areas every two or three weeks throughout the growing season.

ADD ORGANIC MATERIAL
TO THE SOIL

If you have a healthy turf and soil, you might think that the soil would be able to generate its own organic content. Not so. Truly healthy soil has between 3 percent and 5 percent organic material, composed mostly of organic debris such as grass clippings, dried leaves, pieces of sticks and such. It is also made of lots of things that were living in the soil but have died, such as roots, earthworms and billions of dear-departed microorganisms. But few residential landscapes have soil this rich with organic material.

The reality is that the soil under American lawns typically contains less than 1 percent organic material. This is because over

Spiking Tool

a ten- or twenty-year period not only was no new organic material introduced, but the most abundant natural sources, such as leaves and grass clippings, were systematically collected and disposed of in the municipal trash stream.

A healthy soil needs a steady source of new organic material. It is constantly decomposing and yielding nutrients for the grass plants and must be replaced. The black, fibrous material called "humus" that results from the decomposition of grass clippings and other organic material eventually has little food value left. However, it has enormous value in aerating the soil, in storing water and in feeding key microorganisms needed for other tasks.

Also, while leaving grass clippings on the lawn provides some organic material, it is not sufficient to consistently provide 3–5 percent. You must provide more. If you have not routinely spread a thin topdressing, or layer, of topsoil, peat moss, finely chopped leaves or other organic material on your lawn in the past five or ten years, it's high time.

Just as with the aerating task, if your soil is in really bad shape then consider doing this topdressing task every year for the next two or three years to restore the soil humus content

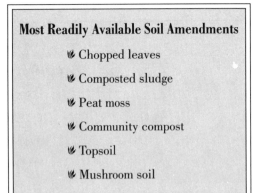

Most Readily Available Soil Amendments

- ❦ Chopped leaves
- ❦ Composted sludge
- ❦ Peat moss
- ❦ Community compost
- ❦ Topsoil
- ❦ Mushroom soil

to the proper proportion. Then adopt a topdressing routine every three to five years.

The ideal soil contains about 5 percent humus; 3 percent is fine. A 1-inch topdressing of peat moss (mixed with dried cow manure) or other organic material spread evenly over the surface of your lawn represents the equivalent of about 5 percent of the first 12 inches of soil. However, spreading a whole inch is not necessary. If you spread only 1/4 to 1/2 inch of organic matter once a year and leave your grass clippings on the lawn all season, you will approach that ideal 5 percent figure in two or three years. Then you can topdress less frequently—every three to five years. If you have leaves on your lawn in the fall and you mow with a mulching mower, you are effectively putting that inch of topdressing on your lawn every year simply by mulching in the leaves while you mow. Leaving about 1/2 inch of mulched leaves each season will produce wonderful soil in just a few years.

Suggested Sources of Organic Material

The most common organic soil amendment for lawns is sphagnum peat moss harvested in Canada. Sphagnum peat moss excels in holding moisture and it also supports the microlife necessary for a healthy soil. It has little nutrient value, however, so it is best supplemented with some dried cow manure or compost. Sphagnum peat moss is available in compressed bales. A 4-cubic-foot bale is most cost effective for lawns; about three bales per 1,000 square feet yield a 1/4-inch layer over the entire lawn. Alternative humus-rich products for topdressing lawns are: compost (either homemade from yard waste or purchased at the garden center), composted municipal sludge, mushroom soil and plain old topsoil. (Though much topsoil these days has precious little organic matter.) These products are not uniformly available in all regions of the country.

We are fortunate to live where both spent mushroom soil and composted municipal sludge are available. If you are lucky enough to live near Milwaukee, Philadelphia, Wilmington (Delaware) or any city with a sludge-composting system, you have a source of topdressing material that is very safe for any landscape application. Made of dehydrated sewage waste that is composted with wood chips at high temperatures, this humus-rich material works magic in regenerating the soil. Lawns show rapid improvement which persists over two or three years.

Spreading any topdressing over the lawn evenly takes some effort. First, cut the grass a bit shorter than normal—between 1 inch and 1 1/2 inches—so that the humus can easily fall down among the grass blades. Jeff prefers to use a regular garden rake to distribute piles of sludge or peat moss roughly over the lawn. Then he shifts to a flexible grass rake to spread the material as evenly as possible while keeping the grass blades from being buried.

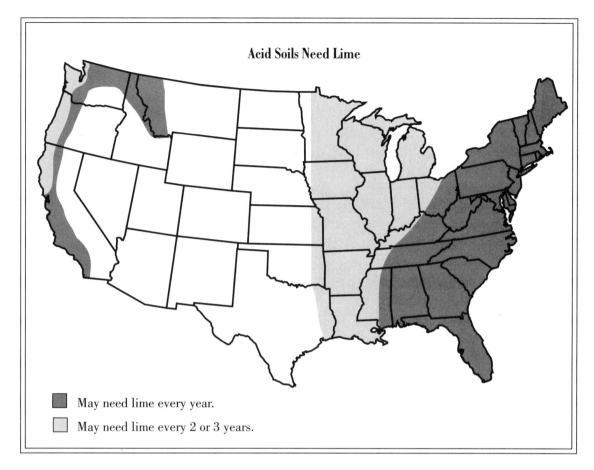

Acid Soils Need Lime

■ May need lime every year.
□ May need lime every 2 or 3 years.

Adding Limestone

Grass grows best in soils that are only slightly acidic, preferring a pH range of 6.0–7.2 (7.0 is neutral). Many soils around the United States are naturally acidic with a pH somewhat below the preferred 6.0 range. Those soils need to be treated routinely to bring the pH up and "sweeten" the soil. Check the map to see if you live in an area that typically has acidic soil. A more accurate source is your local county extension office; experts there will know what kind of soils are common in your neighborhood.

It is easy to treat overly acidic soil even when the lawn is in place by spreading a layer of limestone over the turf. Limestone is naturally alkaline and it buffers the excess acid in the soil sort of like an antacid tablet relieves acid stomachs in humans. The primary reason to have the soil within the preferred pH range is to keep the microbial population happy. An acidic soil discourages microbes and therefore provides fewer nutrients for the grass plants.

In addition to sweetening it, lime does many more good things for soil than people realize. It adds valuable calcium and magnesium to the soil, improves soil structure and enhances seed germination. We recommend that you lime your lawn at least every three years even if the pH is okay; your grass needs the calcium and magnesium and can get it no other way!

There are many types of lime available in garden centers and hardware stores. Choose dolomitic lime in as fine a grind as you can find. The finer the granules, the faster it will take effect. It may be gray or tan or off-white, but it must be labeled as truly dolomitic lime. Some retail outlets sell bags of limestone labeled as dolomitic, but they are basically only ground marble.

Since it takes at least three to six months for limestone to be absorbed in the soil and take effect, the very best time to spread it is the fall. However, it is OK to lime anytime. If your soil is very acidic (below 5.2), then you will want to apply limestone in both the spring and the fall for several years. As the pH works its way up to the ideal level, cut back to once a year or even once every two years. Generally speaking, shady areas of your lawn are more likely to be acidic and therefore will more likely need lime every year.

Sandy soils that are within the proper pH range will need to be limed lightly about every two to three years. Clay soils that are within the proper pH range require heavier doses at least every five to six years.

One last note on lime. Do not spread it on the lawn at the same time you fertilize. The chemical combination produces ammonia gas which releases the nitrogen you want for the grass into the air.

We should note that as this book goes to press, a new product, liquid lime, has become available in garden centers. This liquid calcium is effective in raising the pH of the lawn quite quickly, but it must be applied twice a year to equal the staying power of the granular limestone. We have not had time to try this product, nor are we able to compare the cost of using granular versus liquid.

Pounds of Limestone for 1,000 Sq. Ft.		
Soil pH	Sandy Soil	Clay Soil
Over 6.2	0	0
5.2–6.2	25–50	50–75
Under 5.2	50–75	100–150

We hope we have convinced you that it's worth taking action to improve the quality of the soil under your turf. You will have a healthier lawn and, in the long term, you will have less work. Liz figures if Mother Nature already has a system set up, why not use hers? In these next three chapters we help you learn to mow, fertilize and water properly for a low-maintenance result. However, these steps we just outlined—aerating and topdressing—may be the most important maintenance steps you take.

Chapter Two
Mowing the Lawn

We Mow a Lot

Americans apparently love to mow the lawn. We certainly spend a lot of time at the task. On average, a typical lawn needs between twenty-five and thirty cuts per growing season, roughly once a week between April and October. Of course, in the summer we mow less when heat and drought slow grass growth, but in the spring we may be out there every five days. It balances out, though, and represents an impressive forty hours or so a year behind a lawn mower.

Because we mow often, we rarely give much thought to how we do it. Yet, the act of mowing grass has an enormous impact on the health and appearance of a lawn. We suggest some simple techniques below that are preferable, in our opinion, to traditional practice.

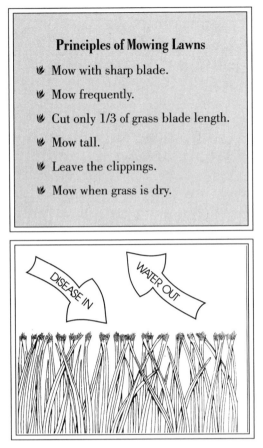

Principles of Mowing Lawns

- Mow with sharp blade.
- Mow frequently.
- Cut only 1/3 of grass blade length.
- Mow tall.
- Leave the clippings.
- Mow when grass is dry.

Before Mowing

Proper, safe mowing actually begins before the machine hits the turf.

KEEP BLADE SHARP

When was the last time you sharpened your mower blade? If you are like most yardeners, you have never sharpened it, even though it has probably been dull since six weeks after you purchased the machine.

Grass is always somewhat damaged and stressed when it is cut. However, cut with a sharp mower blade, individual leaf tips heal much more quickly and the grass plant remains healthy. Dull mower blades bludgeon the leaf tips, causing them to become frayed and turn gray, then brown. These brown, mutilated tips provide ready access for disease-producing organisms.

We were embarrassed to realize that, like many others, we spent hundreds of dollars on a fancy lawn mower and forty hours or more a season using it, but could not seem to find the money and the time to keep the blade sharp. Once we realized the importance of this simple step, Liz sought out a place to take the blade for sharpening. Even better, Jeff eventually learned to sharpen it himself at home.

Sharpen the Mower Blade Twice a Year—maybe first thing in the spring and again in July. We found it easier to buy an extra blade for our mower so that we could rotate them. Twice a season we remove the dull blade for sharpening and immediately replace it with a sharpened one.

Have It Sharpened Professionally—It costs between $5 and $8 if you remove the blade from the mower yourself. If the dealer removes and reinstalls the blade after sharpening, it costs slightly more, around $15. You may find it is even simpler just to buy a new, sharp blade when your existing one gets dull. Brand-new blades for most mowers cost $15 or $20, worth the money to simplify the sharpening process. Any way you handle it, the lawn will certainly benefit from your taking the trouble to use a sharp mower blade.

A Handy Helper

Taking the blade off the mower can sometimes be difficult. There is a great tool on the market to make that job a breeze. Called the "Blade Buster Safety Lock," it clamps onto the mower's deck and holds the blade steady so you can easily remove it for sharpening.

Do It Yourself— Sharpen the mower blade yourself with a file. An excellent safety precaution is to disconnect the spark plug before beginning. Remove the blade from the mower with a socket or adjustable wrench and secure it somehow to a bench or table. A vise is ideal for

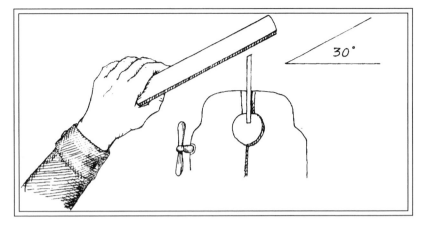

this job, but a single hand-clamp will serve just fine. Notice that the business part of the blade is actually only a few inches at each end. This is the area that needs sharpening.

Use a medium file at about a 25°–30° angle to the blade. The idea is to remove the minor nicks and rounded edge on the blade, not to sharpen it like a knife. If the mower blade has lots of major nicks, it is time to replace it entirely.

Try to sharpen the blade fairly evenly on both ends to maintain the important balance of the blade. Using a grinding wheel for this job is not recommended. It is too easy to take too much metal off the blade. Also, the heat that is generated in the process may affect the metal blade. Take care to fasten the nut tightly when you remount the blade on the mower.

WEAR PROPER CLOTHING AND PROTECTION

Thousands of yardeners are taken to emergency rooms of hospitals every year with lawn mower injuries that could have been avoided by wearing proper clothing. Mowing the lawn is not without risk. By dressing properly, you can minimize the danger. Wear long pants to shield your bare skin, even though shorts may be a lot more comfortable in July. Avoid loose clothing or dangling jewelry that can snag on mower controls. Don't mow the lawn in bare feet or in sandals. Wear sturdy, nonslip shoes that provide good traction and protection.

*Consider Ear Protection—*While you might feel a little silly wearing ear protection devices while mowing your lawn, you might want to consider doing just that. Research has indicated that the noise level of a standard gasoline-driven lawn mower is loud enough to cause some measurable hearing loss when a person is exposed to that noise level for more than thirty minutes at a time. The lawn care industry now recognizes this danger and more and more of the professional companies are providing their workers with proper ear protection for mowing lawns—something to think about for yourself. If you decide on ear protection, do not rely on wads of cotton, or even earplugs. We went to the trouble of buying the type of ear protectors that are worn at firing ranges. They offer truly effective protection for when we use our chain saw and shredder too.

Lawn Mower Does Not Start

What happens if the mower doesn't start on the first few pulls of the cord? There are a few items to check before kicking the mower and taking it to the repair shop.

🌿 Is there gas in the tank?

🌿 Is the starter switch on or baffle engaged?

🌿 Have you primed the mower by pushing the soft rubber button?

🌿 Is anything obstructing the blade?

🌿 Is the spark plug old?

🌿 Is last season's gas still in it? If this is the first start of the season and you left gasoline in the tank all winter, you probably have stale gas and a clogged carburetor and will definitely need to take it to the repair shop. (Next fall remember to remove the gas from the tank after the last mowing.)

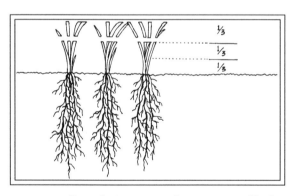

DON'T CUT WET GRASS

If you have a choice, and sometimes we don't, cut the grass when it is completely dry. Walking on wet grass as you mow bruises it. Cutting it wet causes uneven mowing and messy clumps of clippings which tend to mat together and block light from the grass. Try to avoid mowing during early morning hours when there is a heavy dew on the grass. It is tough to persuade lawn care services to do this. They need to cut on schedule, wet or not.

MOW LIGHT AND LOTS

Grass is happiest when it is mowed lightly and frequently. The rule is to take no more than one-third the length of the blade each time you mow. So, to keep the lawn at 2 inches tall, mow when it reaches 3 inches. That is a nice rule, but if the only time many yardeners have to mow is the weekend, the long-suffering grass may be longer than 3 inches. Then you will have to cut either more than one-third of the blade, settle for grass that is 3 1/2 inches tall or—hardly low-maintenance—cut lightly twice on the weekend, maybe Friday evening and Sunday afternoon.

Taking more than one-third of the grass blade at one cutting stresses grass plants. They are thrown into an emergency survival mode because their capacity to receive sun and make energy to grow has been seriously reduced as so much blade surface is removed.

Cumulative stress from repeatedly losing too much grass blade leads to problems with insects, disease and weeds. Finally, if more than 40 percent of the grass plant is amputated at one time, the roots stop growing. All grass energy is devoted to replacing lost foliage. Over the long term, shallow roots reduce the grass's vigor. So mow when you can, but the more often you mow and the less grass you take off each time will definitely make a difference in the health of your lawn.

MOW TALL

We have observed that most yardeners tend to cut their grass much too short. Maybe we do that because that was how our parents used to do it, especially if they had a reel-type mower back in the old days. Those early mowers were not adjustable to 2-inch heights. Or maybe we are trying to achieve what we see at the local golf course. Many share the mistaken belief that short grass grows more slowly.

The height of the cut is one of the most critical issues in keeping your lawn healthy. While each lawn grass cultivar has a recommended clipping height, we feel that we can generalize for almost all situations and say "mow tall"!

Tall Grass Grows More Slowly—When grass is mowed tall, it grows more slowly and therefore needs less frequent cutting. Mowing it too short reduces the amount of foliage surface it has available for photosynthesis. So, the survival response to this emergency is to quickly replace the lost foliage, and the grass then grows rapidly. Taller grass experiences less stress when it is cut because it still has plenty of foliage surface. It doesn't feel so compelled to quickly replace the lost leaf surface.

Tall Grass Reduces Water Needs—Allowing the grass to grow tall encourages the roots to grow deep. Deep roots give grass plants more staying power during times of drought. They have access to a larger area of stored water in the soil. Tall grass also helps shade the soil, reducing evaporation of its valuable moisture and cooling the crowns of the grass plants.

Tall Grass Reduces Fertilizer Needs—Small changes in mowing height make a big difference in lawn health and vigor. Increasing the height of your grass only 1/8 inch results in about 300 square feet more leaf surface for each 1,000 square feet of lawn. Since the leaf blade is the food factory of the grass

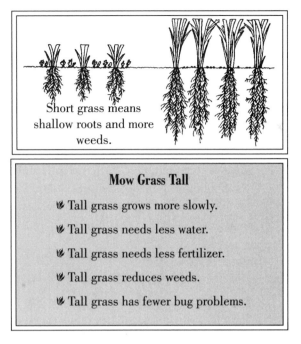

Short grass means shallow roots and more weeds.

Mow Grass Tall

- Tall grass grows more slowly.
- Tall grass needs less water.
- Tall grass needs less fertilizer.
- Tall grass reduces weeds.
- Tall grass has fewer bug problems.

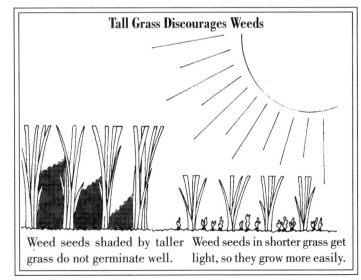

Tall Grass Discourages Weeds

Weed seeds shaded by taller grass do not germinate well. Weed seeds in shorter grass get light, so they grow more easily.

plant, this increased surface for intercepting light means greater ability to produce food and stronger growth of the grass. The more self-reliant grass is in providing its own nutrition, the less work you have to do. Conversely, shearing grass too closely to the soil reduces its ability to metabolize food. Then you must supplement its diet with fertilizer. More work for you!

Tall Grass Reduces Weeds—Mowing northern turf grasses 2 inches high results in a tenfold reduction in weeds over mowing 1 inch high. The longer blades shade the soil, blocking the ever-present weed seeds from the sunlight they need to germinate.

Tall Grass Reduces Disease and Insect Problems—Tall grass is healthy grass and healthy grass suffers much less from disease and insect problems. It can tolerate disease and insect threats better than stressed grass can. In addition, tall grass accommodates a much higher population of beneficial insects such as pests and spiders that will control pest insects for you. They need the protection of the tall grass blades from their own predators.

HOW TO MEASURE

It is all well and good to suggest cutting the grass when it is one-third taller than the height you prefer. How do you know when that is the case? Most folks will just wait until the lawn looks a bit ragged and then cut the grass, especially if they are on the obligatory weekend cycle for cutting the lawn whether it needs it or not. The easiest method for determining

the time to cut the lawn is to use a ruler or make a measuring stick. If the desired standard is 2 inches, then mark the stick at 3 inches. By simply setting the end of the stick down in the turf, it is easy to see if the blades approach the 3-inch mark. Then it is OK to mow.

If measurement shows that the grass is way beyond the 3-inch mark, then the ideal procedure is to cut it twice. Raise your mower so that you cut it at 3 inches, wait a day or two, then lower the mower to the 2-inch height and mow again. This way you are not taking more than one-third of the blade each time.

CUT TOO HIGH?

Can we mow our lawns too high in our enthusiasm to gain the benefits of tall grass? Yes. Lawn grasses cut much above 3 inches fail to form a nice, uniform, close-knit turf. They'll be healthy enough, but they won't look as good as lawns cut somewhere between 2 and 3 inches. They may fall over and mat in rainy weather and then have difficulty drying out.

Seasonal Changes

Northern grasses grow at different rates in different seasons. Because fastest growth occurs in the cool seasons, spring and fall, mowing will be more frequent then. As summer heat slows growth, it is not necessary to mow so often to maintain the desired height. The experts on high-maintenance lawn care have developed a routine for changing the height of the lawn mower,

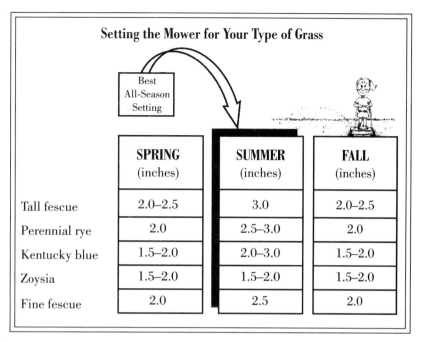

Setting the Mower for Your Type of Grass

Best All-Season Setting

	SPRING (inches)	SUMMER (inches)	FALL (inches)
Tall fescue	2.0–2.5	3.0	2.0–2.5
Perennial rye	2.0	2.5–3.0	2.0
Kentucky blue	1.5–2.0	2.0–3.0	1.5–2.0
Zoysia	1.5–2.0	1.5–2.0	1.5–2.0
Fine fescue	2.0	2.5	2.0

depending on the time of year. They cut a bit closer in cool seasons, and longer in the summer. Our experience is that these changes are not necessary. We are inclined not to take the extra time to adjust the mower and feel the benefits are negligible. However, you may want to experiment with some modest changes.

MOWING IN THE SPRING

The high-maintenance lawn care folks feel that it's best to set the mower lower for the first mowing in spring, about 1–1 1/2 inches for bluegrass-fescue lawns. The logic is that with that first mowing you take off winter-scorched grass foliage and excess dormant vegetation. Our concern is that cutting it risks germination of weed seeds that are lurking in the soil which is newly exposed to light. If weeds germinate, that means more work later.

We recommend a compromise. Lower the mower to 1 1/2 inches for the very first mowing in the spring, but then immediately raise the mower up to the preferred 2 inches for the next mowing and all subsequent ones.

MOWING IN THE SUMMER

You can responsibly keep your lawn at 2 inches throughout the year, but in the heat of the summer, a gradual rise to 2 1/2 or even 3 inches will benefit it. Close mowing in hot weather weakens cool-season grasses. This is the very time when they increase respiration and use nutrient reserves to withstand the heat stress. This is why you see so many brown lawns in high summer. The grass has given up and gone dormant to wait out the stress. It does not make sense to severely defoliate it at this time. So, if you care to take the trouble, we think it is advisable to increase the cutting height of cool-season grasses during the warm, dry summer months.

Mowing in the Fall

As temperatures moderate in September, lower the mowing height to the preferred 2 inches again. Those practicing high-maintenance lawn care make a point of lowering the mower to about 1 inch for the last mowing of the season. The purpose is to encourage the grass to send out shoots from the base of the plants that will thicken up the turf for the following spring. We might consider lowering the mower to 1 1/2 inches, but no lower. Even shorter grass may send out more basal shoots, but that short grass also lets in lots of light for any weed seeds to germinate if there is an Indian summer or a very mild winter.

Mowing Shaded Grass

Grass growing in areas that experience some shade should be mowed higher—by about 1/2 inch—than your grass growing in the sun. This grass needs maximum leaf surface to compensate for the light deprivation.

Dealing with Clippings

Until recently, most Americans have routinely collected grass clippings as they mowed their lawns to eliminate unsightly clumps on the lawn. Clippings tend to clump up on top of the turf if they are long because mowing has been delayed or the grass is damp. Also, if your lawn mower blade is very dull, the clippings will clump. Not only do the clumps look messy, but they foster disease if they are permitted to lie on the turf. If they are not collected, they need to be raked and spread out. Then they are still a nuisance as they are tracked into the house.

There are ways to avoid these problems, yet leave clippings on your lawn. There are lots of reasons why leaving clippings is a good thing to do.

Of course, leaving the clippings on the lawn as you mow is good for the environment because it reduces the pressure on America's landfills. However, the best reason is that leaving nitrogen-rich clippings benefits the lawn, making it healthier and thus more low maintenance.

Leave the Clippings

🍂 Clippings are fertilizer.

🍂 Clippings reduce water needs.

🍂 Clippings are not thatch.

Clippings Are Fertilizer—Grass clippings left on the lawn all season will contribute 30 percent of its total fertilizer needs for the year. Grass clippings contain about 4 percent nitrogen, 1/2–1 percent phosphorus, 2–3 percent potassium and smaller amounts of other essential plant nutrients. They basically constitute a 4-2-

3 fertilizer growing in your yard. Over a season of weekly cuttings, the decomposing clippings add nutrients to the soil the best way—slowly and steadily. And, it is free.

Clippings Reduce Water Need— Leaving clippings reduces the need for water. When you leave the clippings, the soil surface is shaded, which reduces moisture loss from evaporation. Moist soil is cooler soil.

Clippings Are Not Thatch—Grass clippings are not thatch, nor do they promote the development of thatch. (More about thatch later.) You may see them in the thatch when you look closely, but they are there just tem-

porarily. Clippings contain over 75 percent water and will be broken down by the worms, fungi and other resident microbes in about two to three weeks. Since you mow more frequently than every three weeks, there is a constant process of decomposition of clippings going on down at the base of the grass plants. It is a very healthy process.

MOWERS AND CLIPPINGS

The easiest way to avoid the clumping of clippings is to have the right lawn mower. Each of three available types of lawn mowers—conventional rotary, mulching rotary or reel—handles clippings differently.

Both the conventional rotary mower and the reel-type mower cut grass blades once, promptly throwing the severed tips onto the turf. The mulching rotary mower, on the other hand, cuts the blade tips off, then cuts them several more times before they are discharged by the mower to fall onto the turf. The distinctive design of mulching mowers creates a vacuum up in the bell of the mower which suspends the clippings in the area so they can be cut several times by the whirling blade. By the time they are discharged, the clippings have been chopped into small pieces that easily disappear between the growing grass blades.

Grass clippings produced by mulching mowers hardly ever clump unless the grass is outrageously tall. Mulching mowers also chop

The end of the mulching blade is bent slightly.

Mulching Mower

leaves and exfoliated bark that fall on the turf into such small pieces that they, too, fall down between the grass blades. Over time, all this chopped organic material conspires to enrich the soil and improve the health of the grass.

If you own a conventional rotary mower, consider buying a mulching conversion kit from your dealer. Typically offering a new kind of blade and perhaps a device for closing off the side discharge hole, these kits will enable your present mower to solve the problem of clumpy grass clippings so that you can leave them on the turf. Converted mowers are not as effective as dedicated mulching mowers, but they perform better than standard rotary mowers. Conversion kits are available for most name brand mowers and cost around $20.

If you have a conventional mower or a reel-type mower, the only way to avoid clumping of clippings is to mow often enough so that the size of the cut grass blade is within the one-third rule (i.e., small enough to fall down among the remaining blades). You can relieve the problem a bit by overlapping the cutting track as you mow, effectively cutting the fallen clippings again as they lie on the turf. Of course, this means the mowing job takes twice as long, but there are fewer clumps of clippings. If you are using a self-propelled mower, slowing the speed over the ground can reduce its tendency to discharge clippings in clumps.

WHEN TO COLLECT CLIPPINGS

There are a few instances where it is better to collect the clippings in a bag attached to the mower. If the grass is wet and you simply must mow the lawn because of time constraints, collect those clippings or they will clump up for sure. If you've been away and the grass is very, very long, it is easier to simply collect the clippings for that mowing. If, in the fall, you have more than 2 inches of leaves fallen on the surface of the lawn, even a mulching mower

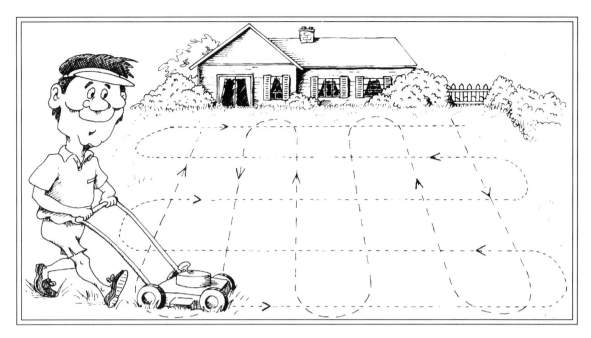

alone won't handle that volume. Use a bagger on the mower to collect those leaves with the cut grass. They make wonderful mulch or compost.

Alternate the Mowing Pattern

While it is not absolutely critical, there is some benefit to alternating the mowing pattern each time you mow the grass. Mowing the same direction every time tends to compact the soil where you walk behind the mower repeatedly and can eventually cause wear patterns. Alternating the pattern is easy. Liz strives for various even designs, but has not yet produced the equivalent of the infield at Candlestick Park.

One routine might be to cut in an east/west direction this week, then use a north/south direction the next time and mow diagonally the next. This strategy produces a "patterned effect" which tends to enhance turf appearance and achieves a more even shearing of the turf over time. If you use a side discharge mower, alternating mowing direction disperses clippings over the lawn more evenly for more uniform fertilization.

Avoid Touching Trees

Don't be shocked, but the sorry fact is that lawn mowers kill trees by the millions. Few yardeners realize the seriousness of what seems like "just a little nick" in the bark of a young tree when the lawn mower (or the weed whacker, for that matter) bumps it. It may take ten years for that tree to die, but in most cases, that "nick" promotes its premature death. Any break in the bark allows disease and insects to gain access to the tender inner wood. Their

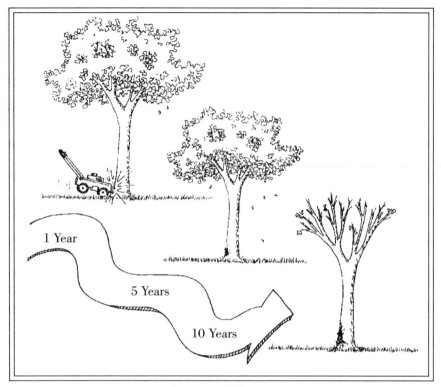

Lawn mowers kill trees.

predations gradually weaken the tree, making it vulnerable to other insects and diseases. Young trees under five years old are particularly at risk to this kind of injury because their bark is not hard. During the late spring and early fall, these injuries are the most harmful.

The simple, strict rule is never, never touch a tree, any tree, with your lawn mower or other yard care equipment. The best way to assure that you keep your distance is to circle the tree trunk with organic mulch or ground cover at least a foot or two wide. This has the added virtue of reducing the amount of lawn to mow a bit, and also helping to nourish the tree. There are also plastic trunk guards available in garden centers and hardware stores that offer some protection to younger trees.

Edging the Lawn

While it is definitely extra work, trimming and edging the lawn after it has been mowed gives your lawn a much more finished look.

Trimming—Mowers usually leave some tall grass in the corners of the lawn and along walls, fences or garden beds. This is often where weeds get their first foothold. While hand shears or clippers will do the job, if you want something larger and faster, try a power trimmer.

Hand-held string trimmers, which cut down weeds and grass with a whirling nylon string, are most popular these days for this job. The electric versions are light, easy to use and ideal for residential scale trimming jobs. Never let the string actually strike tree or shrub stems, for reasons described above. It's best to trim these areas with a hand tool.

Edging—Edgers give a manicured look to your lawn by creating carefully cut turf edges around sidewalks, driveways and patios. While hand edgers do the job, they are high maintenance, requiring a fair amount of time and energy to do the job properly. Power edgers are much easier to use and do a cleaner, faster job. Always wear heavy shoes, protective eyewear and (if gasoline driven) ear protection when operating any power trimmer or edger. Liz insists that we mention here that no one else in the neighborhood has ear protection, so wait to do the job until neighbors are out of bed in the morning.

Mowing Brand-New Grass

When do you mow newly planted grass? It depends. If it is a brand-new lawn started on bare soil, then you must wait until the grass is 3 or even 4 inches tall. Then, for that first mowing, set the mower at 2 1/2 or even 3 inches to take just enough off to give it an even look. Then a few days later, lower the mower to 2 inches and mow again. Setting the mower on the high side will minimize the tendency of the vacuum in the rotary mower to pull the tender new grass plants right out of the ground. If you have a reel mower or can borrow one from a friend or neighbor, use it. A reel mower is best for newly planted lawns.

If the new grass has been overseeded into an existing turf, there is less danger of inadvertently dislodging the new plants with the rotary mower. Mow the newly sprouted lawn when it is time to mow the established grass in which it is growing—at about 3 inches.

🌿 🌿 🌿

Who would have thought that the simple job of mowing the lawn, which you have been doing for years, could take up a whole chapter in a book? We were surprised too. However long it has taken us to discuss these issues, the bottom line is that they are important. By the simple act of mowing the grass properly you are taking the critical first steps in building a healthy, self-reliant lawn.

Chapter Three

Fertilizing the Lawn

Most yardeners use too much fertilizer on their lawns. They harm their grass, they waste money and they waste time. In this chapter, we'll help you develop a fertilizing program that is appropriate for your situation and avoids these problems.

In the best of all possible worlds, turf grass would get its nutrition solely from the soil. However, as we have seen, most soil on residential properties is in such bad shape that it is not capable of sustaining grass plants by itself. Besides, lawn grasses are not native plants long-adapted to soil conditions in our region, so they require some extra attention. Consequently, we have to fertilize some. How much is a function of the health of our soil. To the degree that we can improve the soil, we relieve ourselves of the responsibility of providing nutrition to our grass.

Feeding Options

Fertilizing plants is sort of analogous to feeding humans. A diet that is too rich is harmful, affecting performance and often creating conditions that foster disease. We recommend putting your lawn on a sensible diet. It needs a nutritious main meal or two with optional snacks and "vitamins."

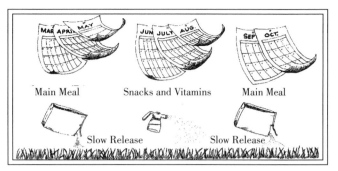

The best annual main meal for lawns is a slow-acting, general-purpose, granular fertilizer spread in the fall and again in the spring. Snacks for lawns are additional servings of fertilizer, liquid or granular, to boost energy at key times in the late spring and early summer. As with people, snacks are optional. Finally, to maximize the effectiveness of this nutrition, you may want to offer some "vitamins" to the lawn. These products, bioactivators such as seaweed or kelp sprays, are not food for plants, but they help plants utilize the nutrition in the soil more efficiently. Vitamins are also optional.

Your choice of fertilizer for the main meal will be greatly influenced by your particular lawn care philosophy. How much time and effort you intend to devote to lawn care—especially soil care—determines what kind and how much fertilizer you will buy.

Fertilizing Philosophy

This book focuses on low-maintenance lawn care. Reducing the time spent on annual maintenance of the lawn while enhancing its health and vigor is our goal. It may, or may not, be yours. However, it is in the fertilizer department where the difference between low-maintenance and high-maintenance lawn care shows up most dramatically. There is little difference in the cost and the appearance of high- and low-maintenance lawns. The difference rests primarily with how much time you must spend to achieve an attractive lawn. We prefer the low-maintenance approach to fertilizing the lawn, because we never seem to have enough time to do all the things we need to do. If we can save time by fertilizing only twice a year, then that's a big plus for us. We recommend this approach to yardeners who want to minimize the time they spend on yard care.

Northern Grass Needs 2–4 Pounds of Nitrogen per 1,000 Sq. Ft. of Lawn		
Nitrogen Source	Four Applications Quick Release	Two Applications Slow Release
Fertilizer	3–5 lbs.	2 lbs.
Clippings	.5–1 lb.	.5–1 lb.
Worms	0	.5–1 lb.
Microbes	0	.5–1 lb.
	3.5–6 lbs.	3.5–5 lbs.

In this chapter we recommend two main meals of fertilizer, one in the fall and another in the spring. We should note that if you follow all the recommendations of this book, and after two or three years have a healthy, dense turf growing in rich, healthy soil, you can maintain that level of health with just one annual application of fertilizer each fall. To get to this once a year program, you must leave the clippings, and you will have aerated, topdressed and overseeded at least once in the past two or three years. You will have encouraged earthworms and the lawn is thick and vigorous. Most yardeners reading this book do not have a lawn in such wonderful condition, so you will need two main meals for a few years.

Before You Fertilize

Before dealing with how to choose the right fertilizer and how to calculate how much is needed, consider three issues—what kind of grass do you have, do you leave the clippings and do you encourage earthworms?

What Kind of Grass?

The various northern grasses have somewhat different requirements for nitrogen, which is the primary nutrient needed by turf. The general rule is that you never give the turf more than a pound of nitrogen per 1,000 square feet in any individual application. You can generalize that in a year's time, most northern grasses are going to need between 2 and 4 pounds of nitrogen (from whatever source) in every 1,000 square feet of turf to grow well. On golf courses, where the grass suffers continual use and stress, the grass might require from 6 to 10 pounds of nitrogen each year for every 1,000 square feet; now that's high maintenance!

As a general rule, if you apply enough fertilizer to provide 2 pounds of nitrogen (1 pound in the fall and 1 pound in the spring), your lawn should look fine. Remember, though, that lawns are not necessarily totally dependent on store-bought fertilizer for their nutrition. The more they can get from natural sources, the less time, energy and money we have to put out.

Leaving the Clippings

Earlier we recommended that you leave the clippings on the lawn as you mow. We make that strong recommendation primarily because grass clippings contain nitrogen. Remember, when left on the lawn all season, they can contribute up to 25 percent of your lawn's seasonal fertilizer needs. Grass clippings are a pretty balanced fertilizer in their own right, usually containing approximately 3–4 percent nitrogen, 2 percent potassium and 1/2 percent phosphorus. A season's worth of clippings represent about 1/2–1 pound of nitrogen for every 1,000-square feet of your lawn. If you don't leave the clippings, you need to provide that pound of nitrogen by means of an (additional) application of fertilizer.

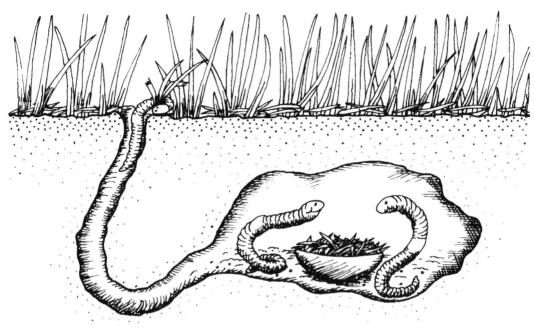

Earthworms reduce fertilizer needs.

ENCOURAGE EARTHWORMS

While they do lots of good things for soil structure, earthworms' greatest role is as a major producer of natural fertilizer. As they go about their business in the soil under your lawn, they excrete their weight in castings every day. Worm castings are an absolutely wonderful fertilizer, providing nutrients in a form all plants can use. In a 1,000-square-foot area, for example, at a density of only five worms per cubic foot (considered a low population), your earthworms will give you over 150 pounds—about 1/3 pound per worm—of top-grade fertilizer during each growing season. This fertilizer contains the key plant nutrients—nitrogen, phosphorus and potassium—plus many of the essential micronutrients plants need to grow and remain healthy. Dead earthworms are also very rich in nitrogen. Earthworm castings offer the equivalent of about 1/2–1 pound of nitrogen per 1,000 square feet per year.

Worms not only produce this valuable fertilizer, they also spread it evenly throughout the top 12 inches of the soil. In many cases they travel much deeper, sometimes as far down as 6 feet. A well-managed soil rich in humus can easily support twenty-five worms per cubic foot, which, in that same 1,000-square-foot area, means at least 800 pounds of fertilizer. That amounts to a lot more than 2 pounds of nitrogen for each 1,000 square feet, all courtesy of Mother Nature.

If you decide to take advantage of the work that earthworms do in your lawn, that has implications as to whether you choose quick-acting or slow-acting fertilizer. Quick-acting nitrogen fertilizer can make the soil more acidic. Research shows that when enough fertilizer is added to a lawn to cause the soil to become more acidic, thatch accumulation goes up and earthworm populations go down, every time. It follows that if you are trying to attract worms to help you with fertilizing the lawn, then you will avoid routine use of quick-acting fertilizers. These products do have their place, but not as main meals for turf where earthworms are invited guests.

At the end of this chapter we tell you how to increase your worm population.

ENCOURAGE MICROBIAL SOIL LIFE

A soil that contains the desirable 3–5 percent organic matter in the top 8–12 inches will have a very active microbial population, assuming there is sufficient air and water available (the soil must not be seriously compacted). Those microbes do many good things, including decompose thatch, control diseases and pest insects and produce nutrients for consumption by the grass plants. One of those nutrients is nitrogen. A healthy microbial population working in a soil with sufficient organic matter will produce 1/2–1 pound of nitrogen per 1,000 square feet of lawn each season, representing about 20 percent of your lawn's nitrogen needs. As with the earthworms, if you choose to use a quick-acting nitrogen lawn fertilizer, you will make the soil more acid and greatly reduce the population of these valuable microbes, eliminating their contribution of nitrogen. Then you have to make up the difference.

Choosing Fertilizer

Whether a fertilizer is technically considered "organic" or not is a distinction that is less important in lawn care than in growing food crops. We feel that identifying fertilizers as either "natural," made from natural materials such as feathers or blood meal, or "synthetic," made from materials created through chemical procedures, is more practical. It more correctly describes the nature of the product and avoids the problem of defining "organic" to everyone's satisfaction. However, even this distinction can be blurry. We believe the primary issue in choosing a fertilizer for lawns is whether it features nitrogen available to be released slowly over many weeks, or quickly within days, not whether the fertilizer is made from natural or synthetic material.

SLOW- VERSUS FAST-RELEASE NITROGEN

Let us state at the outset of this discussion that all fertilizers formulated for lawns provide basically the same nutrients. All provide a proportionally large amount of nitrogen and smaller amounts of potassium and phosphorus. So there is no significant difference in the basic nutrition provided to grass whether you use a slow-release (or "slow-acting") nitrogen lawn fertilizer or a quick-release nitrogen lawn fertilizer.

However, in our experience, there is a clear difference in the impact on the soil, the grass plants and time spent on the task. Quick-acting fertilizers release their nitrogen into the soil rapidly. Such a strong dose may "burn" the soil, driving away microbiotic life and earthworms that normally reside there, losing their value as aerators as well as fertilizers.

Visible greening of grass blades is evident within a day or two of a quick-acting application and lasts up to two or three weeks until the nitrogen becomes depleted. The immediate availability of so much nitrogen stimulates grass plants to grow rapidly above the soil at the expense of strong root development below, increasing the amount of mowing necessary in the weeks following application of the quick-acting fertilizer. To maintain this level of growth and color, repeated doses of fast-acting fertilizer must be provided over the growing season in a timely fashion. Grass that is suddenly deprived of the rich nitrogen suffers stress that makes it prone to disease and insect problems.

Because the nitrogen in slow-release nitrogen fertilizer is gradually released into the soil over many months, there is no danger that it will harm valuable microbiotic life down around grass roots. Grass plants produce both sturdy blades and roots over this time. The slow-release feature also assures that grass plants are not subjected to an overdose of nitrogen when it is first applied only to suffer dramatic deprivation when it is rapidly depleted. Growth is steady and uniform, so periods of frequent mowing after fertilization are avoided. There is also less danger of burning the turf if too much slow-release fertilizer is accidently applied.

Finally, because slow-acting fertilizer releases into the soil slowly over the growing season, there is no need to repeat fertilization several times over the summer. This saves time. The relative cost between the fast-acting and slow-release types of fertilizer, when each is used properly, can be about the same, though the natural slow-release fertilizers tend to be more expensive pound for pound than the quick-acting synthetic fertilizers.

SLOW-RELEASE FERTILIZERS

There are three types of slow-release fertilizers on the market. "Natural" products are made from feather meal, composted sludge or other natural materials. These materials naturally release nitrogen slowly. "Synthetic" products feature nitrogen that is synthesized from chemicals and is then encapsulated, or coated, so it, too, is released slowly over time. These high-technology products are relatively new to the lawn care market. "Bridge" products contain a little bit of synthetic quick-release nitrogen for initial green-up and then mostly natural materials for the slow-release form of nitrogen. The basic difference between the groups is price; the synthetic, coated fertilizers are much cheaper than the products made mostly or all from natural materials.

How Do I Know It's Slow-Release?

Slow-release fertilizers may also be called "timed release," "slow acting" or be described as having "water insoluble nitrogen" (WIN). A lawn fertilizer is considered to be "slow-release" if the nitrogen in the bag is made up of at least 30 percent WIN. Some manufactur-

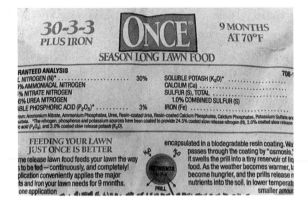

ers play pretty loose with that definition. The only way to be sure is to look at the small print on the back of the bag. Find that part of the label that lists precisely how much insoluble nitrogen is contained in that product. If the product has both soluble (quick) and insoluble (slow) nitrogen, be sure the insoluble is at least 30 percent of the total nitrogen contained in the bag. The better fertilizers, as far as we are concerned, will have 40–60 percent water insoluble nitrogen.

WHAT ABOUT NPK NUMBERS?

There is considerable variety among lawn fertilizer products in terms of their relative percentages of nitrogen (N), phosphorus (P) and potassium (K), the primary nutrients for lawns. The slow-release fertilizers tend to have a lower percentage of nitrogen (although it is still proportionally more abundant than the other nutrients) than do the quick-acting fertilizers. Our recommendation is not to worry about the NPK numbers. Purchase a fertilizer labeled for lawns that has 30 percent or more slow-release or water insoluble nitrogen. Leave the NPK numbers to the professionals who have the expertise to manipulate the various nutrients under certain conditions. As long as the label of the package clearly indicates that the fertilizer is formulated for use on lawns, don't worry about the precise NPK values.

HOW SLOW IS THE RELEASE?

To complicate this discussion ever so slightly, we must point out that some slow-release fertilizers last longer than others. How do you tell, and what difference does that make? Well, you can be sure that most slow-release products are going to last at least eight to ten weeks, or two and one-half months. Eight weeks in the spring and early summer and eight weeks in the fall and early winter are the periods for normal active growth of grass plants. The fertilizer label is likely to announce the duration of release.

As the technology for developing release mechanisms improves, we will see longer and longer periods for the release of nitrogen. Some products now on the market advertise release for up to sixteen weeks and there is one product that lasts for thirty-six weeks! As you can imagine, the longer the release period, the higher the cost, which we feel is reasonable. You are trading money for time. If it lasts longer, that means you do not have to do the job as often. At the same time, it is likely that the cost of those newer products will come down over the years to compete with other products on the market.

WHO DOES THIS JOB?

When deciding whether to hire a lawn service to fertilize your lawn, the ultimate question is whether you feel that the difference in cost between hiring a lawn company and doing it yourself is worth the time you save. Remember, you do not have to blindly accept whatever kind of fertilizer a company puts on your lawn. You can ask them to show you precisely what they are using so you can decide if it fits into your idea of a "good" fertilizer for your particular needs and desires.

HOW MUCH FERTILIZER DO I NEED?

Labels on lawn fertilizer bags indicate how much area their contents are designed to cover, typically 5,000 square feet or 10,000 square feet. Consequently, you need to have a rough idea of the size of your particular lawn.

Pace off the dimensions of each turf area and multiply the length times the width. For instance, a front yard that is 24 by 40 feet is 1,000 square feet. A back yard 33 by 33 feet is roughly 1,000 square feet. Total the square footage of all patches of lawn you have to estimate how much fertilizer to buy. Another way is to measure the outside boundaries of your property, and deduct from the calculation of its square footage an estimate of how much space is taken up by the house, gardens and other nonturf areas.

Our experience is that it's better to buy more fertilizer than necessary, rather than less. Even if you accurately measure your lawn and purchase the correct amount of fertilizer according to the label on the bag, you may not have enough. It is difficult to spread granular fertilizer uniformly and thinly. It takes some experience to learn how to spread it so that it covers the area advertised on the bag. Liz always seems to end up with more lawn than fertilizer, so we buy extra. Any unused product will keep until next year.

WHAT ABOUT LIQUID FERTILIZERS?

We do not feel that fertilizers sprayed in liquid form on the lawn are appropriate as the main meal for a low-maintenance lawn for three reasons. Liquid fertilizers use quick-acting nitrogen and therefore require four to six time-consuming applications a year. Liquid fertilizers are two to three times more expensive than granular fertilizers of the same type. And finally, many of the liquid fertilizers do not provide sufficient nitrogen in each application (1 pound of N for each 1,000 square feet per application) to effectively meet the needs of a healthy lawn. We recommend you use liquid fertilizers only for snacks (see below).

When to Fertilize

Fall is the best time to fertilize a lawn for lots of reasons. At that time, the nutrients go more toward developing the all-important root system of grass plants than toward growing more foliage. Although blade growth in the fall has slowed due to cool temperatures and the

Fall Fertilizing Is Best

❧ Increases grass density.

❧ Increases root growth.

❧ Increases drought tolerance.

❧ Improves fall to spring color.

❧ Decreases weed problems.

❧ Decreases spring mowing.

❧ Decreases summer disease problems.

approach of winter, roots still continue to grow for many weeks. If part of your lawn is under deciduous trees, then feed it after the leaves drop and be sure to remove leaves as quickly as you can to avoid their damaging the grass (remember, mulching leaves into the turf with a mulching mower is one of the best things you can do for the soil).

Spring is the next best time to fertilize, and as we mentioned earlier in this chapter, a second main meal may not even be necessary once your turf is in top condition. You feed in the spring for one of two reasons. Either your lawn is not yet in excellent, dense, healthy condition and needs a nutritional boost at the start of the season, or you want to stimulate the grass to green up sooner than it would naturally. If you have part of the lawn under deciduous trees and you wish to fertilize in the spring, the best time is about a month before the leaves come out.

The trick to fall fertilizing is to time it so the grass is approaching dormancy, but the ground is not frozen. Depending on where you live in the North, the window of opportunity is from late September through early November. Do not fertilize too early in the fall or you may get a rush of green blade growth that is vulnerable to damage from frost. Labor Day weekend is a great time to aerate, overseed and topdress, but too early to fertilize.

If you need to feed the lawn in the spring, early spring is best. You can fertilize before the lawn starts turning green but after the ground has begun to thaw.

Zoysia grass—Unlike northern grasses, zoysia grass lawns are best fed in the spring and summer. April, May and July applications are best.

How to Fertilize

Fertilizer for the main meal on low-maintenance lawns will always be granular. Spreading granular fertilizer by casting handfuls over the turf is easiest if the lawn area is very small. However, it is very difficult to get a uniform application this way. Using a spreader, either a drop spreader or rotary (spinner or cyclone) spreader, is easier for large lawns. The drop spreader is cheaper but the rotary spreader is more effective in getting uniform coverage. The throw pattern of the fertilizer "feathers" out along the edges so that the margins of each pass blend together uniformly.

With drop spreaders, overlaps and skips are common. If you use a drop spreader, the best way to avoid the dreaded and very obvious "fertilizer stripes" is to divide the fertilizer in half and set the spreader to apply at one-half the recommended rate. Then cover the lawn twice, pacing the pattern of the second pass perpendicular to the first pass.

Water It?—It is not essential to water in slow-release nitrogen fertilizer, but it does not hurt. It ensures that the fertilizer will begin working right away. Otherwise, the next rain will take care of it.

Overseeding?—If you are overseeding your lawn in the fall, you can mix the seed and the slow-release fertilizer and spread it at the same time, saving an extra step.

Liming?—Never apply lime and fertilizer to a lawn at the same time. The lime causes the fertilizer to lose much of its nitrogen, which turns into a gas. Do those two jobs at least two weeks apart.

Pest Control?—Do not use fertilizers combined with herbicides or pesticides. If areas of the lawn have weed or pest problems, treat those areas separately and at different times.

USING QUICK-RELEASE FERTILIZER

If you decide to use a quick-release granular fertilizer, the technique is the same as with the slow-release fertilizer, but you need to be very sure you don't spread too much material over any area since the quick-acting fertilizer can burn your turf if it is spread

Rotary spreaders take less time because they cover more area with each pass.

Watch for new product—Just as this book was going to press, the Toro Lawn Mower company released an exciting new device to make fertilizing the lawn a very easy task. Their new "Mow and Feed" hopper sits right on Toro and Lawn Boy mowers and dispenses fertilizer as you mow. It is probably only a matter of time before other companies come forward with a similar product. It is too good an idea.

too thickly. In fact, it is strongly recommended that after you apply quick-acting nitrogen fertilizer to a lawn, you water that fertilizer into the soil immediately. If you do not water in the material right away, much of the nitrogen will escape as a gas, reducing the effectiveness of your effort. A conventional sprinkler system works fine for this job. But don't overwater—there's no sense in leaching a lot of the nitrogen away!

WHAT ABOUT LIME?

Northern grasses prefer a pH level of between 6.0 and 7.0, which is considered just mildly acidic. They do not do well in soils that are more strongly acidic, in other words when pH levels fall below 6.0. Soils in the eastern United States tend to do just that (see map, p. 13), so yardeners in this region should plan on applying lime to their lawn every year or two as a matter of routine. Even if the pH of your soil is OK, lime provides essential calcium to your grass plants, which is not available in lawn fertilizers.

Because lime takes at least three to six months to take effect, fall is the ideal time to spread it on your turf. If you have used a slow-release nitrogen fertilizer, aerated and topdressed, and have been leaving the clippings as well, lime only every other year or so. If you use a quick-acting nitrogen fertilizer you will probably need to lime every year, because that type of fertilizer tends to enhance soil acidity. There are now liquid lime products on the market that work just fine but require two applications a year to provide the equivalent impact of the granular or powdered limestone. In Chapter One we discuss how to apply lime, how much lime to apply and how to avoid liming problems.

Important note—As we noted above but will say again: Never apply lime at the same time you apply lawn fertilizer. The lime will react with the fertilizer and much of your nitrogen will be lost as a gas. It is usually best to fertilize first and then wait several weeks or a month to spread lime.

Quick fast-acting fertilizer snacks will "green up" your lawn.

Giving Snacks
to the Lawn

We consider additional fertilizer in the form of snacks to be optional in the low-maintenance lawn. After all, this job takes more time. However, dedicated yardeners sometimes take the trouble to give their lawn snacks during the long growing season to supplement the main meal applied in the fall and spring. There is evidence that a snack, in the form of a quick-acting nitrogen fertilizer applied in late June or early July (*before* heat and/or drought sets in), boosts the ability of northern grasses to deal with the stress of high summer. If you routinely collect your grass clippings, then a snack or two of fertilizer will help compensate for the nitrogen lost from this source.

A snack of fast-acting fertilizer may also be in order if you are having a major outdoor event at your home, such as a wedding or a party, or if you are about to try to sell your house. A quickie snack will green up the grass intensely for a period of a few weeks when you want some cosmetic improvement of its appearance.

Either granular or liquid quick-acting nitrogen fertilizer is appropriate for a snack. The liquid form is definitely more convenient to apply using a hose-end applicator, but it is quite a bit more expensive.

Giving Lawn Vitamins

Vitamins, either in food or as supplements, improve the ability of people's bodies to make the best use of the nutrition in food. Liquid bioactivators work the same way for grass. These products, containing seaweed, kelp or various synthetic hormones and enzymes, improve each grass plant's ability to absorb macro- and micronutrients from the soil. Acting as a tonic, they also increase the grass's drought resistance, insect resistance and disease resistance. A lawn dosed once or twice a season with these "vitamins" will be healthier than one that gets none. However, you can have a fine lawn and not use any liquid bioactivators; they are definitely optional.

Bioactivator products are almost always sprayed on the turf, even though they may be packaged as dry powder. Diluted with water, they can be applied with a hose-end sprayer or a pressure sprayer of some kind. They can be given to the lawn once, twice or even three times a year. If you choose to use them just once, then early summer is the best time. If you want to give your lawn three applications, spray first just before the grass greens up in the spring to give the lawn a good start. Then spray a second time in early July to improve drought resistance, and spray again in late August to help the grass prepare for winter dormancy.

Providing vitamins for the lawn is definitely optional. Even one dose requires time and effort that moves you out of a strictly low-maintenace mode. While they do benefit turf growth, vitamins are not essential for a wonderful lawn—especially if you leave the clippings and follow our other suggestions.

Feeding Brand-New Lawns

When you are starting a lawn from scratch by planting seed in bare soil, use a fertilizer designed precisely for that situation. The product label will indicate if it is for newly seeded lawns. While "starter" fertilizers come in both slow-release and quick-release form, we of course prefer the slow-release nitrogen products. At the beginning of turf development, phosphorus and potassium are almost more important than nitrogen. The emphasis is on getting new grass plants started properly with strong root systems. The proportion of phosphorus and potassium will be greater in fertilizers for use on new lawns.

Never Feed a Stressed Lawn!

While there are folks who believe that feeding a cold helps get rid of the cold, the same principle definitely does not apply to a lawn. If your lawn is stressed in any way, *do not fertilize it!* Stress can be caused by drought. It can be caused by disease or insect attack. A lawn that is sick should not be fed. Get rid of the cause of the stress and then you can consider fertilizing it.

ᴠ   ᴠ   ᴠ

For those of us interested in the best possible lawn for the least possible effort, fertilizing is an area where we can save a lot of time. By incorporating practices such as leaving clippings, encouraging earthworms and using slow-release type fertilizer, it is possible to build and maintain fertile, nutritious soil that will support vigorous grass plants with only one fertilizing session, rather than three or four.

Read on to discover how to save even more time with good watering practices.

Chapter Four

Watering the Lawn

We suspect that over half of the yardeners in the northern part of the country never water their lawns, and probably most of those lawns would benefit from some water during the dry spells of summer. On the other hand, unfortunately, yardeners who do water their lawns often tend to overwater them, especially in the hottest part of the summer. Either practice can cause unnecessary lawn problems. If you have a healthy turf growing in a very good soil in the North, you need to water only occasionally, and some years not at all.

This chapter discusses how to water effectively, saving time and water yet guaranteeing a healthy turf. Before we discuss how to water, however, we want to discuss ways to minimize the need for watering your lawn. As you might predict, in this as in other lawn issues, a healthy lawn requires less effort on our part because it is more capable of taking care of its own needs.

Principles for
Watering Lawns

🌿 Water infrequently.

🌿 Water deeply.

🌿 Water in the morning.

Good Soil Means Less Watering

We feel it makes more sense to promote conditions in our yard that encourage self-reliant grass so that nature handles most of the watering chores, giving us more time for other activities. To do this, we make sure the soil that supports the grass plants is as healthy and vital as possible.

ORGANIC MATERIAL STORES WATER

We talked in Chapter One about the benefits of having 3–5 percent of your soil made up of organic material such as compost, peat moss or sludge. Organic material is the food for all those billions of microbes that are busy conditioning and enriching the soil. However, that organic material has another very important job: It stores water. Particles of organic matter act like microscopic sponges, soaking up and holding water. Soil that has been enriched with organic matter holds more moisture longer after a rain—two to three times longer—than patches that are primarily plain old dirt with little or no organic matter. The more able the soil is to store water, the longer the grass can go without rain or watering. Thus, the less often you need to wrestle with the hose.

DEEP ROOTS NEED LESS WATER

The deeper the root systems of the grass grow, the more able they are to find water in the soil. They use available water so efficiently that they can withstand longer dry periods without supplemental water from you. As we've noted earlier in this book, the roots of healthy

northern turf grass should be at least 4–6 inches deep. Kentucky bluegrass is capable of generating root systems as long as 8 inches and turf-type tall fescue can produce 12-inch-long roots if soil conditions permit. That is the problem. The grass in most American lawns is trying to survive in compacted, inferior soil. Consequently, typical grass has stunted roots that penetrate the soil only 2 or 3 inches.

Inspect the roots of your grass by digging up a plug or splitting the turf apart with a spade. If the root system of the grass goes down only about 2 inches, be assured that that grass is always going to need watering when the soil gets just the least bit dry. Check Chapter One for the steps to take to develop turf with a deep, healthy root system. Aerating is one of the most important steps in fixing a shallow root problem.

Proper Care Means Less Watering

As you can see in the sidebar, how you care for your lawn makes a big difference in how much additional water it needs to remain good-looking. All of the techniques for managing a low-maintenance lawn will lead to deeper roots and therefore less need for water.

MOW TALL

When you mow grass tall, 2 inches or higher, its roots grow more deeply. As we've mentioned, tall grass shades the soil enough to reduce the normal evaporation of water out of that soil. Therefore, more water is available for use by the plants. When you leave the clippings as you mow, they form a light mulch around the base of the grass plants that also reduces the loss of water through evaporation.

USE A SHARP BLADE

A sharp mower blade cuts grass foliage cleanly. By avoiding ragged, flayed tips which release more moisture from the plant into the atmosphere, sharp blades assure that water is conserved for use by the grass plants.

FERTILIZE LIGHTLY

Adding lots of nitrogen to the lawn causes moisture loss too. It stimulates rapid blade growth above the mowing level and into air currents. The air flow "wicks away" moisture from the tissues of the blades, again reducing moisture available to the grass plants. Experts recommend limiting any single application of nitrogen to less than 1 pound per 1,000 square feet. Overdoses of nitrogen require much more frequent mowing, which, in turn, limits the development of deep root systems. Constantly regrowing blades in response to mowing causes grass to use more water. During drought periods, underdeveloped roots cannot keep up with this demand for water and stressed, wilting grass frequently signals that it needs watering.

GOOD TIMING SAVES WATER

Sometimes all you need to do to reduce the need to water is to time lawn care tasks more carefully.

Avoid Spring Irrigation—Try not to water your lawn at all in the spring. This will prevent the grass from becoming overly dependent on a steady water supply. Slight drying out of the soil in the spring stimulates grass roots to reach deeper into the soil for moisture. Making this effort will pay off for the grass plants later, when the going gets tough in the summer heat.

Factors That Restrict Growth of Turf Roots

- Compacted soil.
- Grass cut too short.
- Too much fertilizer.
- Light, frequent watering.
- Acidic soil.

Factors That Promote Root Growth

- Aerating.
- Mowing tall.
- Adding lime.
- Watering deeply.
- Using slow-release fertilizer.

Avoid Major Maintenance Activities in Summer—Applying fertilizers and pesticides, aerating and de-thatching are all important lawn care activities. However, when performed in the high heat of summer, they put extra stress on grass plants, so they need more water. These tasks are best done in the spring and the fall, anyway. Then it's easier on the yardener as well as on the grass.

Can You Live with Dormant Grass?

All northern grasses will naturally go dormant in the heat of the summer if they do not get enough water, either from rain or from you. Going dormant doesn't mean they are dying. They simply stop growing, turn brown and wait for the rains of fall to turn them green and start them growing again. This is the natural survival mechanism that grasses on the African savannah and elsewhere use too. This does not mean that grass can go completely without moisture all summer and still survive. Even in the dormant stage, grass needs some water to survive into the fall.

If you have a very large lawn, and no easy way to irrigate it, one option is to consider letting your lawn go dormant if summer rainfall is scarce. Yardeners in California and Washington states have had to allow their lawns to go brown in recent years because of restricted water supplies. However, short of water emergencies, our feeling is that the whole point of having a lawn is to have a rich green sward. It enhances the landscape, setting off colorful ornamental plants and linking areas of the yard together into a pleasing landscape. Therefore, we feel that letting the lawn go dormant defeats its primary purpose. If the lawn is too big to water, then maybe you should consider making the lawn smaller.

Kentucky bluegrass and perennial ryegrass lawns are the first to go dormant in a dry, hot summer spell. Tall fescue requires a lot of drought before it gives up. Zoysia, a southern grass, is really reluctant to go dormant in the North, which rarely gets hot and dry enough to discourage it. (However, it is notoriously quick to turn brown the minute warm weather ends.) The long and short of it is that to keep your lawn looking green and healthy throughout the summer, you will probably have to water occasionally. Let's look at when that will occur.

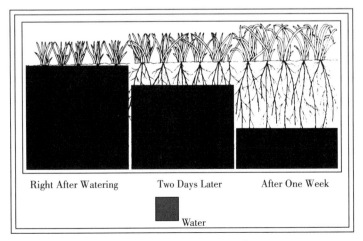

Right After Watering   Two Days Later   After One Week

Water

Water moves downward as it leaves the soil from the surface.

When to Water

You water your lawn when it truly needs water—not before. If you water your grass before it really needs it, you are asking for trouble—

shorter roots, disease-prone grass and insect-prone grass. Lots of terrible things, besides wasting your valuable time, result from premature or too frequent watering.

Usually, watering the lawn isn't necessary until summer arrives and rainfall diminishes. In any case, wait until the grass tells you it needs water. How does it do that?

Signs That Grass Is Thirsty

There are three ways your turf tells you it needs water. The most subtle is that it changes color and texture. When grass gets thirsty it wilts and acquires a bluish tinge. The leaves or grass blades start to curl or fold in along their edges. Once you become acquainted with these signs, you will be able to recognize them more easily.

Meanwhile, the soil gets harder as it dries out. So, if it resists the pressure of a screwdriver punched into the turf soil, that's a likely sign that it needs moisture. If the screwdriver penetrates the soil very easily, then there is sufficient moisture there to support the grass.

The lawn also signals that it is thirsty if, when you walk on it, your footprints linger for several hours. Normally, hydrated grass blades quickly return to their upright posture after being stepped on. Leaves lacking water, however, will remain trampled for a period of time. If your footprints remain, it's time to water the lawn. Remember, lawns mowed with dull mower blades have grass whose tips turn brown. Do not mistake that as a sign of thirst. Just sharpen the mower blade.

Shade and Water Needs

An area of the lawn under trees, even those with high canopies, can be deceptive in terms of watering needs in July and August. Those shady areas often feel cool and comfortable and leave one feeling that watering is not necessary. In fact the opposite is probably true. Lawn grass in partial shade will need watering more often than grass out in the sun. Why? Because that grass is competing with trees for water and the trees will usually win. In fact, these areas may need three times as much water as the rest of the lawn. This is partly because large trees and shrubs are very thirsty, and partly because light rains often fail to penetrate thick foliage canopies and the soil below gets cheated of natural moisture.

Not only do you want to provide enough water for grass and trees, but you also want to avoid inadvertently encouraging the tree roots to gravitate toward the surface of the soil in search of water. So when you feel your summer weather is such that watering may be necessary, check in the shady areas first because that is where you will need to water first.

If You Have a Good Lawn—If your grass has good roots and your soil has a reasonable amount of humus, then you should not have to water in the spring or fall at all. After two weeks without rain during these seasons, look for signs that the grass may be thirsty. Do not be surprised if you do not see any for several more days. In the summer, think about watering if you have not had a good rain (at least an inch) for over ten days to two weeks. Again, let your grass tell you when it is time.

If You Have a Poor Lawn—If you have a lawn that is still in poor shape (shallow root system, compacted soil, etc.), then you will have to be a bit more watchful. Typically, it will show symptoms of thirst within about ten days in the spring or fall, and within a week in the summer if rainfall is scarce. You may have to start watering earlier in the summer. The grass plants may signal that they need extra water as early as May. They are not lying to you. Until you improve the lawn you may have to water much more often than your neighbor who has a healthy lawn with a deep root system.

TIME OF DAY TO WATER

Depending on whom you consult, there are different "rules" about what time of day is best to water the lawn. In our opinion, the best time is when we have the time—morning, noon or night. Now, if your schedule allows you a choice, the morning is really the best time to water. This way, grass starts the day with plenty of moisture, and foliage has lots of time to dry off before evening. If you water in the heat of the day, you will lose water from evaporation. If you water during windy periods, you also lose water to evaporation. If you water in the evening, the grass spends the night in a moist environment that may foster fungal disease. But again, if that is the only time you have in your schedule and you know your grass needs water, water your lawn.

HOW MUCH TO WATER

When the soil does dry out and the grass needs water, the formula is: Water deeply. In order for the lawn to get the water it really needs to stay healthy, water generously enough that the water soaks down into the soil where the roots are—at least 4–6 inches. Too much water leaches past the root zone and is wasted, and too little fails to reach the roots.

TYPE OF SOIL AND WATERING NEEDS

Even if you have added sufficient organic material to your lawn every few years, the type of soil you have will influence the amount of water necessary to adequately hydrate a thirsty lawn. We are not expecting you to be an agronomist, a scientist of soils, and to diagnose your soil type. Just get a sense of whether the soil under your turf is generally sandy, loamy or clay. Don't worry about all the degrees in between those broad categories. In Chapter Five we show you how to determine the type of soil you have.

Different soil types retain water differently even with the same percentage of organic matter. Soil type, therefore, determines the amount of time you spend watering and how much water you need to deliver to grass plants at any one time. The chart shows the difference in volumes of water you need to cover that root area depending on your type of soil. Without worrying too much about being scientifically accurate, we can observe that if you have very sandy soil, you will use much less water in any one application than if you have a heavy clay soil.

FIGURING WATER NEEDS

Technical calculations to determine how much water the lawn needs are not necessary for yardeners. For example, we don't feel it is necessary for you to figure how many gallons of water per square foot your lawn, cut at 2 inches, is transpiring in 85° temperatures for six hours. Understanding some basics is enough. You know that grass needs more water in the summer than in the spring. Grass in clay needs more than grass in sandy soil. Grass in the shade under trees and shrubs needs more than grass in the sun.

MEASURE WATERING IN INCHES AND TIME

The easiest way to determine how much water to give a thirsty lawn is to use the "1-inch rule." Using low-maintenance standards, most northern lawns use about 1 inch of water a week during the spring and fall seasons in loamy soil (more in clay, less in sand). When the weather is very hot and dry during the summer months (no rain for long periods), grass plants might need up to 2 inches of water a week in a loamy soil (more in clay, less in sand). *Note:* While they might need 2 inches for the week, give them only about 1 inch at a time, otherwise you will be wasting water through runoff.

So let's assume we need to give our lawn about an inch of water because it is looking bluish and retains footprints for several hours. While an oscillating sprinkler system produces about 1 inch of water when it runs forty to sixty minutes, it isn't necessary to know this.

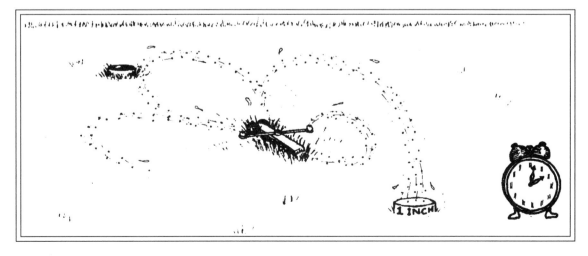

Regardless of the type of sprinkler, if you simply set some empty cans (cat food or tuna fish cans are about 1 inch deep) out in the pattern of the sprinkler device and time how long it takes for them to fill with water as it runs, you'll know about how long to run the system in the future to deliver an inch of water.

For example, after you've determined that your particular sprinkler produces 1 inch of water in fifty-four minutes, then attach a mechanical timer to your system and run the water for fifty-four minutes in each area that needs water. This is the system that Liz uses.

It's very difficult to inspect your soil to see if it has received enough water, since most of us prefer not to dig holes in our lawn. One somewhat unscientific trick is to stick a screwdriver down into the soil after watering. The screwdriver should slide into the soil easily up to its handle. It's not precise, but it gives you some indication.

Watering Problem Areas

Since it is possible that you do not quite have a lawn that handles most of its own watering needs, here are some watering tips to help you compensate.

WATERING COMPACTED SOIL

In some cases, you need to be concerned about whether your soil can absorb water as fast as your watering system can deliver it. If you have a very compacted soil, or if your soil is a dense clay with very little organic content, then it is possible that your watering system can provide water faster than the soil can absorb it. If so, to avoid wasteful runoff, water in steps. Water until it begins to puddle. Turn off the system. Wait fifteen minutes to half an hour and then water some more until puddling occurs again.

Lawn areas that are moist, firm and have no visible puddles are ready for a repeat irrigation cycle. Areas that are soft and produce squishy footprints when walked on are not ready to receive additional irrigation. When they are ready, water a second time to make sure the lawn gets enough water overall.

WATERING LAWNS WITH THATCH

Thatch is somewhat hydrophobic, which means it tends to repel water. Because it is difficult to moisten, it prevents water from passing through it into the soil. The result is uneven moisture throughout the lawn. To counteract this effect, use a wetting agent, called a "surfactant," when watering a heavily thatched lawn.

A surfactant, such as mild dishwashing liquid or a product specifically designed for this purpose available at garden centers, makes thatch able to absorb the water and pass it through to the soil. Spray it on the lawn with a hose-end sprayer, using about half water and half soap, or follow the directions on the labels of commercial surfactants. The best way to solve this problem, of course, is to get rid of the thatch. We explain how to do this in Chapter Twelve.

Watering a New Lawn

Whether your new lawn has been seeded or created with new sod, watering is critical to its success. Most people stop watering a new lawn too soon.

WATERING SEEDED LAWNS

Homeowners almost always fail to water newly planted grass seed sufficiently. To have its best chance for germination, grass seed needs to be kept moist *all the time!* Although turf professionals lightly water new seed beds three to five times a day, most yardeners don't have time to go out and move the sprinkler around the whole new lawn five times a day. So we do the best we can. At the very least, as we have discovered the hard way, newly seeded lawns must be watered at least twice a day. While most of us will be able to manage morning and evening sessions, for those who work at home, midday is actually the best time to water.

Missing only one day of watering new grass seed can reduce germination by 30 percent. If you miss two days (that getaway weekend?) you may lose over 50 percent germination. It is very important to keep the top 1/4–1/2 inch of soil from drying out for the first two to three weeks of a new lawn.

NEW SOD LAWNS

For new sod, watering is just as important. The sod itself must be thoroughly wet throughout its roots and soil, and the soil bed where it is laid must be wet down to an inch or two. Once it is installed, sod cannot be allowed to dry out at all. Water well between pieces of sod and along the sidewalks and driveways where the water evaporates more quickly. They dry out first.

Dealing with Drought
and Watering Restrictions

Unfortunately, drought conditions are not uncommon even in the North, and when a drought occurs, local governments are forced to establish restrictions on the use of water. Often, use of water for irrigating lawns is high on the list of no-no's. (Sometimes they will exempt newly seeded lawns, because moisture is so critical for them.) If your area experiences a drought, you can drastically reduce the use of water without having to lose the entire lawn.

As we mentioned earlier, northern grasses will go dormant in hot and dry weather. This dormancy is a survival mechanism that served the ancestors of our turf grasses that grew in arid prairies in Africa and elsewhere. It works essentially the same way in our yard. However, it does not guarantee that a lawn will fully recover from the water deprivation if absolutely no water is made available during the drought period. So you will need to provide some moisture for your lawn, restrictions notwithstanding. Often, water restrictions allow hand watering in the yard.

While estimates vary, a lawn that has gone dormant will need to receive 1–1 1/2 inches every two to three weeks during the drought period to prevent complete loss of the turf. The grass may not show a noticeable greening, but that amount of irrigation should be sufficient to hydrate the lower plant portions and increase the recovery once adequate moisture is available.

During times of extreme or extended drought, try not to walk on the lawn at all, especially after watering. Drought-stressed grass will not recover from damage as rapidly as healthy grass. More importantly, wet soils will compact to a greater extent than dry soils, even under normal foot traffic.

If drought is a chronic problem in your area and can be anticipated almost every year, adjust your lawn care practices to accommodate that reality. You will reduce overall watering needs in your lawn if you feed your lawn only in the fall and not in the spring and summer. If you have a Kentucky bluegrass lawn, change it to a turf-type tall fescue lawn which, once established, is far more drought resistant.

Once a drought is over, a dormant lawn that has received some moisture every two or three weeks takes about three to four weeks to recover. The brown look gradually gives way to a rich, full, green appearance again.

The amount of time you will spend watering your lawn will be reduced significantly when you've developed a strong, healthy, dense turf growing in a vital soil containing lots of organic matter. The next section of this book tells you how to achieve this goal.

SECTION II

IMPROVING YOUR LAWN

Chapter Five

Assessing the Lawn's Condition and Size

Section I was devoted to a discussion of general lawn care. While reviewing the various routine cultural practices such as soil aeration, mowing, watering and fertilizing, we explained how you can move toward a low-maintenance regimen in lawn care that enhances your lawn as well as your free time. That discussion presumed that your lawn was in reasonably decent shape, so that the remedial low-maintenance practices such as leaving clippings, using slow-release fertilizer judiciously and occasionally aerating and topdressing would upgrade it sufficiently.

However, the typical American lawn is not in reasonably decent shape. More often than not, it is in dire straits and, while the changes in maintenance practices will certainly improve it, they are not sufficient in themselves to truly regenerate it in vigor and long-term health.

In this section we provide you with techniques for diagnosing and correcting severe soil and turf problems that go beyond quick-fix measures. If a lawn is in disastrous shape, like ours was when we moved to our house eighteen years ago, then major structural changes—correction of profound soil problems and replacement of grass—are necessary.

While all this work would seem to contradict the idea of "low maintenance," it is, in fact, part of getting there. Time, money and energy invested at the outset to establish a good foundation for your turf pay off handsomely in the future.

Checking the Condition of Your Lawn

Most yardeners probably don't spend much time worrying about the underlying structure of their turf. The lawn is usually already in place when they buy the house and so they are blissfully ignorant of the condition of the soil under the grass and the condition of grass itself in terms of its age, its variety and general growing characteristics.

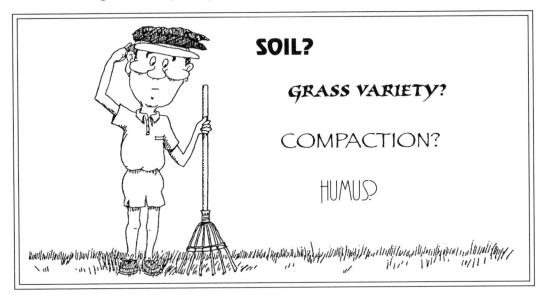

However, this is information that you should have if you intend to have an attractive, low-maintenance lawn. How do you know what the situation is and whether a major overhaul of your soil or grass is necessary? This chapter deals with how to evaluate the condition of your existing soil and grass to determine if major work is needed. Chapters Six, Seven and Eight offer follow-up instructions on how to accomplish this structural rehabilitation of the turf.

Defining "Renovation"

Renovating a lawn means taking steps to make the soil and/or the grass as good as new—renewed and revitalized. While it requires lots of work, it is something you only do once (unless you move!). Once a healthy foundation for your lawn is established, regular care will assure its continued health and beauty. We have found that if you take care of the soil, it will take care of the grass. Moreover, if the grass has the newly developed built-in disease, drought and pest resistance, your lawn can, to a great degree, take care of itself. A healthy soil and the proper grass seed take you a long way toward a successful low-maintenance lawn.

Do You Have Dirt or Soil?

We like to make a distinction between "dirt" and "soil." If you are growing plants in material that has no life, has little fertility and does little to support healthy plant growth, then we say you are growing plants in "dirt." If you have a medium that has sufficient air, water, minerals and microbial life to ensure healthy plant growth, you have "soil." So, are you growing grass in dirt or in soil? If you have dirt, you may need to take some steps to make it soil.

Determining Whether Your Soil Needs Renovation

If you don't want to take the time to check your soil with the various tests outlined in this chapter, you can take this short quiz to learn whether you have dirt or soil under your grass.

You will likely need to renovate your soil if in the past five years:

🌿 You have *not* aerated the lawn.

🌿 You have *not* added organic material to the lawn.

🌿 You have *not* left the clippings on the lawn.

If you find that you do need to renovate your soil, you can skip the soil section of this chapter and go directly to the next chapter dealing with soil renovation. You are growing grass in compacted dirt with little life in it. It needs work.

In the previous chapters we learned that leaving the clippings, aerating the lawn and periodically adding a thin layer of organic material to improve the soil will serve, over time, to recondition the soil. The question is whether your soil needs more intensive care.

You do not have to be a soil scientist to figure out whether your soil needs some renovation. All you need to do is answer three fairly simple questions. Is your soil compacted? Does it have sufficient organic material in the top 12 inches? Is it protected from the harsh effects of wind and sun? In this section we suggest some easy tests to help you answer those questions. You don't have to use all the tests. If two or three tests indicate that your soil is definitely compacted, then don't waste your time with more tests; you need to fix that compaction problem.

IS THE SOIL COMPACTED?

Grass does not grow well in compacted soil. The spaces between particles of soil that normally store air and water are so compressed in compacted soil that little air or water is present. Microorganisms cannot reproduce and generate the nutrients needed by grass plants. Grass roots, seriously deprived of these vital elements (air, water and nutrients), are badly stunted; the grass is stressed. There are a number of ways to determine if the soil under your turf is so seriously compacted that it needs to be repaired.

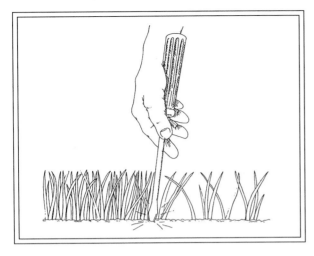

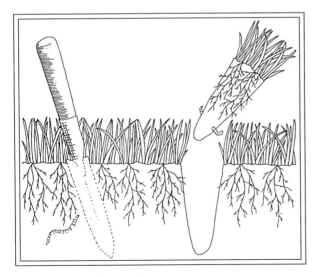

Surface Tree Roots

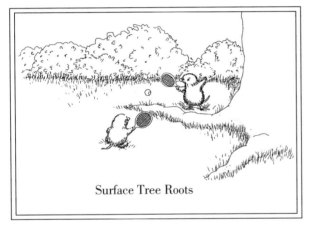

SCREWDRIVER TEST FOR COMPACTION

Test for compaction by inserting a large screwdriver into the turf when the soil is dry. If it is hard to push the screwdriver down into the soil, that suggests a compaction problem. It is relatively easy to push a screwdriver into uncompacted soil that is dry.

INSPECT TREE SURFACE ROOTS

Perhaps one of the most obvious indicators of serious soil compaction is tree roots that are exposed in the lawn. Normally, a tree's feeder roots range through the top 4–8 inches of soil seeking air, water and nutrients. This is, of course, exactly the same area where the grass roots are looking for nutrients, air and water. The limited amount of air in compacted soil not only stunts grass roots, but it also forces tree roots to rise toward the surface of the soil in search of oxygen. So the presence of tree roots bulging above the soil surface signals compaction of the soil. In Chapter Twelve we explain how to deal with surface tree roots.

NOTICE BARE SPOTS

The frequent appearance of bare spots in your lawn, small spots where grass just disappears, suggests a soil compaction problem. Areas of the lawn where there is routine foot traffic often become bare. The weight of passersby gradually compresses the soil, killing the grass in these spots—a good indicator of compacted soil.

CHECK DEPTH OF GRASS ROOTS

The roots of your grass plants will tell you a whole lot about the condition of the soil, especially whether it is compacted. Believe it or not, one single grass plant is capable of generating 375 miles of roots with as many as 14 million individual root strands, having a total surface area of 2,500 square feet. That's just one (healthy) grass plant! Isn't that amazing? Since a square foot of vigorous turf typically has up to 850 of those plants, grass roots are extensive and pervasive in the soil.

The point here is that it takes that many roots to provide a grass plant with sufficient nutrients every day. Only in healthy, active, well-drained soil can grass plants develop such extensive root systems. Grass that is cut too closely and/or grown in compacted soil is not able to do this. It struggles to survive with only a small portion of its potential root volume, which severely reduces its capacity to get nutrients from the soil. So, the depth of the roots of your grass will indicate how badly your soil is compacted.

The best way to check grass roots is to dig a sample core from the turf. Choose a time when the soil is moist. Using a trowel or sharp knife, dig down as far as the tool allows (preferably 4–6 inches) and extract a chunk of sod—turf, roots and some dirt. Examine how deeply the roots penetrate the soil. If they go down less than 4 inches into the soil, chances are it is because the soil is too compacted. Jeff was shocked to discover that our grass roots were only 2 inches deep. We later learned that, unfortunately, that is typical of most lawns.

Measure Thatch Layer

Thatch is the layer of dead organic material that accumulates on top of the soil at the base of the grass plants. It is composed of decomposing grass clippings and shallow-growing grass roots, or "stolons," that have started to grow on the soil surface. A certain amount of thatch, 1/4 inch or less, is desirable and should be no cause for concern. However, as you inspect your core of soil and grass, if there is as much as 1/2 inch or more of thatch in the turf sample, then it is likely that your soil is compacted. Thick thatch 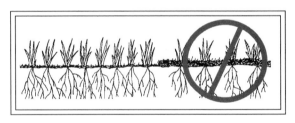 can also indicate overenthusiastic fertilizing and watering. Chapter Twelve deals with how to eliminate thatch problems.

Examine Lawn Weeds

Mother Nature has many ways of signalling compacted soil. Simply by identifying the weeds that are growing most commonly in your lawn, you can get a clue. If you have chickweed or plantain in your lawn, the chances are good that you have compacted soil because those two weeds favor areas that have been cultivated and then compacted.

Check Soil Drainage

Normal, healthy soil manages to simultaneously drain well, yet retain moisture. It is able to do this only because its structure is loose—not compacted—and because of its physical and chemical composition. So, if your soil does not drain well after a rain or your watering, that suggests that it is not healthy. You may need to improve its structure and content. There are several ways to evaluate your soil's capacity to drain efficiently.

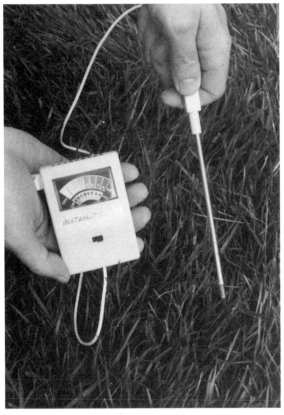

Houseplant Water Meter

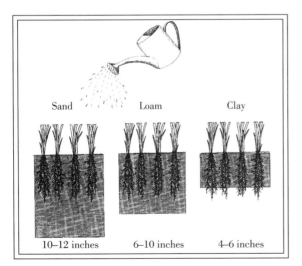

Sand

Loam

Clay

10–12 inches

6–10 inches

4–6 inches

Observe Puddles after a Rain—While puddles may indicate compacted soil, they also indicate drainage problems. Even compressed soil, if it has certain physical and chemical properties, will drain halfway decently. So the puddles may be signalling deficiencies in the composition of your soil.

Check Water Runoff—Like puddles, rivulets of water that run off the turf when it rains rather than soak into the soil are suspicious. Water flowing off the lawn in streams similar to the flow of runoff down the driveway when it rains suggest that soil under your grass may be just as incapable of absorbing water as the paved drive! Obviously, this soil needs repair if it is to support healthy grass plants.

Evaluate Water Penetration—Examine a sample core of turf after a good rain. If your soil's drainage is satisfactory, the core should be moist all the way through its 4–6 inch depth. Another way to determine just how deeply an inch of rain has penetrated the soil is to use a houseplant water meter. Take it outside and insert the probe into the turf as you would into a container holding a plant. Do this at several spots over the lawn area. The meter will register the degree of moisture at each site. Where soil is dry, compaction is likely to be the culprit.

Of course, some soils, by their very nature, are looser and more absorbent of moisture than others. In the next chapter, dealing with soil rehabilitation, we will discuss the differences in sandy, loamy or clay-based soils and how their respective structures can be improved to facilitate drainage.

How Much Organic Material Is in Your Soil?

After looking at your compaction situation, the next issue is whether your soil has sufficient organic matter to be healthy and fertile. Healthy grass needs a soil that provides sufficient nutrition for those plants. As we described in Chapter One, good soil teems with microbial and earthworm activity which generates nutrients in the form that plants can best utilize.

The soil can do that if it has enough organic material and the proper balance of minerals, and is in an environment conducive to releasing those minerals to the plants. Organic matter, or humus, is that stuff that will decompose. It includes old dead roots, decomposing leaves, decomposing grass clippings, dead worms, dead microbes and anything else that was alive and then died and decomposed.

Again, you don't have to take every test listed below. As we noted earlier in the chapter, if you have not left your grass clippings on the lawn and if you have not added any amendments such as peat moss or compost to your lawn in the past five years, you can assume that your soil is quite devoid of organic matter and that you definitely need to add some this season.

Sufficient Organic Material?

🍃 Earthworm count.

🍃 Check humus content.

🍃 Examine the weeds.

Earthworm Count

While not very scientific, the easiest way to check the organic content of your soil is to count its earthworms. Earthworms will not spend much time in soil devoid of organic material since that is the stuff they eat. No humus—no earthworms. To check your earthworm population, dig a hole in your lawn about 12 inches deep and about 12 inches across, roughly a cubic foot of soil. Do this when the soil is not bone dry but rather nicely moist. Worms move out of dry soil.

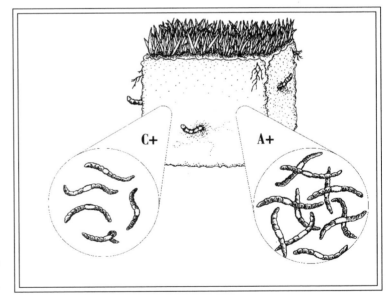

Deposit the cubic foot of soil on a newspaper and break it up to expose its worms so you can take a census. Healthy soil has at least five earthworms per cubic foot. Very healthy soil easily supports twenty-five worms per cubic foot. Soil rich in organic material (5 percent) can support large worm populations. Conversely, soil lacking it, lacks worms.

ORGANIC CONTENT OF SOIL

A healthy soil does not need a massive amount of humus to support healthy plants. The ideal is somewhere between 3 percent and 5 percent in the top 12 inches, not a great amount, relatively speaking. The only accurate way to determine the organic content of this "topsoil" is with a laboratory soil test. However, you can eyeball your soil for a rough indication.

Similar to the earthworm count, dig a hole in your lawn about 12 inches square. Most organic matter is very dark in color, so the darker the upper layer of topsoil (with some exceptions we won't worry about at this moment), the more likely you have a generous percentage of organic matter. If the topsoil is the same light color as the subsoil (the dirt down at the bottom of a 1-foot-deep hole), then you can suspect that you've used up most of the humus or, worse, the topsoil was removed when the house was built and never replaced by the contractor.

Ideally the 3–5 percent organic matter, or humus, is distributed throughout the top 12 inches of soil. So if all the topsoil is in the top 2 inches and all the rest of that 12-inch layer is subsoil, you will have a problem growing healthy grass. Remember, those roots need to go down at least 4–6 inches, and 8–12 inches is better. If you determine that you are growing grass in subsoil, then we suggest you consider a major renovation of the soil.

ONCE AGAIN, THOSE WEEDS TELL A WHOLE LOT

As in the case of compaction and drainage problems, weeds often provide a telltale clue to unhealthy soil. That is because they are adapted to lousy soil. They can thrive in subsoil and soil that is so lacking in structure, drainage and humus content as to be essentially dead. Cultivated plants, such as grass, cannot manage in these conditions, so weeds take over. Clovers, ground ivy and various thistles are weeds commonly found in lawns growing in poor soils.

IS THE SOIL PROTECTED?

It may sound a bit ridiculous to ask whether the soil under your grass is protected from the environment. How can the sun and wind affect soil covered by turf? Well, this issue may not be quite so important for soil under grass as it is for soil in garden beds, but it still deserves your attention. Any soil exposed directly to the sun, wind and rain is adversely affected and is under stress from that environment. *The simple rule is that there should be no bare soil anywhere on your entire property!*

If the grass over your soil is not very dense, then the sun's rays can reach the dirt and dry it out. The wind then blows the dust away, causing minor erosion. Similarly, rain can hit the exposed soil and cause slow but steady compaction. Look beyond your lawn to those areas under trees and shrubs growing in the yard, maybe in the turf. Is the soil under those plants bare or almost

---

Protecting Soil from Environmental Stress

- Grow thick grass.
- Spread ground covers around trees.
- Leave the clippings.
- Mulch any bare soil.

bare? If so, it is suffering from the elements. Soil under trees and shrubs should always be mulched if it is not covered by grass. Here again is another good reason to leave your clippings on the lawn as you mow. Those clippings serve as a mulch for the soil, protecting it from the impact of sun, wind and rain.

In the end, if any or all of the soil in your lawn has been exposed to the elements for many years, then some serious renovation may be in order.

Why Renew the Grass?

After diagnosing possible soil problems that need to be addressed, the next step in determining whether lawn renovation is necessary is to evaluate the grass situation. It may not be enough to repair the soil. You may have to also renew, perhaps even totally replant, the grass.

It is likely that you have "tired" grass which reduces the attractiveness and health of your lawn. Grass plants that have been in place for more than five years have less vigor than recently planted grasses. They lack the drought, pest and disease resistance of the newly developed seed strains. So even if the soil is healthy, and it probably is not, your grass plants are struggling.

It is a relatively simple process to upgrade the lawn by changing over to new grass. Do it quickly by installing a new lawn in one season or do it gradually by patching bare areas or overseeding the existing lawn with new grass seed over a few seasons. Chapters Seven and Eight deal with choosing the right grass and how to improve turf grass. First, you must decide how extensive a job is necessary. No point in doing more work that you have to!

LOOKING AT YOUR GRASS

Can you figure out what type of grass you have? It's not absolutely critical, but it helps to know sometimes. Most northern lawns contain mostly Kentucky bluegrass, especially if they were planted more than five years ago. You may have more than one type of grass; sometimes different parts of the property have been planted with different types of grass such as perennial rye or a fescue. Knowing this, you may wish to change the type of grass to get a more uniform look over all the yard. Then again, you may wish to vary the type of lawn to accommodate its use. In any case, there are some tests you can take in figuring out whether your lawn grass needs minor or major renovation.

Often, homeowners are dissatisfied with the general appearance or look of their lawns. Even though there are no obvious bare spots, there are some indicators that suggest that renewal may be in order. By studying your grass closely you can get a sense of its general condition.

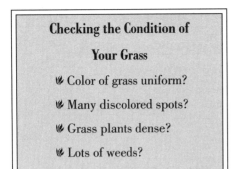

Checking the Condition of

Your Grass

❧ Color of grass uniform?

❧ Many discolored spots?

❧ Grass plants dense?

❧ Lots of weeds?

CHECK THE COLOR OF GRASS BLADES

A healthy lawn should have a nice uniform green color. It is more important that the color be uniform than show a deep, dark shade of green in order to indicate health.

The deep green color that has become the standard, and is promoted by advertising photographs, is typical only of Kentucky bluegrass recently fertilized with a quick-acting nitrogen fertilizer. Then, grass plants are briefly bursting with top growth and are as green as they can get. For this reason this rich color is actually an artificial standard. It is unrealistic to expect grass to look this way all of the time. Grass that is properly cared for and living in healthy soil, rather than being hyped with fast-acting fertilizer, is more typically a medium green color.

The color of grass also varies somewhat according to its variety, the weather over the year and the condition of the soil. For example, while grass tends to be slightly yellow-green in the spring when it newly emerges from dormancy, at other times the same bright, pale green color indicates that it is receiving excessive amounts of nitrogen fertilizer. A lawn suffering from poor soil may have a splotchy look with deep green spots and light green spots. Over time, previous owners may have spot-seeded with different varieties of grass, giving the lawn a mottled look. A healthy lawn has a uniform color of medium green over its entire surface. That is what you are looking for.

EXAMINE DISCOLORED SPOTS IN TURF

Circles or rings of yellow or brown anywhere in the lawn can mean any number of problems. Chapter Nine helps you diagnose whether those spots come from insects, disease or even the neighbor's dog. Usually, dealing with discolored spots does not require renovating the whole lawn. At the same time, once you've diagnosed the problem, you may find you need to change the kind of grass you are growing to one that is more resistant to the insect or disease that is causing problems.

NOTICE THE DENSITY OF GRASS PLANTS

A healthy turf may have as many as eight hundred grass plants in a single square foot of soil. When they are that dense, it is almost impossible to see the soil when you get down on your hands and knees and spread the grass plants apart. If you see soil between the plants in your lawn, then you can assume that something is wrong, because healthy grass normally fills in spaces over time. So, thin grass suggests that either your soil is in poor shape, or your grass is tired and needs replacing. Overseeding with new grass may be all that is necessary.

ESTIMATE THE PROPORTION OF WEEDS

One of the inevitable results of having a thin turf is lots of weeds. Weed seeds need light and space to grow. Thin grass, and grass that is mowed too short, allows sunlight to penetrate to the soil surface and germinate weed seeds that lie in wait for these ideal conditions. Therefore, when you eyeball your lawn and see lots of weeds, it is time to repair the grass. The percentage of weeds present in your lawn actually determines how much work is necessary.

Jeff decided a few years ago that he could live with some weeds in the lawn. It seemed a reasonable trade-off for the savings in time, energy, money and environmental impact that a more low-maintenance lawn—one that tolerates some imperfection— provides. Having made peace with that decision, he discovered that when we achieved an otherwise healthy, dense turf, as many as 10–15 percent weeds, evenly distributed throughout the grass, were barely noticeable. The cost of trying to attain a perfect lawn, one that is virtually weed free, does not seem to us to be worth it.

> **How Many Weeds Are Tolerable?**
>
> ❧ 10–15% weeds is OK.
>
> ❧ 20–50% needs treatment, but renovation is optional.
>
> ❧ Over 50% means renovation.

However, when the percentage of weeds in a lawn sneaks over 20 percent, it is time to reevaluate. Depending on the type of weed, this larger proportion of weeds is likely to become obvious, even to the casual observer. It may be time to take some remedial measures. There are a couple of strategies.

If the weeds in your lawn are noticeable, but do not comprise more than half of the green turf area, solve the problem by killing just the weeds with an appropriate herbicide, then overseeding the lawn with new grass seed to fill in the spaces and thicken the turf to discourage new weeds. If weeds comprise more than half of the green turf area, we have found it's worth it to kill the entire turf and install an entirely new lawn. We describe how to do each of these procedures in detail in Chapter Eight.

Measuring the percentage of weeds does not have to be precise. Just look at a small section of your lawn and guess. You are the final judge. If you think it looks OK, then that is all that matters. If it doesn't look OK, then you know you need to address the problem.

How about the Size of the Lawn?

While you are evaluating your lawn, we suggest you spend some time thinking about its size. That has a whole lot to do with how much work is involved in its care. Most yardeners live with the lawn that comes with the house at the time of purchase. It is just simpler to go with whatever the builder determined would be turf area. Occasionally the addition of a pool, patio or deck may reduce the lawn size, but mostly only homeowners with some gardening experience set out to deliberately turn lawn areas into beds of ground covers or other ornamental and landscape plants, simultaneously reducing the area they have to mow.

One of the keys to a low-maintenance lawn, however, is size. The smaller the turf area, the less time it takes to care for it. Ask yourself some questions: Do we need to have a lawn this big? What do we use it for? Do we use the lawn in the front of the house just for appearance's sake? Could another ground cover besides grass achieve the same purpose? Is the backyard bigger than necessary? Are there remote areas in the "back forty" that we never use except to mow every week? Are there steep slopes or other difficult terrain that we would like to avoid mowing?

> ### Ways to Reduce Lawn Size
>
> ❦ Add patios, pools, gazebos.
>
> ❦ Plant trees, groves of shrubs.
>
> ❦ Plant beds of flowers, vegetables.
>
> ❦ Establish paths for traffic patterns.
>
> ❦ Plant evergreen ground covers as grass substitute.

"Hardscape" features such as pools, patios, gazebos, tennis courts, children's play equipment areas, dog runs and the like take up space otherwise devoted to turf. So do various plantings—clusters of shrubs, small trees encircled with mulch, and flower and vegetable beds. Significantly, there are many ground cover alternatives to lawn grass that are attractively green and low growing, but take little or no

work once they are established. Unlike grass, they require no fertilizer, special watering or regular mowing.

Why not take this opportunity to evaluate your landscape and determine if a lawn the size of yours is justified. Consider gradually reducing any large lawn areas over the next year or two. You might start with the heavy-traffic areas—those lawn areas that always turn into hard dirt paths because they represent major walk-throughs on the property—and turn them into permanent paths. Wood chips, gravel or even stone or brick, if they are available, make attractive walkways.

Using Ground Covers

There is no doubt that grassy turf plays an important role in most residential landscapes. It provides a soft-textured area in contrast with coarser-textured larger plants. It connects areas of the yard, uniting the elements of the landscape into a whole. It makes a wonderful soft carpet on which to walk and play.

However, ground covers other than lawn grass can do many of these same things. Plants such as pachysandra, English ivy and vinca are green too—and not just in the summer. They offer a variety of textures in a low-maintenance environment. They, too, serve as effective visual links between a handsome grouping of shrubs, the front walk and the facade of the house. They offer effective erosion control on steep banks and, as a bonus, crawl up and over unsightly landscape features such as old stumps, utility boxes and crumbled walls.

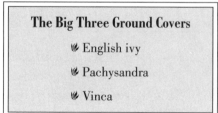

The Big Three Ground Covers

🌿 English ivy

🌿 Pachysandra

🌿 Vinca

Ground covers can also soften property boundaries and reduce weeds on undeveloped or remote areas on the property. Planted around trees and shrubs, they serve to reduce the lawn size and simultaneously protect trees and shrubs from damage by the lawn mower or weed whacker. A large circle of mulched ground cover, such as pachysandra planted around a tree trunk, requires watering only during very serious droughts. This measure also eliminates that ugly "surface root" problem that messes up the appearance of so many properties where trees sit in the middle of turf.

If this is the time that you are going to renovate the lawn, its soil and grass, maybe this is an opportune time to install some patches of ground cover.

More about the Big Three Ground Covers

English ivy (*Hedera helix*)—Ivy is basically a vine that will either climb vertically or creep horizontally as opportunity permits. As a ground cover it spreads rapidly over the soil by trailing stems, which root periodically as they progress. Ivy will take sun or shade in most climates. It has three to five dark green, lobed leaves about 2–4 inches long. Some types have leaves with variegated patterns of cream and green. Ivy grows most vigorously for short periods in the spring and fall.

Pachysandra/Japanese spurge (*Pachysandra terminalis*)— A most satisfactory ground cover for shaded areas, pachysandra's foliage stays dark green even in severe winters. Its elongated leaves are finely toothed at the tips and grow in whorls at the top of 6- to 8-inch stems. It produces a simple white flower in the spring, which is a favorite of honeybees. Pachysandra spreads by underground runners. It prefers slightly acidic soil and needs little watering once it is established.

Vinca/Periwinkle/Myrtle (*Vinca minor*)—This evergreen, trailing vine has a finer texture than the other two ground covers. Small oval leaves grow in pairs opposite each other every inch or so along its creeping stems, forming a mat of foliage about 6 inches tall. It sports small blue (also purple or white) flowers with five petals that have distinctive squarish tips. They appear in the spring and sometimes again in the fall. Vinca is happiest in light shade and moist soil but will cope with less ideal conditions.

Which Ground Covers?

Almost any low-growing plant can function as a ground cover. There are ground covers that are appropriate for shade, others for sun. Some provide mainly foliage, while others offer flowers too. Almost any plant that is relatively low-growing and that spreads to form a mat to cover the soil can be used as a ground cover to replace turf.

Woody, shrublike plants such as creeping juniper, wintercreeper, certain cotoneasters, barberry and rosemary varieties serve this landscape purpose. Perennial flowering plants such as various types of phlox, sedums, bellflowers, geraniums, lily of the valley and hosta, as well as numerous flowering annuals, are also useful. Some ground cover plants even resemble grass— lilyturf, mondo grass, ribbon and dwarf blue fescue ornamental grasses are examples.

This said, however, there are three plants that are, hands down, the most versatile and easiest to grow ground covers. For nongardening homeowners whose experience with plants is limited, these are fail-safe. You can hardly go wrong with pachysandra, ivy and vinca (aka periwinkle or myrtle). They are attractive, usually evergreen and virtually carefree. In addition, in most parts of the country they require little or no watering, a significant advantage over lawn grass.

MULCH AROUND TREES

Another fine way to reduce the size of a lawn is to spread some kind of attractive organic material over the soil under trees instead of growing grass there. A large circle of wood chips, shredded bark, pine needles, chopped leaves or bark nuggets at the base of each shade tree substantially improves tree health. Tree roots no longer have to compete with grass for soil nutrients and water. The soil around the roots is improved as the mulch gradually breaks down and provides humus to the soil.

There is some disagreement among professional horticulturists about how deep the layer of organic mulch around trees and shrubs should be. There can be too much of a good thing. If mulch is piled too high, it will cut off the roots' access to air, essentially smothering them. However, if the mulch layer is too thin, it will fail to suppress weeds. We find that a mulch layer from 2 to 4 inches deep works fine. Liz keeps an eye on it over the season, and adds some as it breaks down into the soil. She is really careful to keep the mulch away from the bark of the trunk too.

Your lawn size is reduced to the degree that you spread the mulch out from the trunk of each of your trees. Because tree and shrub roots extend under the soil well beyond the edge of the leaf canopy, or "dripline," it is likely that you will not cover all of them anyway. We spread mulch at least 12 inches out from the trunks of small trees, and even farther out from large ones. Because our intention is to reduce the lawn size as well as nurture our trees and shrubs, we spread mulch widely.

No doubt, by now you are looking at your lawn with new eyes—and probably new respect too. Hopefully, close examination of both your soil and your existing grass has yielded enough information to enable you to decide how extensive your renovation efforts should be. We can not stress enough how valuable rehabilitation of the soil and repair and renewal of the grass are in creating an environment to support a low-maintenance lawn.

If your evaluation confirms that renovation of your turf—treatment of both the soil and the grass—is in order, then consult the next several chapters for details on how to accomplish this task. Perhaps you are among the lucky homeowners who discover that their soil and grass are in pretty good shape. The maintenance program outlined in Section I may be sufficient to maintain this desirable state of affairs.

Chapter Six
Rehabilitating the Soil

In the previous chapter we described various tests to help you evaluate the condition of the soil under your lawn. In the likely event that they revealed serious deficiencies in soil structure and chemistry, it is time to decide on a strategy for correcting the problems. One alternative is to fix the soil while the grass is still in place. Another, the more ambitious one, is to start from scratch and dig up the lawn. In this chapter we explain each of these alternatives. Remember, this is a one-time job. Once you have rehabilitated your soil, proper routine lawn maintenance as described in the first four chapters will assure continued soil quality—fertility, drainage and microbial activity—for as long as you own your lawn.

Improve Soil with Grass in Place

It is relatively simple to improve soil; it just takes some patience. When soil has been mistreated for ten, twenty, even forty years or more, it takes a few years to restore it to a state of full health, no matter whether you take the gradual approach with the grass still in place, or the quicker approach by starting all over again. If you wish to upgrade your soil with the grass in place, expect the transformation to take two to three years.

DEAL WITH COMPACTION

People live at cross-purposes with lawns. While grass grows well only if its roots do not live in compacted soil, people establish lawns to walk and play on, and these activities compact the soil. Even if we don't routinely walk on the front lawn, years and years of walking behind a lawn mower—or worse, driving a mower—every ten days or so will cause compaction. Of course, starting out with damage from the weight of the builder's heavy equipment doesn't help either. Unless you have taken measures over the years to loosen the soil in which your grass grows, then it has simply gotten more and more compacted.

So, are we fighting a losing battle? Not at all. We just need to do what the golf course and athletic field turf managers have been doing for decades; we need to aerate the lawn once or twice every year until the soil's air capacity is improved. We don't have football teams or thousands of golfers tromping on our lawns, so once the soil compaction is treated and the mailman and the kids are reminded to use the sidewalk, you can get by with aeration only every two or three years.

AERATE TO REHABILITATE THE SOIL

Thorough core aeration is the cornerstone of soil rehabilitation. As we described in Chapter One, core aerators are hollow-pronged tools that puncture the turf and draw out a plug of soil, leaving a little hole about 1/2 inch in diameter and about 3–4 inches deep. The soil plugs are deposited on the turf where they gradually break down in rain. Power-driven aerating tools that will do 2,000 square feet in an hour or two are available for rent. Hand-aerating tools are available at home and garden centers for about $20.

If your soil is badly compacted, then you definitely need to use a gas-powered core-aerating machine the first few times you aerate the lawn. Hand aerating is great for maintenance and for taking care of tight little corners where the big machine can't reach, but power aerating is the only way to get that first level of rehabilitation done properly. When you are going to do a major aerating job, it is best to cut the grass a bit shorter (1–1 1/2 inches) than usual. Choose a cool day when the soil is damp but not wet. The soil should not be dead dry. Most core-aerating machines can be adjusted for the depth of the core hole. Set your machine so the hole is 3–4 inches deep or as deep as it will go. Most machines will core down at least 3 inches.

Most yardeners don't aerate thoroughly enough. Don't be timid. Run the aerating machine over the lawn repeatedly—in two or even three directions. Run it east and west, then north and south, and then run it diagonally. Three or even four passes over the entire lawn are necessary to do a thorough job.

Of course your lawn is going to look awful. As the aerating prongs puncture the soil they also tear up a lot of the turf and the lawn becomes littered with plugs of soil and battered grass plants. Resist the impulse to fire off angry letters to us for at least three or four weeks. By then you will see an almost miraculous change come over your turf.

The rain breaks down the soil cores and they disappear. The holes gradually fill in and the grass greens up all by itself now that there is air down in the soil to fuel microbiotic activity. We find that if we spread a thin layer of organic material such as peat moss, compost, sludge or topsoil on the turf after we aerate, it falls into the holes, making them less obvious. It does not obstruct the air access down into the soil.

Lawns that have never been aerated will benefit from this kind of intensive aeration twice a year for a few years. Do it in the spring, and again in the fall. After two or three years, that effort will undo the long-term damage. Then shift to a once every two or three years maintenance aeration schedule. That is frequent enough to compensate for the normal everyday compaction of residential turf.

Try Products with Humic Acid

There is also a nonmechanical way to deal with compacted soil. There are several liquid products on the market designed to treat compaction caused either by compression of the soil from weight or from innate soil structure such as that found in clay soils. Their key ingredient is humic acid, which is usually combined with safe chemicals and enzymes that loosen soil. Packaged as sprays, they can be used instead of or in conjunction with aeration. Follow the instructions on the product label. For chronic compaction problems in certain areas, routinely use humic acid once a year.

Deal with Drainage

If you have some drainage problems in parts of your lawn, they will be difficult to solve while trying to leave the turf in place. However, aerating goes a long way to improve the drainage of any soil. By using the humic acid products discussed above or some of the biostimulant products discussed below, you will see some improvement on minor drainage problems. Major drainage problems usually require significant landscape reconstruction, as we'll discuss later in this chapter.

Optimum Soil pH Range by Type of Grass

Grass	Soil pH Range
Tall fescue	5.5–7.0
Kentucky blue	5.8–7.5
Perennial rye	5.8–7.4
Fine fescue	5.6–6.8
Zoysia	5.5–7.0

DEAL WITH pH

In the last chapter we described how to determine the pH of your soil. The chart below shows the pH level favored by various types of grass. Even if you are not sure what kind of grass you have, the soil pH will need adjustment if you determine that it is either too acidic (pH less than 5.8) or too alkaline (pH more than 8.0). As the chart suggests, most grasses fall comfortably between these numbers.

CORRECTING ACIDIC SOIL

Often, soil pH is simply a function of the natural composition of the soil in the area where you live. For that reason, more often than not, lawn soil is too acid in the eastern and midwestern parts of the country (see map on p.13).

Many other factors promote acidity in soil. Acidic soil may be partly a function of the action of plant roots which release hydrogen as they take up nutrients from the soil. The accumulation of hydrogen over time increases the acidity of the soil. Also, acid rain may contribute to the problem, leaching out those elements in the soil, like magnesium and calcium, which help neutralize soil acidity. Also, your choice of fertilizer may influence soil pH. Quick-acting nitrogen products tend to acidify soil. Even too much watering can affect soil acidity. Excessive water leaches out other soil minerals that act as natural buffers against soil acidity.

Causes of Acidic Soil

🍂 Regional soil composition

🍂 Plant roots and microorganisms

🍂 Acid rain

🍂 Quick-acting nitrogen fertilizers

🍂 Excessive rain or irrigation

ADDING LIMESTONE

It is easy to deal with overly acidic soil even when the lawn is intact. Spread limestone on the grass. As we detailed in Chapter One, it is naturally alkaline and it buffers the excess acid in the soil. As a bonus, it also adds important calcium and magnesium, improves soil structure and enhances seed germination.

Because lime takes three to six months to take effect, pH correction will happen as quickly as compaction correction. If a soil test reveals that your soil is extremely acidic (below 5.2), plan to apply limestone in both the spring and the fall for several years. As the pH gradually works its way up to the ideal level, cut back to once a year or

Pounds of Limestone for 1,000 Sq. Ft.

Soil pH	Sandy Soil	Clay Soil
Over 6.2	0	0
5.2 –6.2	25–50	50–75
Under 5.2	50–75	100–150

even once every two years. Typically, sandy soils that are within the proper pH range will need a light-maintenance liming roughly every two to three years. Clay soils that are within the proper pH require heavier maintenance doses of lime every five to six years.

CORRECTING ALKALINE SOIL

It is also possible that some yardeners will find that their soil is too alkaline to support grass plants. Again, the imbalance may simply be a function of the natural character of the soil in your region, in which case your neighbors are probably also struggling with their lawn. More likely, it may be due to the leaching of cement, mortar, stucco or similar construction material into the soil in certain areas, especially near house walls and sidewalks. This might explain why grass grows well in some areas of the lawn and not others.

If a soil test indicates that the soil in the lawn is excessively alkaline (pH above 8.0), acidify it by adding ammonium sulfate, iron sulfate or elemental sulfur. These products, usually in powdered form, are available in local garden/home centers and some hardware stores. Spread them on the grass by hand or with a grass seed spreader and let the rain soak them into the soil. Read and follow package label instructions carefully.

Pounds of Sulfur for 1,000 Sq. Ft.		
Soil pH	Sandy Soil	Clay Soil
Under 7.5	0	0
7.5–8.5	10	7
Over 8.5	20	15

Do not add sulfur to the lawn at rates exceeding more than 5 pounds per 1,000 square feet on any single occasion. To meet suggested amounts, you may have to make two or three applications over the season. The best time to spread sulfur is in the spring or fall, rather than during the summer months. It will begin to take effect in about one month.

DEALING WITH SOIL FERTILITY

The more organic matter incorporated into the soil, the greater its capacity to hold water and air, and thus deliver nutrients to plants. While it is easy to add valuable humus to the soil in flower gardens and vegetable beds, it is a bit trickier when there is an established lawn over the soil. However, there are a number of ways to boost the organic content of soil under turf.

LEAVE THE CLIPPINGS

Yes, we are going to say it again! Leave the clippings when you mow. On an average lawn, these green clippings make available over 200 pounds of nitrogen-rich organic material for every 1,000 square feet over the season. It's a nice gradual way to maintain the humus content of the soil. Consult Chapter Two for a detailed explanation of the benefits of leaving the clippings on the lawn.

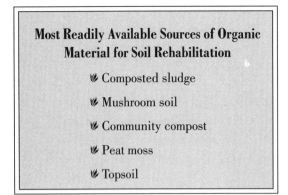

Most Readily Available Sources of Organic Material for Soil Rehabilitation

❧ Composted sludge

❧ Mushroom soil

❧ Community compost

❧ Peat moss

❧ Topsoil

ADD A LAYER OF ORGANIC MATERIAL

In addition to leaving grass clippings on soil to increase its humus content, spread some organic material such as peat moss or topsoil over the turf once a year for at least two, and even three, years. In Chapter One we recommend a layer of topdressing of 1/4–1/2 inch every two or three years to simply maintain healthy soil. To remedy really poor soil, we recommend that the topdressing be as thick as 1 inch for at least two years in a row. This extra dose of organic matter will jump start microbial activity in the soil. The sooner the microlife is in high gear, the faster the soil will improve and the quicker the lawn will look better.

The materials available for restoring turf soil are exactly the same as the materials we recommended for the periodic maintenance of the soil. If a soil is in pretty bad shape, composted municipal sludge, mushroom soil or compost are the best choices if those materials are available to you.

Composted Municipal Sludge—Municipal disposal plants in over one hundred cities across the nation are processing sewerage into sludge products. More properly called composted municipal sludge, this product is available in enormous amounts for use in public, corporate and residential landscapes. It offers rich, dark, coarsely textured organic material that nourishes and conditions soil in a spectacular manner. Early technical problems related to the presence of heavy metals in sludge have been overcome, making it ideal for lawns and other ornamental uses.

Sludge is inexpensive enough so that annual applications to the lawn are feasible. If you are lucky enough to reside near a city where sludge is produced, make every effort to get some. Yes, it does have a slight smell, especially in a pile that gets wet in the rain, but the smell dissipates rapidly once it is spread and/or dry. Liz found it to be about as objectionable as fish emulsion newly sprayed on plants in the yard. It is nowhere near as bad as manure-spreading time in Amish farm country! Unless it rains, it is all over in a day.

Mushroom Soil—It is our good fortune to live in a mushroom-producing region, so we have access to richly organic mushroom soil. That is why it is included on our list. The composted residue of the straw and manure that is used to grow mushrooms in commercial operations, the "spent" soil, still rich in organic content, is usually mixed with some regular soil to increase its volume. Although mushroom soil that is freshly removed from the mushroom houses very likely contains a fair percentage of residual pesticides, many farmers compost this industry by-product for three to six months. This effectively eliminates most pesticide traces. Look for this "aged" mushroom soil to put on your lawn to increase its organic content.

Compost—Commercial compost sold in garden centers is generally too expensive to even consider for this job unless you have a very small lawn. However, more and more communities are composting the leaves they collect and are making the resulting compost available to residents free or very cheaply. Composted leaves or leaf mold, as it is sometimes called, is excellent organic material for lawns.

> **Amount of Sludge or Compost to Use**
>
> As a general rule, apply 250 pounds of compost per 1,000 square feet on sandy soil, 400 to 600 pounds on loamy soil and 1,200 pounds on clay soil.

Peat Moss—Canadian sphagnum peat moss is the most widely available product for turf topdressing. A 4-cubic-foot bale of peat moss costs about $9 and will cover anywhere from 200 to 500 square feet of lawn, depending on how thickly it is spread. Its water-holding capacity is legendary. Boost its nutritional content by adding a 50-pound bag of dried cow manure to every bale of peat moss, and it becomes a pretty good compost substitute. Some yardeners mix regular topsoil with peat moss about half-and-half. This is another way to get some nutrient value into the topdressing material.

Chopped Leaves—The increased popularity of the mulching mower gives the yardener a magnificent tool for topdressing the lawn at zero expense. A dedicated mulching mower can reduce a 2-inch layer of leaves to a 1/2-inch layer of confetti-sized pieces of very valuable organic material on the lawn. Chopped leaves are the favorite food of earthworms. They will immediately begin pulling those leaves down into the soil. They consume some of those leaves, making nutrient-rich fertilizer and distributing it, along with the chopped leaves, throughout the top 4–6 inches of soil. The leaves become the food that fuels a microbial population explosion. After three or four years of leaving a 1/2-inch layer of finely chopped leaves on the lawn, almost any soil—even heavy clay or heavy sand—will turn into gorgeous black, nutrient-rich, water-retaining topsoil.

If you don't have a mulching mower, you can chop dried leaves finely enough with a leaf shredder and then spread them over the lawn by hand, making sure to rake them down to the soil level so they don't sit on top of the grass. If you don't have any deciduous trees to provide free leaves, throw a party in October requiring all guests to bring five bags of leaves as a house gift. Your neighbors will think you are nuts, but fear not; your lawn will look better than theirs in just a few years.

Topdressing with Organic Material

Whatever material you choose to increase the amount of organic matter in your soil, plan to spread it on the lawn in either the fall or the early spring. Achieving a uniform layer is easier said than done.

First, cut the grass a bit shorter than normal—from 1 to 1 1/2 inches—so that the organic particles can easily fall down among the grass blades. Then haul the supply of topdressing material around the yard in a wheelbarrow, strategically depositing piles of it on the turf every few yards. Then go back and distribute the piles evenly over the grass with a rake. Jeff does this in two steps. He uses a regular garden rake to distribute piles of sludge or peat moss roughly over the lawn, then he shifts to a flexible grass rake to spread the material as evenly as possible.

Rain settles the organic material down into the turf pretty quickly where soil organisms, especially earthworms, transport it out of sight down into the soil. By the first spring mowing, most of a fall topdressing of peat moss, sludge or compost is no longer visible. It will already be incorporated into the soil. Because fall is also a prime time to overseed the lawn to help thicken up the turf, consider doing this job in conjunction with the topdressing operation. See Chapter Eight.

ADD THE MAGIC

Over the past ten years, technology has yielded an overwhelming assortment of new products that are designed to improve the soil in which we grow grass. These products are coming thick and fast and will continue to proliferate for the next several years. Unfortunately, because they are sophisticated and new, it is easy to become overwhelmed—even a bit intimidated—by the bounty on store shelves.

Some new products feature microorganisms. We must take on faith that they are in there, because there is no way to see them. How can we be sure that they are still alive? Other products feature humic acid, enzymes or "trace" elements. How can we be sure they will bind to soil particles as advertised? We can't see enzymes improve a plant's ability to absorb nutrients. So buyer beware, but be adventurous. Don't avoid these exciting new products just because you don't understand them. Try them and watch for results; improved soil quality as evidenced by nice, healthy grass will tell the tale. We can cover only a few of your new product options here. Believe us, in five years there will be twice as many. Soil improvement was never so easy.

Adding Microorganisms to the Soil

If your soil has been in really serious shape for some time, there is some value in introducing additional microorganisms into it to reinforce those that are already struggling there. However, unless you upgrade their soil environment so they have sufficient air, moisture and organic material to thrive, they won't be much help. So, it is a good idea to topdress with organic material (described above) at the same time you apply any product containing microorganisms to make sure things get off to a good start.

Products containing these microorganisms are available by mail order and in garden and home centers. Usually they are sold as added ingredients to slow-release lawn fertilizer. Sometimes they are called "bioactivators" and are often packaged as stimulants to the decomposition rate of a compost pile.

Usually bioactivators are packaged as a dry powder, which actually contains live microorganisms (as many as a billion per tablespoon). Once they are spread on top of the lawn by hand or with a fertilizer spreader, the microbugs enter the soil on their own. It helps to water the lawn right after applying these products to give the microcreatures a good start. It doesn't matter whether you use bioactivators in the fall or in the spring; the micoorganisms winter over. Either way, they are poised to get busy in the spring as the soil warms up. This gives the lawn a jump start on the season.

The microorganisms tackle the organic matter you have added to the soil, gradually breaking it down into nutrients for the grass plants throughout the entire season. Expect a rapid green-up of the grass in the spring soon after adding these biological soil builders. However, unlike the fleeting flush of green that follows a dose of quick-acting nitrogen fertilizer, this healthy glow remains.

Adding Biostimulants

There is a relatively new family of products on the market called "biostimulants" or "bioactivators" which do not necessarily contain microorganisms, but do contain hormones, enzymes and other natural chemicals designed to serve as a tonic for your lawn. These products are not fertilizers as such, but they enhance the lawn's general health and condition. Acting much like a catalyst, they help the grass plants absorb nutrients more efficiently from the soil. It makes the fertilizer you use more effective. These products are often made from a kelp or seaweed base.

Biostimulants work, but they require extra time and money to apply. Therefore, we usually consider them optional in the normal maintenance cycle of our low-maintenance program. On the other hand, they make an excellent addition to any soil rehabilitation regimen, and in that role are highly recommended.

Rebuild Soil from Scratch

Perhaps you are moving into a newly constructed home or have a lawn situation that is just so serious that you feel it is irredeemable. Then, starting from scratch is probably the best way to approach building good soil. This means sacrificing the grass, or what passes for grass, and digging up the soil. It is a major undertaking. Fortunately, done properly, it will not have to be done again. The fall is the best time to do this job.

MAJOR DRAINAGE RENOVATIONS

A complete rehabilitation situation presents an opportunity to correct major yard problems. Proper mulching of trees, construction of terraces, beds and berms and other engineering projects are best done now. Common problems such as grade irregularities or drainage difficulties are also easily addressed now. Solving drainage problems often requires major earth moving (and heavy equipment which compacts the soil) which you want to complete before you start fixing the soil.

We can't help you a whole lot with drainage problems. Often they are more complex than they appear. There are only two ways to deal with a serious soggy area in a lawn: either raise the height of the lawn or lower the water table. Both those steps often require some technical knowledge and skills that are far beyond the scope of this book.

If there is a serious drainage problem on your property, we recommend that you consult a professional. Landscape architects have the engineering expertise to properly evaluate the situation. The whole problem might be solved very simply, but you want a professional to assure you of that. On the other hand, moving earth, laying pipe, excavating swales and generally playing in the dirt "big time" may be advisable. This can cost a lot of money, so mistakes are to be avoided.

Later in this section we'll discuss some products that can be added to improve the drainage and water storage capacity of your lawn's soil.

WATER

HUMUS

CLAY

SILT

SAND

Employ the jar test for soil types.

WHAT KIND OF SOIL DO YOU HAVE?

While it is not absolutely necessary, it is very helpful to have a rough idea about whether the soil under your grass is mostly clay, mostly loam or silt, or mostly sand. The necessary amounts of various products, such as fertilizers and lime, vary depending on the type of soil they are to be used on. Usually, a professional soil test (see next section) will indicate your type of soil.

If you know nothing about soils, perhaps the simplest approach is to ask a friend or neighbor who is a gardener. They may not be experts, but experienced gardeners often know in general terms what kind of soil is in the area.

An easy way to get a rough indication of your soil type is to perform your own test. Use a glass jar with a screw-on lid such as a mayonnaise jar. Fill it half-full with soil taken from several spots around the lawn, taking soil between 2 and 4 inches from the surface, the primary root-growing area for the grass. A tablespoon is good for this job. Dig up a divot of grass and roots with a trowel and then scoop out a bit of soil with the tablespoon. When the jar is half-full of dirt, fill it to the top with water and put the lid on tightly. Shake the jar vigorously for fifteen to thirty seconds and let it sit overnight, or even a few days, until the dirt begins to settle and the water clears up.

The soil particles will settle in layers. Sand gravitates to the bottom of the jar; then silt particles settle on it, followed by the clay particles nearer the top. In most cases, each layer is a slightly different color. The very top layer of soil particles will be a thin dark layer of organic material on humus. In fact, some of this organic stuff may still be floating in the clearer water near the top of the jar.

Measure the height of the combined layers of soil in the jar. Then, when you measure the thickness of each individual layer you can calculate the percentage of sand, silt and clay of the whole. Collectively, these bottom three layers represent the mineral components of the soil. Obviously, the organic content is represented by the topmost layer or floating particles.

Typically, in healthy, fertile soil the sand layer represents between 10 percent and 50 percent, the clay layer represents between 10 percent and 25 percent and the balance is the middle layer of silt.

Do You Need a Soil Test?

If you are having serious problems with your lawn, and you are unable to readily diagnose their causes, a soil test by a professional laboratory is a very good step to take. Many county extension services offer a soil-testing service for about $5 per test.

Check the blue pages of the phone book under "Government Offices" for your county. Call the number for "Agricultural Extension" and ask them if they offer soil-testing services. The kit they will send to you includes instructions for how to collect the soil for the test. It requires that you take samples from many parts of the lawn to get an approximation of the soil conditions in the entire lawn. There are private laboratories that will give you a soil test, but their charges range from $20 to $50. Inquire at your local garden center about soil-testing services in your area.

A soil test is important for learning about the availability of phosphorus and potassium in your soil—you may have too little or too much. It also tells you precisely what the pH of your soil is and gives you some idea of the type of soil you have (clay, loam, sand) and how much organic matter is present.

Soil pH

The pH of the soil refers to a measure of how acidic or alkaline a soil happens to be. Why is that important? Grass plants growing in a soil that is either too acidic or too alkaline will be unhealthy and will not thrive primarily because in those extreme conditions the roots of the grass plant cannot take up certain kinds of nutrients, even though they are present in the soil.

For example, grass growing in soil that is too acidic will have great trouble absorbing the all-important calcium and magnesium. At the same time, acidic soil causes the plant to take in too much aluminum and manganese, which can be toxic to the plants. On the other end of the continuum, grass growing in soil that is too alkaline has trouble getting nitrogen, phosphorus, iron and other essential nutrients. The pH of the soil is very important to the ability of grass to grow well.

Another very good reason to worry about the pH of the soil is that, when it is too acidic, earthworms tend to move somewhere else. Microbial activity is greatly reduced, causing reduced decomposition of that important organic material, which, in turn, leads to thatch problems. At the same time the population of helpful bacteria declines, the population of fungal spores explodes, promoting more lawn disease problems. Dollar spot, brown patch and snow mold are much more common in lawns growing in overly acidic soil.

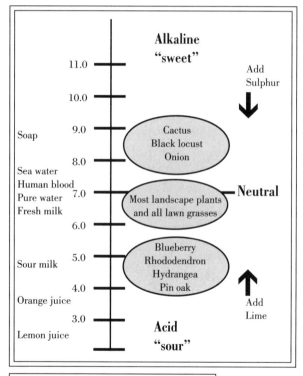

The degree of soil acidity or alkalinity is expressed on a continuum from 1 to 14, and is referred to as the "pH" of the soil in gardening and lawn care books. A perfectly neutral soil registers a pH of 7. The lower the pH number below 7, the more acidic the soil. The higher above 7, the more alkaline. Like all plants, lawn grasses prefer some types of soils over others. They do best in soil that is just slightly acidic (pH 6.0 to 7.0). If the soil is too acidic (below 5.8), as is often the case in the North, it is necessary to add limestone to it to "sweeten" it—make it less acidic (see map, p. 13). Bluegrass and ryegrasses, a bit less able to handle soil acidity, need more lime than fescues or zoysia grasses. Consequently, it is really helpful to be aware of the type of soil on your property.

Determining Your pH

The easiest way to get a reading on the acidity or alkalinity of soil is to consult that friend or neighbor who is an experienced gardener. Most serious gardeners know the pH of the soil in the area, and while it can vary even within the neighborhood, it is not likely to vary much. Simple pH meters designed for home use are available in some garden centers and from various mail-order catalog firms. Although they give only a rough indi-

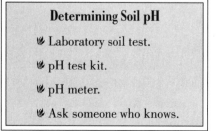

Determining Soil pH

🍃 Laboratory soil test.

🍃 pH test kit.

🍃 pH meter.

🍃 Ask someone who knows.

cation of possible extremes in pH, they are useful to alert homeowners to possible problems.

GETTING ALL WORKED UP

Starting from scratch means that you do not save the existing grass. You plow up the soil in order to directly add all the ingredients necessary to bring it back to life. Some books advise that you scrape up the existing turf as chunks of sod before you rototill the soil. We don't agree with this approach. We believe that if you use a tiller that is powerful enough to do the job correctly, working the old turf into the soil makes a major contribution to its organic content right off the bat.

Rent a heavy-duty tiller (about $50–$100 a day) for this job. Till the soil as deeply as the machine will work, probably 4–6 inches. Do not till directly under any trees as you will seriously damage their feeding roots; dig that area by hand.

IMPROVING THE SOIL AS YOU TILL

Not only is this a good time to tackle chronic drainage problems, but using a

pH Meter

tiller makes short work of breaking up compaction in the soil. The whirling tines of the tiller loosen and fluff the soil down at least 4 inches, introducing lots of air into it.

Jeff usually likes to go over the lawn once with the tiller to break up the sod and to surface nuisance rocks to discard. Then he spreads layers of organic material of some sort, slow-release fertilizer and materials to improve water storage (if needed) over the lumpy, disheveled soil. Finally, he works all that stuff into the soil by running the tiller again.

IMPROVE SOIL TEXTURE AND FERTILITY

The rototilling operation is a good time to add as many of the things necessary for healthy soil as possible.

Add Organic Material—Spread a 1-inch layer of composted municipal sludge, regular compost, Canadian sphagnum peat moss or mushroom soil. This is the time to add some microorganisms if you wish; add them to the layer of organic material to assure an abun-

dance of energetic microlife in your new lawn at the outset.

Add Slow-Release Fertilizer—Many companies now sell a granular slow-release nitrogen fertilizer intended expressly for brand-new lawns. Called "starter" fertilizer, it is designed to meet the needs of young grass plants. However, any slow-release lawn fertilizer in the amounts indicated on its label for new lawns is OK.

Add Water Storage Materials for Sandy Soils—If your soil is very sandy, this is a good time to add some material designed to store water and maintain air spaces in soil. For the past ten years, absorbent polymer crystals, sometimes called "hydrogels," have been used extensively in the dry Southwest to give predominently sandy lawns some more water storage capability. These products look like granulated sugar, but when brought into contact with water, they act like little sponges, absorbing up to four hundred times their weight in moisture. Water stored this way in soil is available to roots for a week or two past the time when sandy soil normally drains dry. These hydrogel crystals last for about ten years and then biodegrade into harmless components.

The only problem with hydrogels is determining the correct proportion to use. There is a danger of overdoing, causing soil to become too water absorbing and turning squishy after every rain. If instructions on the product package are not clear, avoid overuse by using this rule of thumb: Add no more than 5 pounds of hydrogel crystals (dry) per 1,000 square feet of lawn area. Till them into the soil.

Add Air Storage Materials to Clay Soils—If you have a particularly heavy clay soil, you may want to add some kind of material that will provide more air space, such as very coarse sand. It is amazing how much sand you can use for this job. A reliable local contractor is your best advisor for determining how much sand is needed in your neck of the woods.

INSTALL SPRINKLER SYSTEM (OPTIONAL)

If you intend to install a lawn sprinkler system, this is a good time to have that job done. These systems can be very convenient. Professional installation is the best way to be sure they will perform as you desire. A certain amount of digging is necessary to lay the pipes, so doing this now avoids damaging the new grass in the future. Before taking on this expense, remember that your new lawn will be quite drought resistant. Unless you live in the South, you may not need the system.

WHAT ABOUT SURFACED TREE ROOTS?

If you have trees growing in your lawn that have developed "surface roots," be careful about how you treat them. Surface roots are usually caused by compacted soil, so we can assume that in this rehabilitation project you have solved that compaction problem. Now what do you do with those roots still sitting up on top of the soil? *Do not cover them up with soil!* Surface roots will die if covered with more than an inch or so of soil. It is far better to plant the area with ground covers. If you insist on planting grass, then cover those roots with no more than 1 inch of soil.

FINAL GRADING

When you finish thoroughly rototilling all the added materials into the top 6 inches of the soil in the lawn area, smooth the soil surface with a hard-pronged garden rake. Notice areas where soil is a bit high or a bit low and rake the soil to adjust the level. Be sure that soil is not piled any higher over nearby tree roots than it was before.

The more even the surface of this potential seedbed, the less likely dry spots and wet spots will appear in the lawn a year from now. Fill in the low spots with topsoil and smooth out the high spots. If you have a lawn roller, it is useful at this point for spotting low and high spots you might have missed. It is not an essential tool, but if you have easy access to one, then use it for this job. Just fill it half-full with water and roll it over the soil to find high and low spots. If it is too full and heavy, you risk compacting the soil again. Now the seedbed is ready for seed, *but do not plant seed just yet!* There is one more very, very important step!

Germinating Weed Seeds—As you till the soil, you inadvertently bring up thousands and thousands of weed seeds that reside in the top 6 inches of all soils. If you plant grass seed before dealing with those surfaced weed seeds, you will have a lawn that is half grass and half weeds. This is always a cruel disappointment to yardeners who neglect this next step.

Water the freshly smoothed soil every day for a week to get all the weed seeds to germinate. Then, when the seedlings are a couple of inches tall and show some leaves, spray them with the herbicide, Roundup. This glyphosate herbicide will kill them in about a week. Then sow grass seed right on the soil without disturbing it again.

Now the Soil Is Terrific!

Taking the steps recommended in this chapter will substantially improve the soil in which you are growing grass. A rehabilitated soil is well on its way to self-sufficiency. Freed from dependence on costly fertilizer fixes and your constant labor, it will support the vigorous growth of grass plants over the whole season.

The kind of grass you should have is another important consideration. Upgrading the quality of the grass in the lawn, either gradually by overseeding or immediately by starting from scratch, will definitely improve the look of your lawn. It will complete the renovation process that begins with building healthy soil. That is what the next two chapters are all about— renewing the grass. We describe how to choose the appropriate seed in Chapter Seven and how to plant it in Chapter Eight.

Choosing the Right Grass

While establishing healthy soil is fundamental to a successful low-maintenance lawn, it is not the only factor in its success. The type of grass plants that grow in that wonderful soil is important as well. Whether you decide to simply overseed your existing lawn with new grass seed to revive it, or to kill all your grass and plant an entirely new lawn, selecting appropriate grass seed is very

important. In order to avoid problems down the road, take time now to choose the proper grass for the site. That decided, be sure to use premium quality seed.

This whole chapter is basically everything you ever wanted to know about grass seed but were afraid to ask. Perhaps, like us, you assumed that all grass seed was pretty much alike and kind of ho-hum. We have discovered that enormous advances in research over the last ten years have yielded major improvements in the varieties of grass and their ability to withstand drought, disease and pests. These new products are anything but ho-hum. In fact, modern grass varieties are one of the key factors in a truly low-maintenance lawn. Plan to integrate them into your turf.

The Best Grass Seed Costs More

Plan to spend more money for this modern grass seed. Buy the most expensive grass seed (of the type that you want) on the garden center shelf. The slightly higher prices reflect the costs of the development of new seed technology. There is no doubt that you will be getting your money's worth in the long run. The less-expensive grass seed on the shelf is the older, unimproved kind. A few cents saved at the store translates into lots of work and many problems—in short, the old high-maintenance lawn.

Even if you hire someone to install a new lawn, whether they use seed or sod, you must insist on the highest-quality grass. Why spend $1,000 for the job and end up with an inferior-quality grass that was developed twenty-five years ago?

What's Available?

Aside from high quality, the other most important consideration in choosing grass seed is the type or variety of grass. There are many types of grass plants—bluegrass, fescue, zoysia, ryegrass, St Augustine, buffalograss—which have been bred for use as turf. Some of these do best in warm climates, others in cooler regions. It is important to select a kind that is appropriate to the climate where you live. This is not as difficult as it sounds, because garden centers and hardware stores in your region routinely stock seed that is the right kind for your area.

SEED MIXTURE VERSUS SEED BLENDS

When you look closely at the label on a box or bag of grass seed, it usually lists percentages of seeds of several grass types. Almost all grass seed sold in retail outlets in this country is packaged as a "mixture" or "blend" of two or more varieties of one or two, or even three,

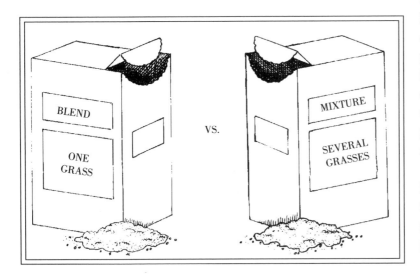

types of grass. The various kinds of seed are mixed in different proportions depending on whether the seed is to be used in sunny areas or in areas that have some shade during the day. So the package may say "shade mixture" or "shade blend."

A "mixture" means the box contains more than one type of grass—perhaps bluegrass and perennial rye. The package label indicates the percentage by weight of each type of grass represented in the mixture. A Kentucky bluegrass mixture is one where bluegrass seed predominates and there are small percentages of perennial rye or fescues of some kind.

A "blend" means that the package contains only one type of grass—such as bluegrass. However, the blend contains a number of varieties of bluegrass such as, 'Baron', 'Nassau', and 'Abbey'. Each different variety has certain desirable traits and, collectively, they improve the quality of the lawn. However, if you use a blend, all of the grass plants in the lawn are basically of the same plant species.

Whether you use a mixture or blend, there is a value in having more than just one single variety of any type of grass in your lawn. Combined varieties or types of grass produce more attractive lawns that are more drought hardy and disease and pest resistant.

Which should you buy—a mixture or a blend? On the theory that the more genetic diversity in a lawn, the more vigorous and self-reliant it is, we recommend using the highest-quality mixture available in your retail store. We feel that mixtures provide a more balanced combination of plants, each having unique strengths that offset the vulnerabilities of the others. A high-quality blend has the advantage of more uniform texture, since all the plants are the same type, and are perfectly fine for situations where the "look" of the turf is critically important. However, blends lack the broad genetic diversity that is a hedge against disease.

So in this chapter, when we refer to Kentucky bluegrass we mean a mixture where Kentucky bluegrass represents the largest proportion of the total mix. The same goes for the other grasses we describe in this chapter. If you buy the highest-quality grass seed and select the package labeled for the situation you have (shade, heavy use, etc.), you will be getting a mixture that has been determined best for your area of the country for that particular situation.

Know What You Buy

How can you be sure of the quality of the grass seed in a package? As we have indicated, price is usually a good clue. The front label is not a reliable guide. For example, if the label says "Ecological Mixture," you don't really know what you are buying. Check the side panel or back of the package for a little chart that lists the specific types of grass by type and/or variety as a percentage of the total. Every box or bag of grass seed is required to display this information.

Ingredients are listed as "pure seed" and "other ingredients." A package of grass seed will list the percentages of various grass seed types or varieties. Look for generous percentages of one or more of the main seed types for cool climates that we have mentioned—Kentucky bluegrass, tall fescue or perennial rye. They should represent 90 percent or more of the contents of the package. Avoid seed mixtures that include annual ryegrass.

The other ingredients listed are inert matter, other crop seed and weed seeds. While traces of these seeds are unavoidable, the higher the quality of the seed mixture, the lower the percentage of "other ingredients" it will have. Since the fall of 1993, packages of high-quality grass seed sport a special seal of the Lawn Institute that indicate that the seed meets certain minimum quality standards.

Technology Is Minimizing the Differences

There are really just three grasses available and appropriate for most lawns in the North—Kentucky bluegrass, turf-type tall fescue and perennial ryegrass. Ten years ago, there were significant differences between these three types of grass. Each had its assets—bluegrass had the best color and texture, tall fescue was tough and perennial rye germinated quickly and reliably. Of course, each had its respective liabilities as well—weak in heat, slow germination, disease-prone.

In recent years, advanced breeding techniques have minimized differences between these types of grass. Color, texture, germination rate, heat and drought tolerance, and disease

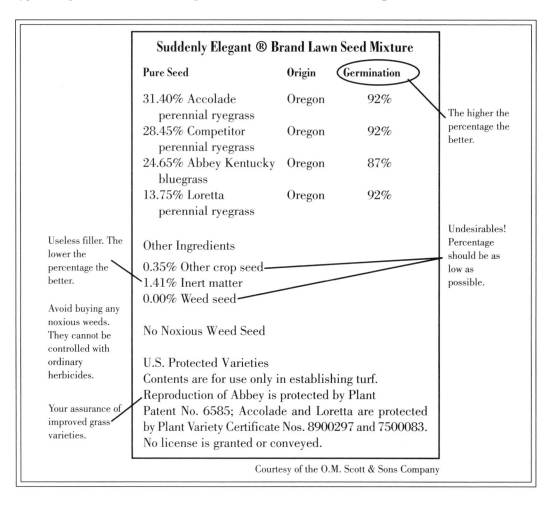

Suddenly Elegant ® Brand Lawn Seed Mixture

Pure Seed	Origin	Germination
31.40% Accolade perennial ryegrass	Oregon	92%
28.45% Competitor perennial ryegrass	Oregon	92%
24.65% Abbey Kentucky bluegrass	Oregon	87%
13.75% Loretta perennial ryegrass	Oregon	92%

The higher the percentage the better.

Other Ingredients

0.35% Other crop seed
1.41% Inert matter
0.00% Weed seed

Useless filler. The lower the percentage the better.

Avoid buying any noxious weeds. They cannot be controlled with ordinary herbicides.

Undesirables! Percentage should be as low as possible.

No Noxious Weed Seed

U.S. Protected Varieties
Contents are for use only in establishing turf.
Reproduction of Abbey is protected by Plant Patent No. 6585; Accolade and Loretta are protected by Plant Variety Certificate Nos. 8900297 and 7500083. No license is granted or conveyed.

Your assurance of improved grass varieties.

Courtesy of the O.M. Scott & Sons Company

resistance have been improved in all of them. There are still some differences between the three grasses, but the industry is working all the time to improve the weaknesses of each type of grass while maintaining its strengths.

Consequently, the three grasses are now almost indistinquishable by color. All are approaching the legendary fine, uniform texture of bluegrass. All have improved germination, getting closer and closer to the germinating benefit of perennial ryegrass. The development of insect resistance, disease resistance and drought tolerance in each type of grass is well underway. There are still some differences in performance between the three grasses under specific circumstances, which may mean that one is more appropriate for where you live and the conditions you have in your yard. However, those differences are no longer major. We will review them in the next section.

To sum up, when you purchase a "mixture" of high-quality grass seed, you are generally gaining the benefits of two or even three types of grass in combination. Your lawn will have the capacity to endure lots of problems because any one problem might only affect a portion of the grass plant population in your turf. The other plants will keep right on growing, giving your lawn a nice overall look of good health and vitality.

Grass Choices in Northern Regions

In this section, we describe the basic choices you have among northern grass types. In the next section we suggest three key questions to ask when you make your final choice for your yard.

As we've noted, the three most common lawn grasses for the North are Kentucky bluegrass, turf-type tall fescue and perennial ryegrass. In addition, for shady areas there are what are called "fine fescues." These grasses include hard, sheep, spreading, creeping and chewing fescues. So if you see any of these terms on your seed label, you will know they are all considered part of the "fine fescue" family.

Extensive research and product development is being conducted nationwide by all the large seed companies. They are

> **How Types of Grass Differ**
>
> ❧ Color
>
> ❧ Texture
>
> ❧ Disease resistance
>
> ❧ Insect resistance
>
> ❧ Shade adaptability
>
> ❧ Drought tolerance
>
> ❧ Maintenance requirements

constantly improving the quality of the grass they are selling. We are writing these paragraphs in late 1994. By 1995, much of what we say here may need revision because the technology of grass development is moving so quickly. So consider these descriptions as a general guide rather than as scientifically precise and immutable.

KENTUCKY BLUEGRASS

For decades, Kentucky bluegrass *(Poa pratensis)* has set the standard for beauty in the North. Bluegrass grows best in the area of the country north of a line drawn connecting

Kentucky Bluegrass

🌿 Good for lawns for show.

🌿 Spreads very easily.

🌿 Good for sun or part shade.

🌿 Needs water in hot summer.

🌿 Best planting time in fall.

Where Kentucky Bluegrass Grows Best

■ Best growing area.
□ Does well, but requires more work
▨ Only with irrigation.

Where Tall Fescue Grows Best

■ Best growing area.

Washington, D.C., and St. Louis. Below that line, it needs to have some shade to help it endure summer heat. For best results, Kentucky bluegrass should always be planted in the fall, not in the spring.

Kentucky bluegrass spreads easily and uniformly, so that in a few years it creates a very dense, even-textured turf. It prefers full sun, but the newer varieties are able to tolerate part shade as well. While it requires considerable moisture to look its best during the hot summer months, greater drought resistance is being developed in bluegrass seed.

If you decide to use a Kentucky bluegrass mixture, be sure to purchase the newer type of seed. Many of the older Kentucky bluegrass mixtures used in full sun are vulnerable to the fungal disease, leaf spot. When bluegrass is used in partial shade, powdery mildew can be a problem. The older variety, 'Merion', is quite susceptible to stripe smut. The newer varieties of bluegrass are much more resistant to these problems.

We have sown a modern Kentucky bluegrass mixture in our front yard. While it takes a bit more attention during the hot Philadelphia summers, we feel it makes the best impression on passersby and our neighbors.

TURF-TYPE TALL FESCUE

Tall fescue *(Festuca arundinacea)* has come a long way over the past decade. Originally considered a weed, in its new incarnation it is preferred for lawns that experience heavy-duty use. Tall fescue is so tough it is often used as the primary grass for football fields. It can withstand fairly heavy use and continue to look good. Heavy use does not mean having damage such as divots or chunks being pulled out. Once damaged, it will not repair itself as well as Kentucky bluegrass, but then no grass is capable of enduring unlimited heavy and hard wear. Any living plant will suffer from being continually stepped upon.

As with Kentucky bluegrass, tall turf-type fescue should always be planted in the fall for best results.

Aside from its toughness, tall fescue's greatest asset is its drought resistance. It actually needs just as much water as does Kentucky bluegrass, but because its roots grow almost twice as deep as those of Kentucky bluegrass (assuming it is growing in good soil), it has twice the volume of soil from which to extract its water. Therefore, tall fescue seldom needs to be watered.

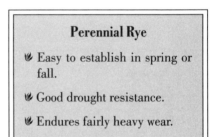

Tall Fescue

🍃 Very drought resistant.

🍃 Tolerates heavy wear.

🍃 Needs less fertilizer.

🍃 Best planting time in fall.

🍃 Not good in Far North.

Perhaps the most dramatic progress made in turf-type tall fescue over the years has been in its appearance. Its original coarse, very rough-textured, light green blades and clumpy growth habit have evolved into finer-textured, deep green blades with a more uniform growth habit. The tall fescue we have experimented with in our backyard looks just as nice as the Kentucky bluegrass in our front yard. Furthermore, it holds up beautifully under Liz's constant back-and-forth with the mower, spreader, loaded garden cart and other foot traffic.

On the down side, pythium is fairly common in tall fescue lawns during periods of high temperatures and humidity. Tall fescue is also somewhat susceptible to brown patch.

PERENNIAL RYE

Perennial rye *(Lolium perenne)* represents a nice middle ground between tall fescue and bluegrass. It is nearly comparable to either grass in appearance, in durability, in toughness, in drought resistance and in level of maintenance.

Perennial Rye

🍃 Easy to establish in spring or fall.

🍃 Good drought resistance.

🍃 Endures fairly heavy wear.

🍃 Not good in Far North.

Where it offers a distinct advantage is in how easily it germinates and grows. Both Kentucky bluegrass and tall fescue are best sown in the fall, because their roots develop more slowly. They need several months to mature before they can handle summer heat. Perennial ryegrass, on the other hand, germinates and develops rapidly. It is ideal for sowing in the spring and even in the early summer, as well as in the fall. Use it for patching bare spots throughout the season.

Because perennial rye germinates faster than the other two grass types, it is often part of both bluegrass and tall fescue mixtures. It provides

Where Perennial Rye Grows Best

☐ Best growing area.

some welcome green in newly seeded patches or lawns while the other seeds are taking their good old time to germinate. If you must do something to improve the appearance of your lawn in the spring, then use perennial ryegrass as the primary grass. It will stand some shade, but works best in mostly sunny areas.

Perennial rye grows best in areas of the North that have moderate climates. It's happiest growing in the area bounded by Pittsburgh on the north and Raleigh on the south. Grown too far north, it suffers from the severe winters; grown too far south, it suffers from the prolonged, hot summers. These stresses make it much more vulnerable to disease problems.

When you buy a perennial ryegrass mixture, look for a product which has from 15–40 percent bluegrass in the mix. It upgrades the durability and general appearance of a turf composed mainly of improved ryegrass varieties.

Pythium is common in ryegrass lawns when the temperature and the humidity are high. These grasses are also susceptible to brown patch and red thread. If perennial rye is mixed with other types of grass in the lawn, however, an attack of one of these fungal diseases will not ruin the entire lawn.

Fine Fescue

🌿 Tolerates shade better than any other grass.

🌿 Tolerates poor soils.

🌿 Has nice color and fine texture.

🌿 Does best with normal wear.

FINE FESCUE

As we mentioned earlier, the term "fine fescue" refers to a collection of fescues that tend to be fine-textured with thin blades. They generally do quite well in shade, even though they thrive in sun as well. Fine fescues include what are called hard fescue, creeping red fescue, chewing fescue, sheep fescue and spreading fescue.

Fine fescues are seldom used by themselves, but represent an important component of many mixtures that feature bluegrass or tall fescue. They generally tolerate normal wear but do not recover quickly from serious injury.

A COMMENT ABOUT ZOYSIA

Conspicuous by its absence in our discussion of northern grasses is zoysia grass *(Zoysia japonica)*. This is because it is essentially a warm-climate grass. Many northern homeowners, however, have been attracted to it because it is extremely drought tolerant and, once established, weed resistant.

Even though it enjoys a certain popularity in the North, we hesitate to include zoysia in this

Where Fine Fescue Grows Best

▨ Best growing area.

▢ Does well, but requires more work.

▨ Only with irrigation.

chapter because it is only green for about three months out of the year.

Early in the fall it goes dormant, bleaching out to form a mat of dry, beige turf. It remains this color until very late in the spring. From our perspective, a grass that is brown most of the year is hardly a suitable or attractive year-round turf. We are definitely biased against zoysia.

Zoysia is planted as plugs (rooted sprigs of young grass) inserted in the ground at intervals of 3–6 inches. The plugs

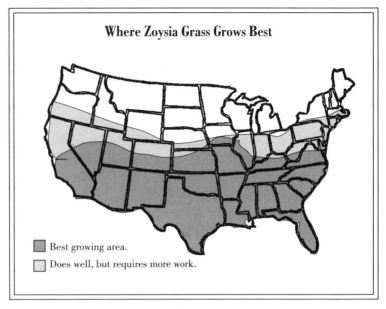

Where Zoysia Grass Grows Best

■ Best growing area.

□ Does well, but requires more work.

spread by sending out stolons, or runners, filling in to become a dense, matted turf in three to five years. Aside from its long dormant period, a major drawback is that it is invasive. Its spreading doesn't stop at your property line. Zoysia slowly insinuates itself into your neighbor's lawn and flower beds, and makes its way on down the street if measures are not taken to control it.

Zoysia does not do well in partial shade, preferring full sun at all times. To give it its due, it needs little or no watering or fertilizing—good low-maintenance credentials. However, these are offset every time you try to mow a zoysia lawn. It is very difficult to push a mower through its dense foliage. Excessive buildup of thatch is also a major problem with zoysia grass and is almost impossible to prevent in cooler climates. So, while zoysia has certain undeniable virtues, our feeling is that, all things considered, it does not qualify as a desirable turf grass for northern regions.

Current research suggests that in a year or two homeowners may be able to purchase sod composed of both zoysia and tall fescue, which offers the best of both their worlds. Theoretically, the lawn will be green in the off-season, thanks to the presence of the tall fescue. It will stay green in the hot summer without extra watering because of the zoysia. If you are a zoysia enthusiast this may be good news.

To achieve this same balance, it is possible to overseed an existing zoysia with tall fescue. To accomplish this, consult the next chapter where we discuss how to overseed existing lawns.

Some Questions to Ask

So now that we've reviewed the alternatives, it's time to select grass seed. Determining the answers to three key questions will help you make the right selection. Where do you live? How much shade do you have? How do you use your lawn?

WHERE DO YOU LIVE?

The first question is "Where do you live?" It is not enough to answer, "In the North." There is a considerable difference between the weather in Boston and the weather in Chicago, yet both are northern cities where planting northern grasses is appropriate. Grass seed mixtures suited to each of these areas will vary somewhat.

Fortunately, you don't have to worry about these variations when buying seed for your particular area. All the reputable grass seed companies have done extensive research to determine what is the best mixture of which grasses—even which varieties of those grasses—for optimum success in your area. Your local garden centers and other retail outlets routinely stock those mixtures that are suitable for your area.

GRASS CHOICES IN THE FAR NORTH

In the Far North, the choice of tall fescue or perennial rye is in part dependent on whether you can predict a good snow cover for most of the winter, most every year. These two grasses will suffer winterkill in unprotected Far North lawns. People living in more northern sections of New England, New York, Michigan, Wisconsin and Minnesota need to consider this problem in choosing a grass. If you do live in the Far North with little hope of predictable snow cover, then a mixture of Kentucky bluegrass and a fine fescue is probably the best choice.

GRASS CHOICES IN THE PACIFIC NORTHWEST

While experts differ, most feel that a good seed mixture for the Pacific Northwest would feature perennial ryegrass as its major component. Then it would also have some Kentucky bluegrass and/or fine fescue. Yardeners in the Northwest might look into a mixture of fine fescue and colonial bentgrass for a lower-maintenance lawn, a mixture recommended by some professionals.

GRASS CHOICES IN THE TRANSITIONAL ZONE

For yardeners living in what is called the transitional zone between the northern and the southern regions of this country, choosing lawn grass is a bit more complicated. As you can see on the map, there is no simple dividing line between the North and the South, above which only certain grasses can be grown and below which others are best suited. Rather, there is a fuzzy transitional belt that spans the country (see map) in which either northern grasses or southern grasses will grow well.

This zone is roughly a hundred miles wide astride a theoretical line drawn between Norfolk, Virginia, and Tulsa, Oklahoma. A general guideline is that cool-season varieties are likely to be better for the higher elevations and mountainous areas in this zone and warm-season southern grasses are better for lower elevations. The grass choice that works pretty well in both situations is turf-type tall fescue. It can handle the heat of the lower regions in the transitional area.

Our advice is to talk with experienced neighbors and with staff in a local garden center, home center or hardware store. After years of selling quality grass seed, they will know whether your particular property will do best with the northern grasses we've described above, or more appropriately should have the southern grasses which we do not cover in this book. Southern grasses include Bermuda grass, St. Augustine grass, centipede grass, zoysia and others.

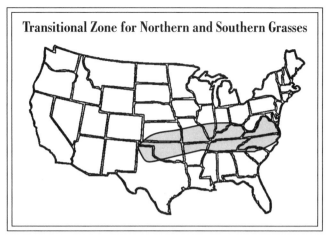

Transitional Zone for Northern and Southern Grasses

If you buy grass seed by mail order, check to be sure the company will forward to you a product that is appropriate for your local climate, soil and general conditions.

How Much Shade Do You Have?

As we have indicated, certain types of grasses do better than others in reduced-sun situations. If your lawn area does not receive sun all day, then it is important to choose a mixture that is formulated of grasses that can handle some shade. Sun-loving grasses may survive in reduced light, but they will be stressed. Their reduced vigor will make them vulnerable to disease and pests. Again, if you buy top-quality grass seed that is labeled for shade, you make the best choice. Bear in mind that grass seed labeled for shade must have some sun and bright light during each day.

So, how do you evaluate the light situation in your yard? For

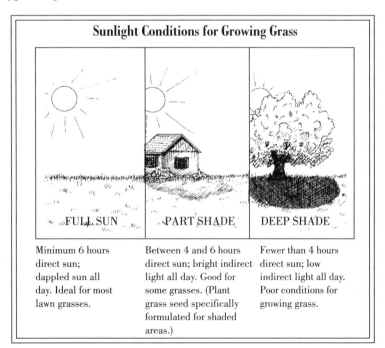

Sunlight Conditions for Growing Grass

FULL SUN

PART SHADE

DEEP SHADE

Minimum 6 hours direct sun; dappled sun all day. Ideal for most lawn grasses.

Between 4 and 6 hours direct sun; bright indirect light all day. Good for some grasses. (Plant grass seed specifically formulated for shaded areas.)

Fewer than 4 hours direct sun; low indirect light all day. Poor conditions for growing grass.

purposes of choosing grass seed, we have devised some simple guidelines.

A site that receives direct sun at least six hours a day, or dappled sun (as through a tree's canopy) almost all day, is basically a *sunny* site. These are ideal light conditions and lawn grasses thrive in these sites.

A site that receives limited sunshine—at least four but fewer than six hours over the entire day—is in *partial shade.* Some spots may not receive sun, but may enjoy bright indirect light a good bit of the time. In all these areas, it is advisable to plant grass seed formulated and labeled for shade areas.

A site that receives miminal sun—fewer than four hours a day, or low light (under thick tree canopies)—is in *deep shade.* We recommend that you not even attempt to grow turf grass on these sites. Instead, plant sturdy, evergreen ground covers such as pachysandra or ivy. These plants are very low-maintenance and promote tree health. While it can be done, growing turf grass in deep shade is an extremely labor-intensive project, hardly the kind of thing yardeners want to get into, unless, of course, they need a time-consuming hobby!

How much light falls on a given site in your yard may have a lot to do with the trees you have there. Sometimes an area can be rescued from deep shade by judicious pruning. By cutting out small limbs, suckers and twigs from within tree canopies and/or by pruning large lower limbs from the trunk to raise the canopy, you can encourage more light to reach the soil beneath the tree. Do not top trees or "head back" major limbs to reduce the size of the leaf canopy. This maims the tree, reducing its life expectancy. These measures may create partial-shade conditions where grass can grow. When Jeff took some lower limbs from our sycamores, our whole side yard became eligible for grass.

HOW DO YOU USE YOUR LAWN?

Various types of grass play different roles in a residential landscape. Your front lawn serves a different purpose from your back and side lawns.

For instance, usually the front lawn is basically ornamental. It is there to look attractive and welcoming all season long. It is not normally subjected to wear and tear and foot traffic, except maybe by the mail carrier. Any of the modern Kentucky bluegrasses, tall fescues or perennial ryegrasses show to excellent advantage under these circumstances.

The lawn in the backyard is often another situation altogether. Family leisure activities, children's play and foot traffic to utility areas all take a toll on turf. In this situation, a grass that can take some abuse is desirable. Here, tall fescue or perennial rye might be more appropriate than Kentucky bluegrass mixtures. Tall fescue is especially appropriate in these situations if you live in a more southern climate with a hot, dry summer, or where irrigation and fertilizing are not used to help maintain the turf.

Perhaps the previous owner planted bluegrass over the whole property. If you have small children, it may make sense to change the type of grass in areas that are getting increased

wear. In most cases, simply buying a grass mixture advertised for play areas and overseeding it into your existing turf in the fall will improve the durability of the lawn.

Super Grasses

As we've noted several times, the technology of grass seed development has made enormous strides in recent years. Consequently, within ten years we expect to see what we are calling "super grasses" on the market. They will have an innate ability to fight off insects and to feed themselves. They will establish easily, grow very, very slowly and seldom need watering. Sounds great, doesn't it? Although we probably won't be throwing our mowers away, we'll find that lawn maintenance will get a lot easier by the turn of the century. Here's a glimpse of some of the latest advances. Evidence of this new technology will begin to appear on grass seed package labels in the very near future.

PRESOAKED OR "PRIMED" GRASS SEED

Very soon, "primed" grass seed will begin to appear on store shelves. Pretreated so that it needs less moisture for germination, this seed germinates almost twice as quickly as regular, untreated seed. Primed seed also produces plants with deeper root systems than regular seed. It will cost more, but the benefits of rapid, dependable germination are worth the extra expense.

Nitrogen-Fixing Grass

Soon grass will be able to supply for itself most of its critical nutrient, nitrogen. Scientists have found a naturally existing bacteria *(Azospirillum brasilenseis)* which, when added to grass seed, gives the grass plant the ability to collect its own nitrogen from the air and "fix" it in the soil, where it is available to the plant roots as food. This bacterially enhanced seed is just now appearing in the marketplace in limited amounts. In the next few years, we should see nitrogen-fixing grass seed becoming very common.

So, choosing grass seed is a bit more complicated than simply reaching for the first package you spot on the store shelf that has a low price. However, it is not as complicated as the length of the foregoing discussion might suggest. Just bear in mind the key points. Plan to spend a little more money to assure that you are getting the best quality of seed. Take into account the region of the country you live in and be sure to choose grass that is best adapted for its climate. Determine whether your lawn area qualifies as "sunny" or "partial shade" and choose seed appropriate to the light conditions. Finally, consider how the lawn will be used and choose grass seed that will flourish in that situation.

Now that the mental work is done, it is time to discuss the physical-work part of renewing your lawn.

Chapter Eight

Planting Grass

Getting Ready

After analyzing the turf situation on your property, taking steps to revive and repair the soil and then selecting an appropriate grass seed, it is time to get out there and plant grass! While you are doing it, take the trouble to do it correctly so that you avoid complications later on.

An unavoidable fact of life is that it takes at least two years to get any lawn in good shape, even longer to build the "perfect" low-maintenance lawn. Not only does it take some time for infertile, compacted soil to recover its health, but it also takes more than one annual seeding to get an attractive, "dense" turf. So in lawn renovation, as in so many other areas of life, patience is a virtue.

GOING FOR THICK GRASS

A "dense" turf is the goal because it not only looks great, but it contributes to low maintenance. The thicker the grass is planted, the less opportunity for weeds to intrude. The ideal turf supports at least six grass plants in every square inch of soil. This requires from ten to twenty seeds on every square inch of bare soil if you are starting from scratch. Roughly ten seeds per square inch is sufficient if you are overseeding an existing turf.

These estimates of the amount of seed needed in either situation reflect the discouraging fact that you can expect a low germination rate. Homeowners are lucky if 50 percent of the seeds they sow germinate and if 50 percent of the grass that does germinate survives the first season. This is not the fault of the seed, especially if it is the high-quality type that we recommend. Poor germination is mostly caused by insufficient moisture.

Grass seed needs to be constantly moist if it is to germinate and sprout. Miss just one day of watering the seedbed and you may reduce germination by 30 percent; skip two days and only half the seeds will germinate. There are several ways to keep the new seed moist after a rain or your watering, which we will discuss later in this chapter.

EQUIPMENT AND SUPPLIES

To sow grass seed correctly you will need to have a few supplies and tools on hand. Whether you are simply patching a few bare spots in the lawn or you are going "all the way" and starting from scratch, a lawn rake and a hose or watering can are essential. A slow-release fertilizer and some kind of topdressing or mulching materials are optional. If you have a mechanical seeder of some sort, that is preferable to casting the seed by hand, but it is not essential. We will cover the necessary supplies for each specific situation further in this chapter.

When to Plant Grass

Timing for planting any grass seed is critical because new, tender grass plants need time to develop roots and gain strength before either very hot or very cold weather arrives. The ideal planting time for all northern grasses is the late summer/early fall period. While most seeds may germinate just fine in the spring, only perennial rye seedlings are able to handle August heat. Kentucky bluegrass and tall fescue seedlings need the cool fall weather to become strong and established for next year's heat. Another reason to avoid seeding in the summer is that all turf grasses are susceptible to pythium fungal disease when they are seedlings. Pythium strikes seedlings when it is hot and humid, the chronic conditions of high summer.

FALL IS FOR PLANTING GRASS

Obviously, grass planted in the fall has nine months to get its roots deep and to get more established before having to face that summer heat. It is much better able to survive its first year than grass planted in the spring. There is another good reason for fall planting.

In the North, annual weeds—crabgrass and others—complete their life cycles in the fall and die out, so they aren't there to compete with the new seedlings for space, water and soil nutrients. Common

Time to Plant Grass Seed

Late Winter	Late Spring	Summer	Early Fall
TRICKY	IN SOME CASES	USUALLY NOT	BEST TIME
Can work but not terribly reliable.	Perennial rye is most reliable. Avoid planting Kentucky blue or tall fescue where summers are usually hot.	Perennial rye can be planted for patching but that's about it.	Absolutely the best time to plant any northern grass seed.

chickweed, mayweed and peppergrass do compete with grasses in early spring, though. However, they, too, stop growing in the fall and pose no problem then to young grass seedlings.

Calculate when to sow grass seed in the fall by counting back four to six weeks prior to when the first light frost is usually expected in your area. For example, if first frost is October 15, then September 1 or thereabouts is the best time to sow. Grass that germinates in early September has roughly three months of growing time before the soil freezes in most parts of the North. Its roots develop below soil surface during this period, even though its foliage has gone dormant.

IF IN THE SPRING YOU MUST...

If you cannot sow your lawn in the fall, then do so just as early in the spring as the passing winter allows. Try to time it so that you plant before you see leaves on the lilacs. Once lilacs bloom in your area it is getting too late. Any other time during the growing season prior to Labor Day is a poor time to sow grass seed. You can patch bare spots during the growing season, but use perennial ryegrass for that task.

One of the tricks you might consider if you are anxious to improve your lawn without waiting until fall is to overseed with a perennial ryegrass mixture. It has the best chance of surviving the heat of the summer and will renew the color and texture of your existing lawn for the season. If you prefer a lawn of primarily tall fescue or Kentucky bluegrass, plan to overseed with that in the fall. This gives you a green lawn during that first year, and a nice dense turf of your favorite grasses over a period of two years.

WINTER SEEDING

It is possible to sow grass seed over your lawn while it's still winter. During the late winter and early spring, the soil alternately freezes, thaws, then freezes again, creating shallow "honeycomb" crevices in the soil. This condition makes an ideal seedbed, allowing seeds to lodge snugly in the soil without any soil preparation. You can sow seed even if the crevices have a slight covering of snow. Planted this way, the seed will wait to germinate until temperatures are constantly in the 60° range and above. With this timetable, Mother Nature pretty much takes care of everything, including moisture supply. However, for best results, remove thatch and kill existing weeds the previous fall.

A Note about Feeding and Watering New Grass

Many yardeners do a nice job of planting and growing grass plants from seed, and then they inadvertently harm their new grass babies with improper care. So before we go any further …

TO FERTILIZE OR NOT TO FERTILIZE?

While it is OK to sow grass seed without simultaneously fertilizing, including this step is beneficial in most cases. It is important to use the right type of fertilizer. Choose a product that is labeled as "slow acting" or features a "slow-release" form of nitrogen.

Almost any brand of fertilizer formulated with over 60 percent of its nitrogen as slow release will work fine with a seeding program. If in doubt, look for a fertilizer designed specifically for starting new grass, often called "starter fertilizer." After your grass has emerged and has been growing for about four to six weeks, an application of a liquid fertilizer for lawns will give the young seedlings a gentle energy boost. From this point on, follow the annual fertilizing program discussed in Chapter Three.

HOW MUCH MOISTURE FOR HOW LONG?

As we have indicated above, continuous moisture is critical for germinating grass seed and sustaining young seedlings. So before we get into the steps for planting grass, we must stress this point. When you plant grass seed, you must be committed to keeping it moist from that time on, right through germination and its infancy as a plant.

For best germination and survival rates, the seedbed must be moist all the time. If it dries out for even a few hours, germination rates are reduced and seedling survival is jeopardized. In the absence of regular rain, you will have to provide the water. While you will not water for long (it doesn't require very much water at any one time to keep the top 1/2 inch of soil moist), you will have to water often.

Turf professionals water new seedbeds at least four times a day. Who has time for watering four times a day? No one we know. The bottom line is, however, that if you are not able to water new seedbeds at least twice a day in mild sunny weather, so little seed will grow that you are essentially wasting your time planting grass seed. It is as simple as that.

Plan to water before going to work and immediately upon returning from work. If it is possible to hire a high school kid to sprinkle the area after school, all the better. Conscientious use of topdressing and mulches will help prevent drying out, but try not to miss even one day. If seedbeds are permitted to dry out just for one day, germination can be reduced by 30 percent. Two days without moisture can reduce it by 50 percent.

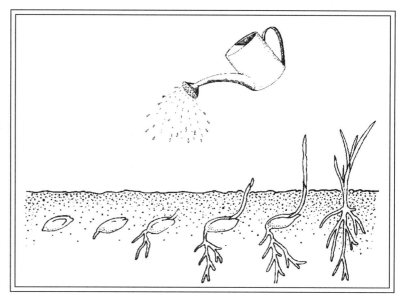

Water from seeding until grass is established.

Do not stop watering when little grass blades begin to appear. Because your seed is a mixture of several grasses, some of which are slower to germinate than others, seeds will continue to germinate successively over a three- or four-week period. For best results, continue to keep the area consistently moist.

Choosing Seed or Sod

Most of this chapter deals with starting grass from seed because we believe that for yardeners that is the most time- and cost-efficient way to rebuild turf. Sod seems to offer a very easy, "instant" lawn, but it takes skill, time and a lot of hard work to lay it and nurture it. Furthermore, sod needs watering for an even longer period of time than grass seed because it takes so long for grass roots to penetrate and establish themselves in the base soil.

Sod is also very expensive. Here again, you must go for the highest-quality grass. Don't even think about using cheap sod; it will be a disaster from the day you install it. A discussion of how to install sod is included below, but we feel it is more of an undertaking than most yardeners are willing or able to handle. If you have the money, the best way to go is to have a professional landscape firm install the sod and maintain it through the first season.

What follows next is a series of discussions on how to plant grass in various situations. We begin with the simplest job—patching a bare spot—and end with the most expensive and complex job—sodding a new lawn. Refer to the section that offers step-by-step instructions for your particular project.

Patching Bad Spots

Most lawns develop trouble spots from time to time. Bare spots or weedy areas seem to turn up while you are not looking. In these localized situations, restoring viable turf involves "patching" the damaged area with new grass.

First, determine the cause of the bare spots. Typical causes are spilled fertilizer, foot traffic, poor drainage, dog urine or wet leaves. Once grass is killed in an area, for whatever reason, weeds rush to fill the space, so they are a sign that something is wrong. Once you've figured out the cause of the problem, solve it before reseeding the spot. Try to divert foot traffic or the dog from the area, add organic matter to improve drainage and aerate or spike compacted spots. Then proceed with the patching job.

It is important to properly prepare even the smallest seedbed. Remove any weeds. Loosen the soil down about an inch or two, mixing in a small handful of slow-release fertilizer if you wish. Then rake it smooth and gently tamp it down. Water this area so that the soil is wet down at least 6 inches. Then sprinkle seed generously over the bare soil and cover it with a thin 1/8–1/4-inch layer of topsoil or peat moss.

Steps for Patching a Bad Spot

1. Clean out weeds and debris.

2. Loosen soil down an inch or so.

3. Add slow-release fertilizer.

4. Sow seeds.

5. Mulch or topdress lightly with peat moss.

6. Water twice a day.

Many homeowners like to cover the newly seeded spot with some sort of mulch to discourage moisture evaporation and protect the seed fom birds. Traditionally, a thin layer of hay or straw has been used for this purpose. Cheesecloth makes a good mulch for patched areas no wider than 3 feet. Available in grocery stores, hardware stores and fabric stores, it lets in plenty of light, air and moisture while protecting the new seed.

Cut out a piece of cloth the shape of the patch and peg it down snugly over the newly sown seed with some wooden pegs made of any scrap wood or even from little branches. Cut the pegs off so they project only an inch above the soil. The new grass will grow up through the cheesecloth and it will gradually become invisible as the grass matures. Professional turf managers leave the cheesecloth in place until it rots and disappears into the soil in about six months. Cheesecloth mulch will improve germination rates by preventing the new seed from drying out so quickly, and by protecting the soil from harsh sun and heat while the tender new grass plants struggle to become established.

Now the all-important watering regimen begins. Remember, water two or three times a day, minimum. For small patched areas, a watering can suffices for this job. After all, the soil only needs to be moist, not drenched. If it is sunny, water four times, if possible. Just don't let that dirt and seedbed dry out, ever. Keep watering for two weeks after the grass seed has germinated.

If you have a number of spots or a path to fix, you may prefer to use sod rather than seed to establish grass in these areas. Be sure to buy high-quality sod. See the discussion later in this chapter on how to prepare the soil for sod. It is important to loosen and prepare the soil more deeply. Establish the planting bed below the level of the surrounding turf so the new sod will be even with the level of the existing grass. Again, watering is the key to success. Water it more deeply than you would new seed so that the soil beneath the sod stays moist. In this case, it will take longer to water properly. Water daily (if it does not rain) for at least a month to be successful with sod used for patching.

Overseeding a Lawn

For some reason, overseeding has never been a common lawn care technique for homeowners. Professional turf managers routinely overseed their athletic fields and golf courses almost every year. It is a great way to assure a dense, thick turf which discourages weeds and looks terrific. It is also a good way to revitalize tired grass by introducing new seed periodically.

It is not as big a deal to overseed as the list of tasks that follows below seems to suggest. A proper job for a 7,000 square foot lawn takes only two days, spread ten days apart. Anyone can do it.

Just because there are weeds in your present lawn does not mean you must dig up the entire lawn to renew it. If the space they take amounts to less than 40 percent over all of the turf area, it is easier to keep the existing grass and overseed the whole area with a vigorous, modern grass.

The best time to overseed northern lawns is in the fall, six weeks before the first frost. Grass planted by overseeding tends to germinate faster than grass sown on bare soil. Assuring that it has good contact with the soil is critical. This is a bit more difficult to achieve when overseeding because

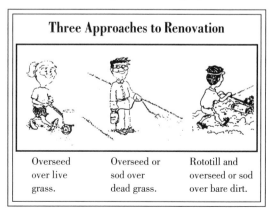

Three Approaches to Renovation

| Overseed over live grass. | Overseed or sod over dead grass. | Rototill and overseed or sod over bare dirt. |

Steps for Overseeding

1. De-thatch if necessary.

2. Pull or kill obvious weeds.

3. Aerate (optional).

4. Mow grass very short.

5. Remove all debris.

6. Roughen soil surface.

7. Fertilize (optional).

8. Sow grass seed.

9. Rake to get soil contact.

10. Spread topdressing (optional).

11. Begin watering.

12. Mulch (optional).

of the existing living turf. Even if is cut very short, it still can prevent the seed from contacting the soil directly. Follow the steps outlined below for best results.

DE-THATCH IF YOU HAVE THATCH

Thatch is an accumulation of surface roots and other debris on the soil at the base of the grass plants. While a thin layer of thatch does not normally present a problem, it must be removed before overseeding to expose bare soil for the new seed. Consider renting a de-thatching machine or a "power rake" to loosen the thatch and simultaneously scarify the soil without pulling out existing plants. A very close mowing of the lawn and brisk raking with a garden rake will accomplish the same thing. Either way, rake up the loosened thatch and discard it on the compost pile.

PULL OR KILL OBVIOUS WEEDS

Many annual weeds will be dying out as the fall approaches, so they are not a problem when overseeding at this time of year. However, if your turf shows a significant number of broad-leaved weeds, which are often perennial and will return next year, they must be removed or killed before overseeding. Judicious use of the herbicide "2,4-D" will efficiently rid the turf of dandelion, plantain, ground ivy and their ilk. Because the vigorous, dense turf that results from overseeding will discourage future weeds of this kind, this is likely to be the only time you will need to use this herbicide. Apply it at least a week or ten days before you plan to sow grass seed. Spot treat each weed or weed cluster. It will have begun to break down after ten days, so new grass seedlings will not be harmed.

- Here are the basic steps for the safe use of herbicide 2,4-D:
- Read the label carefully and follow the instructions.
- Spray when weeds are actively growing (by late summer weeds have abundant, mature foliage).
- Skip one mowing before spraying so weed foliage offers maximum surface for the herbicide application.
- Plan to spray ten days before the date scheduled for overseeding.
- Do not spray when rainfall is expected within six hours.
- Do not spray if winds exceed 5 mph to avoid drift onto other plants.
- Do not walk on, or allow pets and children to walk on, sprayed area for at least twelve hours; a twenty-four-hour wait is better.

Broad-leaved weeds will start to turn brown in three or four days and be completely dead by the end of the ten-day wait. What remains is bare soil to be overseeded. For help in dealing with all kinds of weeds found in lawns over the growing season, consult Chapter Ten on weed control.

AERATION (OPTIONAL)

Aerating the lawn is always beneficial and, if time and energy permit, while preparing for overseeding is a good time to do it. It is not essential to the success of overseeding, though.

MOW LAWN AND REMOVE DEBRIS

Since the grass seed needs to contact the soil and the new grass seedlings need lots of light to grow, it is necessary to mow the existing grass very short. Set the mower to cut at about 1/4–1/2 inch to remove as much foliage as possible. Try to avoid scraping the ground and damaging the crowns of the grass plants.

Collect the clippings in the mower bag or rake them up so that bare soil shows around the live stubble.

ROUGHEN THE SOIL SURFACE

To achieve best germination, break up or scar the surface of the bare soil so that the new seed contacts it. The easiest way to do this is to rent a power-slicing or vertical-cutting tool that cuts the surface of the soil down about 1/4–1/2 inch while it removes thatch. A hand spiking tool or garden rake also does the job. The latter alternatives involve some hard work, but they save the $50 rental costs of power machinery. Of course, the size of your lawn probably will influence your choice here.

SPREAD FERTILIZER

It is a good idea to spread a granular, slow-release nitrogen fertilizer when you are overseeding. Be sure that at least half of the nitrogen in the package is the slow-release variety. A good alternative is "starter fertilizer," which is designed specifically for use with grass seed on new lawns.

There is no need to spread lime on the lawn when overseeding. Since it takes six months for lime to begin breaking down and affecting the pH of the soil, it will not influence the environment of the newly germinated seed. Besides, it should never be spread at the same time fertilizer is.

SOW GRASS SEED

Finally, it is time to sow the grass seed. Many seed package labels prescribe different amounts of seed for overseeding and for brand-new lawns. We suggest you ignore the distinction and use the greater amount recommended for brand-new lawns. Why? Because yardeners like us do not have the luxury of time to water and care for newly sown seed that turf professionals have. We can assume that we will not have optimum germination. By using more seed than necessary, we can hedge our bet and compensate for some of the loss.

To determine how much seed you need, estimate the size of your lawn in terms of 1,000s of square feet. Recommended sowing of Kentucky bluegrass, for example, is 2 or 3 pounds for every 1,000 square feet. At that rate, it will take 20–25 pounds of seed for an 8,000-square-foot lawn. Note that the chart specifies different amounts of seed per 1,000 square feet for the different types of grass.

While it's certainly possible to sow grass seed by hand, the best way is to use a cyclone seeder. A drop spreader will also do the job, but the rate the seed is released is more difficult to control. If you are sowing by hand, take only an ounce or two of seed in your hand at a time and cast it in a semicircular motion from side to side ahead of you as you walk over the lawn. Try to cover as much area as possible, as evenly as possible. Walk over the area several times in different directions to assure even, overlapping coverage.

When using a seeding machine, divide the total amount of seed you will use in half. Spread the entire lawn with the first half, and then go over the entire lawn again in different directions with the second half of the seed. That reduces the chances of missing any spots in the lawn with the new seed. If you are using Kentucky bluegrass, which is a very small, light seed, borrow a trick from turf professionals. Give the seed some heft by mixing it with another material, or "carrier," such as sawdust, sand or fine vermiculite. Again, seed half the total amount of seed in one direction and then half in the other direction.

Rake Seed for Soil Contact

The job is not over when you've spread the seed. It is important to insure that the seed is at least in contact with the soil, and, better yet, that most of it is covered with a thin layer of soil. So the next step is to lightly rake over the lawn surface to bring the seed into contact with the top 1/8 inch of soil that has been loosened by the de-thatching process. Using a garden rake for this purpose takes more time, but it gives your seed better soil contact than a grass or leaf rake does. Ideally, only about 10 percent of the seed should remain visible, with about 90 percent covered by loose soil. This is sufficient to protect the seed while it germinates, but, to be on the safe side, you may prefer to take an extra step and topdress the overseeded lawn.

Spread Topdressing (Optional)

Topdressing means to spread a thin layer (no more than 1/4 inch) of topsoil, compost or peat moss over the turf that you have overseeded. A even covering about 1/4 inch thick does not require much of the material, but there is enough to protect the new seed and help keep it moist. Some yardeners like to lightly tamp the topdressing over the new seeds by going over the area once with a lawn roller filled about 1/3 full with water. For small lawns, simply walking on the topdressing does the trick. This slightly tamped soil will hold moisture near the seed longer. If you choose not to topdress your overseeded lawn, simply water more often to assure that the new seed does not dry out.

Water, Water, Water

Earlier in this section we emphasized how important faithful watering is to grass seed germination. So, after overseeding the lawn, begin watering. A thorough, gentle watering is essential to get things off to a good start. Then move into a watering routine as best you can. Try for twice-daily watering, minimum, if there is no rain. The idea is to keep that top 1/4 inch of soil moist. Be sure to cover the entire overseeded area each time.

If new grass appears in four or five days, don't be fooled into thinking that the watering routine can be suspended. Keep watering. Most quality grass mixtures include a "nurse" grass, such as perennial rye, that pops up quickly. It is there to protect the other seed—the tall fescue and/or Kentucky bluegrass types—which take from ten to twenty interminable days to germinate. This early nurse grass also helps the morale of the yardener who is invariably encouraged to see results so soon from such hard labor! Keep watering.

Use a Mulch (Optional)

A mulch over your newly overseeded lawn is helpful but is definitely optional. The existing turf stubble serves as an effective mulch, as does a topdressing if you choose to spread one. But if you feel you want the extra measure of protection that mulch offers, spread some mulch as the last step in overseeding. Rather than use the hay or straw often used to cover the bare soil of newly seeded, brand-new lawns, try the white, polyspun garden fabric called "floating row cover," Reemay or "agricultural fleece." Available in garden centers and hardware stores for a variety of landscape and garden uses, it is ideal for covering new grass seed.

Agricultural fleece helps protect the seed from drying out. It also discourages birds from going after the new seed. When you cover the newly overseeded lawn with fleece, the germination will be more complete and it will happen more quickly. This fabric allows air, light and water through, so water right over it. In fact, leave it in place until the existing grass outgrows its close shave and needs mowing. That will be in two or more weeks.

When Can You Mow?

Special care must be taken when mowing a newly overseeded lawn. Normally, you should be mowing your grass when it is at 3 inches or so (cutting it to 2 inches), but here we make an exception. When the older, established grass recovers from its close cut and grows to about 2 inches, mow it and new grass to 1 or 1 1/2 inches. Here, a reel mower has an advantage over a rotary mower because it is gentler on the new grass seedlings. In any case, for the next six weeks (or the remainder of the fall) keep the grass at 1 or 1 1/2 inches.

Normally, we recommend that you leave your clippings, but again we make an exception. Collect your clippings for a month or two. Mowing more closely and collecting the clippings helps the new grass seedlings get more light to encourage good strong growth.

Starting from Scratch

Overseeding works well as long as there are not too many weeds in your existing lawn. If they have virtually overtaken the grass throughout most of the lawn, a complete overhaul may be necessary. The fact that the weeds are able to make such inroads into the turf suggests that the existing grass is too weak to compete, and it is only a matter of time before weeds totally take over. In this case, there is no advantage in keeping any of this exhausted grass.

LEAVING TURF VERSUS GOING TO BARE SOIL

The easiest way to renew a totally lousy lawn is to start from scratch and plant all new grass. There are two ways to do this. One way is to kill all the existing grass and weeds with a glyphosate herbicide (Roundup) and then follow all the steps in the overseeding process just described above. This approach is very effective and takes the least amount of time because you do not disturb the soil. Raked and/or de-thatched, the dead existing turf stubble provides a base on which to seed the new lawn.

The other way to start from scratch is to remove the existing weed-infested sod layer to expose the soil below. Then dig or rototill the soil to loosen and prepare the seedbed. This is obviously a lot of work and can damage the soil structure. Usually there is no need to resort to this method unless serious underlying drainage, grade or soil problems need correction. Yardeners usually hire professionals to install a new lawn by this method, and it is not cheap.

SEEDING VERSUS HYDROSEEDING VERSUS LAYING SOD

If installing a completely new lawn is necessary, there are alternatives to the conventional seeding practices described above in the overseeding section. One is "hydroseeding," a relatively new technology for residential situations.

Hydroseeding is a process whereby seed that has been mixed into a slurry of water, fibrous material and fertilizer is power sprayed on the site through large hoses. Available only through a professional service, this high-pressure application quickly coats the soil with a 1-inch layer of wet material. The seed is sown, watered, fertilized and mulched in one step. While the lawn may still need watering every day, the fibrous material in the spray keeps the grass seed moist, just as a topdressing of soil would.

Hydroseeding assures an even distribution of seed and fertilizer. To hydroseed an existing lawn, kill the grass with Roundup, mow the grass down as low as the mower will go, de-thatch the turf to expose the bare soil between plants, if necessary, and then hydroseed right on top of the dead stubble. Hydroseeding costs more than traditional seeding but less than laying sod. Be sure the company you hire sprays a generous layer of slurry to ensure a dense turf.

If basic problems necessitate removing the turf and exposing the soil under your lawn, installing a new lawn with sod is an attractive alternative to seeding. Bare soil is always vulnerable to erosion from heavy rain, and even the best seeding and mulching job yields stands of grass of varying thickness that will definitely need follow-up overseeding in six months to achieve uniform coverage.

In contrast, sod offers an instant, weed-free, dense turf that is immediately attractive and forestalls erosion problems. However, sod laid by either you or by a professional is definitely the most expensive way to install a new lawn. It is also not always as foolproof as the advertisements suggest. It takes skill and lots of very hard work, as well as the same conscientious watering as other methods.

In the next three sections we describe the techniques for installing a completely new lawn. Review them and then choose the method that fits your needs.

	Sodding	**Seeding**
Pros	Provides instant green lawn. Can be installed most any time during the season. Works on side hills. Smothers weed seeds on bare soil. Can be planted over poor turf.	More varieties of grass. Less expensive. Can be sown quickly over large area.
Cons	Higher cost. Limited choice of grasses. Needs frequent watering longer. Takes more time to install.	Has weed competition from beginning. Hard to plant on slopes. Can't be installed in midsummer. Usually needs second overseeding.

INSTALLING A NEW LAWN OVER DEAD TURF—MINIMUM WORK

If more than 40 percent of your existing lawn is weeds and exhausted grass, start over again by seeding the whole lawn area. Follow the steps of the overseeding technique, except kill the entire lawn first (not just the broad-leaved weeds). Use a glyphosate herbicide such as Roundup. It is "nonselective," which means it kills virtually any plant it is sprayed on. Used according to label instructions, it is safe for humans, pets, the soil, birds and the rest of the environment in general.

At least eight to ten days prior to the scheduled lawn installation, spray Roundup over the lawn that is to be replaced. Take care that the spray does not accidentally get on nearby flowers or small shrubs because they will die as well. Choose a day when there is no breeze and use a sprayer that allows you to direct the spray close to the surface of the lawn, to avoid any drift.

Dress properly when spraying herbicides.

After ten days to two weeks, the old lawn will be dead or dying and you can proceed to seed the area. Follow the steps outlined above for overseeding: Mow the dead lawn very short, remove the debris, roughen the soil, spread the seed, topdress the seed and water, water and water some more. With an all-new lawn, you can delay mowing the new grass until it grows to about 3 inches high. Plan to overseed this new turf again next year, and the result will be an attractive, healthy, dense turf.

INSTALLING A NEW LAWN ON BARE SOIL—MAXIMUM WORK

If you have serious drainage, soil or grade problems in your yard, address them as part of your lawn renewal. In these situations, it is usually necessary to physically remove all the existing turf to get at the soil underneath. Because lifting the chunks of sod is a major job, it is a good idea to hire professional help if you can afford it.

EXPOSE THE SOIL

There are two ways to get rid of the existing turf. Going over and over the lawn with a heavy-duty Rototiller will break up the turf and work the sod down 8 inches into the soil. Tilling in the sod adds beneficial organic material to the soil while simultaneously getting rid of the old turf. While you are at it, also till in limestone (50–100 pounds per 1,000 square feet) and a layer of compost or peat moss. These amendments will improve the ability of the critical top 6 or 8 inches of soil to support the new grass plants.

Adjustment in the grade of your lawn can easily be made at this time. Once the soil is loosened, rake it to eliminate sunken areas and uneven patches. As a rule, soil should slope slightly down and away from the foundation of the house. It should also be about 1 inch below the level of driveways and sidewalks.

The other way to get rid of the existing turf is to lift it out in chunks and discard it. Because this backbreaking job requires some special tools, we encourage yardeners to hire a professional to do it. We do not favor this method, as a rule, because the soil loses the benefit of the addition of the old sod, which is rich in organic material. After the sod is removed from the soil, add lime and organic material and rototill as described above.

Take note! When soil is disturbed, as in rototilling, weed seeds long dormant deep in the soil are brought to the surface. Here they enjoy light and moisture, so they sprout right along with the newly planted grass seed. To prevent your new lawn from being half weeds, let the freshly tilled soil lie bare for two weeks. Allow the inevitable weed seeds to germinate— water the soil to encourage them—then spray the interlopers with Roundup. After a week's wait for the herbicide to do its job, begin seeding with grass seed.

If you prefer to avoid using herbicide, take the backside of a garden rake and uproot all the weed seedlings. Try not to break the soil surface deeper than 1/2 inch, otherwise you just bring up more weed seeds. If by week's end some weeds begin to show again, repeat the rake attack. After you do this weeding job, it is the time to work in slow-release nitrogen fertilizer or the "starter" fertilizer sold for this purpose.

Spread the Seed

Divide your seed in half and spread one batch over the entire area, pushing the seeder as you would your mower. Then spread the second half of the seed by walking the seeder perpendicular to your original passes.

Rake the Seed to Contact Soil

Drag the back edge of a garden rake over the seedbed lightly to cover the seed with loose soil. Then firm the soil over the seed with a lawn roller or the back of a rake.

Mulch (Not Optional)

It is essential to mulch grass seed that is on bare soil. Spread a thin (1/4–1/2 inch) layer of straw over the ground to help keep the soil around the seed moist. Try to mulch so lightly that the soil is still visible through the mulch. This assures that the new grass seedlings will be able to see the sun. One bale of hay should be sufficient to cover 1,000 square feet of new seedbed. Mulch not only retains moisture, but it also breaks the fall of raindrops, allowing water to sink in instead of running off in little brooklets which, in turn, cause rill erosion and utlimately wash the seed away.

Straw mulch does not need to be removed later because it will eventually rot. Take time to spread it properly. Avoid clumps or bunches which shade new grass seedlings and interfere with mowing later on. Good alternative mulches are cheesecloth, hard-to-find tobacco netting and the agricultural fleece we described in the overseeding section above. In addition to preventing erosion, mulching fabrics slow evaporation of soil moisture and prevent birds from eating the seed.

All mulches except the agricultural fleece can be left in place to decompose. The first mowing will chop them up and convert them into good organic additions to the soil. Remove the fleece when the new grass grows to 3 inches and is ready for its first mowing.

Water, Water, Water

Follow the instructions given in the overseeding section above. When there is no rainfall, water the new lawn two, preferably three, times a day. Keep it up for several weeks and avoid the temptation to relax when the seedlings first appear.

When to Mow?

Mow the new grass once it has grown past 3 inches. A very sharp blade on your rotary mower will minimize possible damage to the tender seedlings.

Are We Finished Yet?

Truth to tell, after all this hard work to install a new lawn over bare soil, you may be disappointed in its appearance. The procedure we've described above is actually only the first phase of the job. Because it is started from scratch, with no existing grass to help fill in thin areas, a newly seeded lawn always needs overseeding the next year or two to develop a uniformly gorgeous, dense turf. Follow-up overseeding is relatively simple, since the soil has already been rehabilitated.

Using Sod to Renovate

Some yardeners prefer to use sod rather than seed. They are tempted by the prospect of an instant, ready-made lawn. As we warned earlier in this chapter, it is more expensive and very hard work.

Sod can be installed successfully in either the spring or the fall, regardless of the type, and it is available in all the northern grass seed types. Best of all, if it is high-quality sod, it will be nice and dense and weed free.

Select Best Sod

Choosing a good-quality sod is not as easy as it might sound. Even in the better garden centers you might not be able to find out exactly what varieties of grass are included in the sod. As with grass seed, the most expensive sod will likely have the newest varieties with their added insect, disease and drought tolerance. Choose a sod that has a lush, uniform green color and is thoroughly moist. Beware of dried-out edges and thick layers of thatch. A thick matrix of grass roots should be visible in the soil. Sod is usually sold in strips 2–10 feet long and 1–2 feet wide. The soil part should be no thicker than 1 inch; 1/4 inch works best (the sod must

> ### Steps to Take When Sodding
> 1. Select best sod.
> 2. Prepare soil.
> 3. Apply fertilizer.
> 4. Dampen soil.
> 5. Install sod.
> 6. Roll sod.
> 7. Water, water and water.

be thick enough—and knit together sufficiently—to survive handling without tearing). Do not actually buy sod until the soil is all prepared, so it can be laid immediately. If you must store it for a day or so, pile it in the shade and keep it covered to protect it from heat and light. Keep it moist by watering it from time to time if necessary.

Prepare Soil

Prepare the soil for sod just as we described for a bare-soil seeding operation (see description above). Use a heavy-duty Rototiller to incorporate the existing turf down into the soil at least 6 inches. Add at least an inch of compost, peat moss or mushroom soil while you are at it to improve the organic content of the soil. Whether you do this job yourself or have a professional do it, do not lay sod on that bare soil without first rototilling it and adding some organic amendments. Otherwise, the chances of that sod establishing itself well are very slim.

Apply Fertilizer

While raking the tilled soil smooth with a garden rake, work some slow-release nitrogen fertilizer or "starter" fertilizer into the top inch of soil. It will encourage grass roots to extend deeper into the soil and the sod becomes established more quickly.

WATER SOIL

Lay the sod on moist, but not muddy, soil. To assure that the soil is not overly soaked when installation begins, water it thoroughly the day before the big job so it can drain overnight. It should be moist down at least 6 inches. One or 2 inches of water should be sufficient.

INSTALL SOD

Working with sod is similar to laying carpeting or tile. You put down pieces, cutting them to fit as you work and paying special attention to the seams where two pieces meet. When installing sod, have at least one helper to bring pieces to you as you work. Teenagers are ideally suited for this task. With this system, you do not need to be constantly getting up and down.

Lay the first strips of sod along a walkway or place a 2-by-4 on the ground to establish a straight edge. Use a large knife or even a hatchet to cut sod strips or crop them to fit irregular areas.

As you lay sod strips, adjust them as bricklayers fit bricks so the end seams of one row are not flush with those of the next row. Fit strips together as tightly as possible. Avoid stepping on the prepared soilbed by placing a board on the first sodded strip to kneel on and move it forward as sodding progresses. Snug the edges of each strip against adjacent ones and press down on them lightly so they make uniform contact with soil. The idea is to prevent the edges from drying out, as they are very prone to do. Prevent air pockets under the new sod by using the kneeling board to avoid repeated walking or kneeling on it while working or just after watering.

Have a bucket of good topsoil nearby to use to topdress the seams where sod pieces abut. Sprinkle the soil along the cracks and brush it in with a broom or the back of a wooden rake—a good job for a helper.

When laying sod on steep slopes, position strips at right angles to the slope rather than parallel to it. This prevents erosion of the soil between the pieces of sod from rain or watering. Hold the sod in place with wooden pegs driven at right angles into the slope.

ROLL SOD

While a roller may be an optional tool in seeding lawns, it is essential to a sodding operation. One or two passes with a lawn roller filled one-third full with water assures good contact between the sod and the soil surface; that contact is critical to encouraging the roots of the sod to penetrate the soil.

WATER, WATER, WATER

Water within thirty minutes of installing sod. Drying out is the greatest danger to new sod. It tends to occur quickly along the edges—first along seams where it meets the sidewalk or the driveway. Provide at least an inch of water on the new sod at least once a day. Unlike seedbeds, sod needs the water to penetrate deeply. It must soak several inches into the soil to maintain an attractive environment that encourages the roots in the sod to grow into the soil. Continue this daily watering routine without missing one day for at least two weeks; three weeks is better. Even after this period, a newly sodded lawn needs more watering attention than an established lawn.

Keep a close watch on the sod along the edge of the driveway or sidewalk and the seams between strips. Brown edges signal that you've slipped up on your watering chores.

WALKING, MOWING AND FEEDING SOD

Do not walk on or use newly sodded turf for at least three weeks—a month is better. Any stress while those tender new roots are growing into the soil seriously retards the establishment of the turf.

A month after it is laid, the new sod might appreciate a snack. Use a liquid fertilizer designed for spraying through a hose-end sprayer. Use only fertilizer (not fertilizer/pesticide combinations) and follow the instructions on the package carefully. This snack, combined with the slow-release fertilizer applied just prior to laying the sod, provides all the nutrition the new lawn needs until the next regular spring or fall feeding.

Wait as long as possible before mowing your newly sodded lawn for the first time. Mowing requires walking on the turf, which can harm the new roots connecting to the soil. It is a good idea to let the grass grow to at least 3 inches, and 4 is better. Mow just a little off the top first, then come back two or three days later and take it down to 2 inches.

What Went Wrong?

We hate to admit it, but we have made a number of mistakes over the years as we tried to learn how to have a "perfect" lawn. As it turns out, our mistakes were fairly typical. So just in case you've followed our advice in this chapter and the results fall short of your expectations, we'll share what we believe to be the most common mistakes that might be responsible.

1. Failing to water often enough and long enough.
2. Poor contact between the seed/sod and the soil, or too much soil covering the seed.
3. Failing to use enough grass seed.
4. Grass planted at the wrong time of year.
5. Fertilizer had weed killer in it.
6. Seed washed away from heavy rains because not mulched.
7. Area was too shady.
8. Seeded/sodded area walked on too soon.

By now you are probably thinking maybe a nice green ground cover like pachysandra might be better after all. Planting grass or laying sod may seem to be a lot more complicated than you anticipated. All we can say is that if you want to save time, effort and money on lawn care in the future, it is necessary to spend some time, effort and money now. While you will be overseeding and patching from time to time over the years, if you install a new lawn properly you will not have to do that major job again (unless, of course, you move!).

While we would like to be able to assure you that your renovated lawn will be so low-maintenance that it is virtually trouble free, we cannot do that. There will be occasional problems, even in the healthiest turf. We discuss the most common ones in the next chapter.

SECTION III

LAWN PROBLEMS

Chapter Nine

Dealing with Problems

It is a rare lawn that does not have some problems now and then. Brown patches, weed invasion and yellowed or chewed grass foliage are just a few of the possibilities. Sometimes a lawn is just subpar, even though there are no obvious trouble spots. In either situation, the challenge is to figure out what is causing the problem. Until that is clear, it is impossible to come up with a proper solution. While that seems pretty straightforward, diagnosing the cause of lawn problems is not always so easy.

How to Diagnose a Problem

Diagnosing a lawn problem can be very difficult, even for professional turf specialists. Problems in lawns are caused by a number of things. Grass plants, like other plants, are vulnerable to pest insects, various diseases, damage from animals and general inattention

from us. A patch of dying grass may be under attack from grubs in the soil, a fungal disease or the neighbor's female dog.

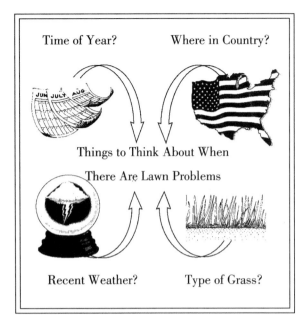

Time of Year?   Where in Country?

Things to Think About When

There Are Lawn Problems

Recent Weather?   Type of Grass?

A major complication is that often the cause of a problem occurred years before, maybe even as the house was built. It is quite important that we know whether the problem is caused by some outside agitator or maybe (blush) by our own oversight or neglect. If you assume that sod webworms are causing the dead patches in the lawn and then spray the grass with a powerful insecticide when, in fact, the problem is a fungal disease, you will compound the problem. Better to take pains to accurately determine the cause of the problem. Here there is great value in being patient.

How to diagnose lawn problems? It turns out that the time of year, the type of grass you have, the part of the country in which you live and the current weather pattern all play key roles in determining which problem you are confronting. While these factors seem to make accurate diagnosis more complicated, in fact they don't. By understanding them and taking them into account when you analyze your turf problem, you can probably rule out a whole lot of possibilities. This chapter and the next three chapters are set up to help you try to sort out all those variables without having to become a turf expert.

TIME OF YEAR AND LAWN PROBLEMS

Very few lawn problems are potential threats over the entire growing season. Some problems occur only in the spring, others in the summer and yet others only in the fall. Some problems even develop exclusively in the winter. The chart on the opposite page shows some of the most common problems that tend to surface only during certain parts of the season. This means that when you spot something wrong, the first question to ask is who are the possible bad actors for the current season.

TYPE OF GRASS AND LAWN PROBLEMS

Most yardeners do not know what kind of grass they have in their lawn, unless of course they planted it themselves. If you don't know for sure, assume that yours is Kentucky bluegrass. Prior to five years ago, most lawns were planted with this grass. In any case, as you can see in the chart, some types of grass are more vulnerable to certain problems than others. So if you have a perennial ryegrass lawn and it develops areas where the blades have a gray coating, then you can be pretty sure it is mildew because that disease is most common in ryegrass lawns. However, that same symptom in a bluegrass lawn might indicate leaf smut instead.

PART OF COUNTRY AND LAWN PROBLEMS

While pests and diseases do not exactly read maps, they do thrive in some geographical regions and not in others. Knowledge of these locally occurring pests and diseases helps narrow the possibilities when it comes to diagnosing a problem. You can assume that because your area is the favorite home of only certain unwelcome

Typical Problems of Different Types of Grass			
Type of Grass	**Insects**	**Diseases**	
Kentucky blue	Chinch bugs	Dollar spot	Leaf spot
	Billbugs	Pythium blight	Necrotic ring spot
	Cutworms	Summer patch	Powdery mildew
	Grubs	Red thread	Rust
	Sod webworms	Leaf smut	
Tall fescue	Cutworm	Pythium blight	
	Grubs	Summer patch	
	Sod webworms	Snow mold	
	Billbugs	Leaf spot	
Perennial rye	Cutworms	Dollar spot	Rust
	Grubs	Brown patch	Snow mold
	Sod webworms	Pythium blight	Red thread
	Billbugs	Summer patch	

pests, it is highly likely that a problem in your lawn is due to one of these. In these final three chapters, we help you to determine whether any of the insects or diseases we describe like to live in your neck of the woods.

WEATHER AND LAWN PROBLEMS

One of the most subtle variables that influence the incidence of lawn problems is the weather. Humidity, precipitation and heat all have enormous impact on disease and insect populations. Extreme or sudden weather variation sometimes triggers a population explosion of pests, causing a serious destructive problem in your lawn. You might not be able to figure out what is happening; it's just another good thing to blame on the poor weather forecaster.

There is no need to memorize all the possible problems that can occur with all the variables in the weather. What we suggest, though, is that when a problem shows up, don't assume that it will persist indefinitely. It may be just a function of some quirky weather and once the weather changes, the problem will go away. Again, in these final chapters we try to identify those problems that are particularly related to weather conditions.

Stress As a Fundamental Cause of Problems

Before addressing the list of all the potential lawn problems, let's take a closer look at what really constitutes a problem. It is important to understand that the types of problems we have been referring to so far—pest insects, diseases, weeds—are often actually symptoms of some more pervasive, subtle underlying condition, something you might be overlooking.

Any strategy you devise to deal with lawn problems must take into account the fact that there is a reason why your grass is suddenly vulnerable to an insect or disease that it resisted two days ago. That reason is likely to be that the environment of the grass plants has changed in some way over those two days. As we have seen, an environmental shock such as a sudden change in typical weather fosters problems. Other environmental changes may be severe mowing of the grass blades, compacted soil under the turf, a change in available light or shade because a tree has been cut down or even the application of a powerful insecticide.

In each case, the environmental change creates stress for the grass plants. Under normal conditions, grass is able to defend itself against the pests, bacteria, spores and viruses that are part of the diverse population of living things in your yard. But when something in its environment is altered, grass plants' natural defenses are weakened. Plants of any kind under stress (and people too, for that matter) are less able to resist disease. Such plants become more attractive to pest insects, which have an uncanny ability to zero in on plants that are struggling.

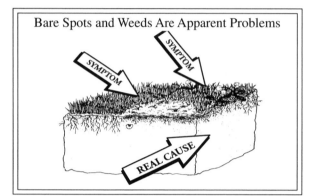

The real problem is the stress caused by compaction.

While it may not be true 100 percent of the time, it is safe to say that most of the times your lawn suffers some kind of insect, disease or weed problem, you have that immediate problem because your grass has an underlying problem—stress!

For instance, sod webworms are an immediate problem, but they are also a symptom of an underlying problem. Lawns fall victim to sod webworms because excessive thatch has built up around the crowns of the grass plants because they are growing in compacted soil. Although the thatch fosters webworms, it is the compacted soil that is the true culprit in this case. It distorts grass root development, which stresses the plants. Eliminate the cause of stress, the compacted soil, and the webworms are not likely to return.

So, when insects, weeds and disease invade your turf, they are signals that the grass is suffering a less-visible problem as well. Rather than simply taking measures to combat the pest, consider also what underlying environmental factors may be at work. Unless you address them, the pest or disease will probably return, and who needs that?

This relationship between pest problems and plant stress means that effectively dealing with lawn problems is usually a two-step job. First, address the immediate problem to control the damage done to the lawn. For example, kill the sod webworms. Then, determine the cause of the plant stress that encouraged the sod webworms in the first place. In this case, it was probably compacted

The Five Most Common Causes of Stress in Your Lawn

- ❧ Compacted soil.
- ❧ Infertile soil.
- ❧ Old or inappropriate grass.
- ❧ Bad cultural practices.
- ❧ Weather.

soil. Aerate the lawn and topdress it with some organic material to reduce the compaction. By altering the turf environment to favor vigorous, healthy grass development, you ensure that the sod webworms will not find desirable conditions in your lawn in the future.

The sidebar lists the five most common causes of stress in a lawn which, in turn, promote insect, disease or weed problems. Notice that four out of the five causes of stress are situations that you can do something about. There are even things you can do to relieve the stress caused by the weather. Although you can't really control the weather, if it is dry you can at least water. What this suggests is, that by addressing these known causes of stress in your lawn, you can preempt most pest and disease problems! An investment in upgrading the lawn and its soil is the most effective way to deal with potential problems.

Encourage Nature's Pest Controls

In the first two sections of the book we discussed the importance of healthy soil and modern grass seed in achieving an attractive lawn. In the process, we described techniques for caring for the lawn and renovating it. We frequently mentioned the critical role that the microorganisms that live in the soil play in keeping soil and grass plants healthy. Now, in the context of controlling pest problems, it is again important to focus on the teaming microlife in the ecological arena that we call a lawn. Micro- and macroorganisms, fungi, earthworms, minute bugs, tiny wasps, ants, spiders and a myriad of other beneficial creatures in the grass and near the soil surface form a natural first line of defense against pests and diseases.

Let us introduce you to the "good guys" in your lawn. Mostly— although not exclusively— insects, these beneficial creatures go a long way toward keeping all the pest insects in a lawn under control. While there are always some grubs, some sod webworms, some fungal spores for brown patch and lots of weed seeds in any lawn, beneficial organisms are there too. They feed on the bad guys, establishing a natural balance of their respective populations so that the harmful creatures are under control. As we have seen, however, environmental events, such as periods of severe or unusual weather or mowing the grass too short, will upset this balance between pest and beneficial insects, and the pests will get the upper hand.

Nature's Insect Controls

Few yardeners appreciate the variety of beneficial insects that inhabit a healthy lawn which has not been routinely assaulted with some all-purpose, broad-spectrum insecticide annually. This is not surprising, since the lawn care industry itself has only recently begun to undertake serious research on beneficial insects in lawns. There is a lot to learn and appreciate. One interesting finding is that ants, spiders and other beneficials will consume 70 percent of the eggs laid by the moth of the sod webworm within forty-eight hours of when those eggs are deposited in the ground.

You would be astounded if you could count the number of beneficial insects found in a healthy lawn. Within every 1,000 square feet of 2-inch-tall grass there are likely to be several thousand

Beneficial Creatures in a Healthy Lawn

🌿 *Spiders* and *ants* eat eggs and larvae of all pest insects as well as the adults themselves.

🌿 *Predatory mites* kill spider mites, thrips and other small pest organisms.

🌿 *Parasitic wasps* kill pest insects by getting into their eggs to lay their own eggs, which hatch into larvae that kill the pest insect.

🌿 *Ladybugs* and their larvae eat aphids.

🌿 *Songbirds* eat all pest insects above the surface of the soil, and robins and starlings pull grubs up from below the surface.

🌿 *Ground beetles* eat spider mites, snails and many pest insects.

🌿 *Rove beetles* eat all pest caterpillars above the surface.

🌿 *Lacewings* attack aphids, mealybugs, white flies, caterpillars, leaf-hoppers, thrips and mites.

🌿 *Soldier bugs* eat all pest insects above the surface.

🌿 *Wasps* and *hornets* kill caterpillars, chinch bugs and other lawn pests.

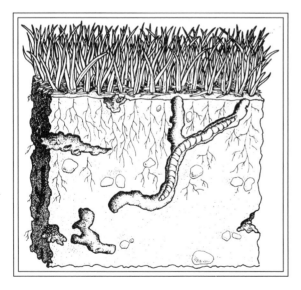

spiders and another several thousand ants alone. The population and the diversity of beneficial insects increases closer to garden beds, ground covers and fence rows. Insects that normally live in those places will range out into the lawn in pursuit of food, but then return to their homes in the mulch or under the ground cover. This is another good argument for avoiding huge expanses of nothing but turf. Not only are there great numbers of beneficials in a residential yard, but there is a great variety of them. The more diverse the plantings in your yard, the better the odds are that you have a healthy diversity of beneficial residents too.

Various beneficial insects reside in the soil as well as in the grass. The first few inches of healthy soil typically host predatory (beneficial) mites, centipedes and some of the friendly beetles. Microbes such as predatory nematodes and beneficial fungi work as fighters against insects such as grubs and chinch bugs. These beneficial allies appear in the spring two or three weeks *after* the pest insects emerge. Mother Nature works things out this way so the newly hatched beneficials have something to eat.

Obviously, the key to maintaining a healthy lawn is to help its natural defense system stay in balance. That means avoiding using insecticides that kill good and bad insects indiscriminately, cutting the grass tall, aerating the soil and taking pains to minimize other environmental stresses on the lawn.

NATURE'S DISEASE CONTROLS

There is now growing evidence that the same kind of balance we seek among pest insects and beneficial insects in the grass and in the first few inches of soil can also be achieved between disease pathogens and beneficial microbes found in a healthy soil down as deep as 12 inches. Researchers have identified beneficial fungi that actually control disease fungi, preventing the disease from ever becoming a problem.

While this is still an area where much more research is needed, it has been clearly shown that a topdressing of compost, municipal sludge or mushroom soil adds billions of these disease-fighting fungi to your lawn's soil. This is an easy way to reinforce the natural defenses already in place. There are also some naturally occurring chemicals in these topdressing products that suppress disease pathogens. So, aerating and topdressing your lawn not only improves the quality of the soil from a nutritional point of view, but it also inoculates the soil against many potential disease problems.

NATURE'S WEED CONTROLS

The simplest natural control of weeds in a lawn is a very healthy, dense turf which shades the millions of ever-present weed seeds in the turf soil. Denied access to the sun, they will not germinate. Keeping the soil well aerated so that grass roots grow deeply to produce thick grass helps fight weeds. Weeds thrive in compacted, infertile soil, so any measures that fight soil compaction also fight weeds.

Songbirds are also allies in the fight against weeds. Sparrows and other birds eat enormous numbers of weed seeds in a season. They are particularly busy gleaning seeds in the late fall, winter and early spring when the grass is dormant. Some insects such as sow bugs, millipedes and earwigs, which facilitate the decomposition of organic material in and on the soil, also break up many weed seeds as they help process the debris in the turf into humus.

KEEPING THE GOOD GUYS AROUND

Obviously, a lawn with virtually no pest problems is low maintenance. By allying with the natural defense system that nature has established, you can let beneficials do most of the pest and disease prevention work, reducing even further the time you spend maintaining the lawn. By focusing your efforts on attracting beneficials and keeping them happy in their work— reducing wherever possible any stressful environmental conditions that might sabotage their efforts—you can do less while accomplishing more. Now that's low maintenance!

Simple Steps to Attract Lawn Beneficials

🐛 Avoid preventative spraying of broad spectrum insecticides.

🐛 Mow grass at 2 inches or higher.

🐛 Plant ground covers to encourage spiders and ground beetles.

🐛 Plant wildflowers to lure parasitic wasps.

🐛 Plant flowers with flat head of florets (yarrow) or daisylike bloom (black-eyed Susan).

🐛 Landscape with rocks (5 inches in diameter or bigger) and landscaping logs to protect ground beetles.

DON'T USE PREVENTATIVE PESTICIDES

Just one "preventative" spray of a broad-spectrum insecticide over the entire lawn indiscriminately kills all the insects in its path. Products containing carbaryl (Sevin), pyrethrum, Dursban, rotenone or diazinon not only kill pests, but eliminate the majority of the beneficial insects for two to four months as well. These insecticides kill the spiders, ants, lacewings, ladybugs and all the other beneficial insects that prey on pests. After such a holocaust, some beneficials gradually reappear over the next few months, but in the interim the pests will likely have returned and started to prosper in the absence of natural defenses. Ultimately, it will take upwards of a year for the lawn's natural ecosystem to totally restore its balance. Of course, by that time, many yardeners are ready to apply another dose of preventative insecticide.

Evidence that diazinon applied in granular form also kills songbirds that mistakenly eat the granules illustrates one more way in which broad-spectrum insecticides undermine the natural pest control system in your yard.

The irony here is that homeowners are investing extra time, money and effort in a spray program that they are not sure they need in the first place. Then, having sprayed, they unwittingly bring about the very thing they are trying to prevent. This high-maintenance step actually invites the type of environmental stress that promotes problems and leads to more high maintenance. Lawn care companies love this cycle since it means more work and money for them.

DON'T MOW TOO SHORT

In Chapter Two we offered a whole bunch of good reasons why lawns prosper if grass is cut to a minimum of 2 inches tall. Keeping the lawn's beneficial insect population strong is another one. Grass sheared to 1 inch does not provide enough protective cover to the spiders, ants and beetles. They will move to more hospitable areas if the grass is so short, leaving your already-stressed grass relatively defenseless.

PLAN AND PLANT YOUR LANDSCAPE WITH BENEFICIALS IN MIND

The name of the game is diversity. The more different kinds of beneficial organisms you lure to your yard, the more likely the ones you'll need to combat a particular disease or pest will be present and on duty. Since various beneficials each have their own idea of the best food and shelter, try to provide a range of choices for them.

Beneficials such as the tiny predator wasps need nectar from flowers, so plant a variety of wildflowers and annuals to attract these allies. Other beneficials, such as spiders and various beetles, prefer to hole up under stones in pathways, or in wood chip or bark nugget mulches and among ground covers, so have these features in your landscape.

Let's Talk about Pesticides

We have had our say against the use of preventative, broad-spectrum insecticides in previous paragraphs. That does not mean that we recommend against the use of all pesticides at all times under all circumstances. It is our belief that pesticides (insecticides, fungicides and herbicides) are tools for maintaining a lawn and landscape, just as rakes and mowers are. However, whether "natural" or "chemical," they are by their nature powerful tools to be used with restraint and respect. We see them as a last resort. We turn to them only when other, more benign means fail. Like powerful antibiotics for humans, pesticides may have undesirable side effects.

Use pesticides as an emergency measure—Use pesticides when a specific insect or disease is so established that it overwhelms the natural defense system of beneficial organisms. In this situation, it threatens to destroy grass plants over a wide area, possibly the entire lawn. Follow up with measures for long-term control of the insect or disease through cultural and natural practices that reduce grass stress.

Use pesticides as temporary solutions—No matter what the lawn care company tells you, pesticides should not be regarded as a substitute for good lawn maintenance practices. They should not be used routinely. They are intrinsically high maintenance. Used routinely, they waste time, money and energy. Use them, if necessary, while you are in transition to a low-maintenance lawn. For instance, we have recommended the use of a herbicide to deal with weeds when you rehabilitate or install a lawn. However, once established, the thick, healthy turf should take over weed control duties for the most part.

Use pesticides for specific problems in a limited area—To avoid the wholesale destruction of all the insect life in the lawn—friend and foe alike—use pesticides only when a specific problem is identified. Choose a product that is specifically designed to solve this problem. Limit the use of the product to the particular area where that problem exists. If a lawn care service wants to spray your lawn with an insecticide, ask to see the insect, weed or disease symptom and insist beforehand on knowing what will be sprayed. Do not permit any spraying beyond the affected area.

Use pesticides alone—Do not use a pesticide product that is packaged along with fertilizer or other lawn product. Buy the appropriate fertilizer for your lawn's needs. Buy the appropriate pesticide only when you need a pesticide for a specific problem.

Use less-toxic pesticides first—Soaps and horticultural oils, organic powders and even beneficial insects purchased and released to address the immediate problems are often very effective, especially if the problem is caught before it gets out of hand. Resort to the more toxic products only when all else fails.

And always, always, read the label—Before using any pesticide read the instructions on the label and accompanying brochures on the use, storage and disposal of the product. Buy pesticide products in small quantities so that there is not a lot left over to present disposal problems.

CHOOSING THE RIGHT PESTICIDE

Obviously, we are reluctant and cautious users of pesticides. In the next three chapters we provide more specific guidelines and information about pesticides for various situations. We believe in using the least-toxic product available that will do the particular job. In some cases, one insecticide is best for light infestations of a problem, but a more powerful one may be necessary for heavier ones.

Inherent in the recommendations above—and throughout this last section of this book—is our concern about the personal and environmental safety of all pesticides, especially the toxic ones. After all, the reality is that if something is toxic enough to kill certain living organisms (whether it be "organic" or not), it is undeniably poisonous and potentially dangerous to other living organisms.

We mention only those products that we have had experience with. We have researched them carefully to satisfy ourselves that the best available information indicates that, used judiciously, they are safe for people, pets and the environment. We recognize that despite rigorous testing and study there are things that even the experts may not yet know and understand about pesticides and their interaction. That is true of medicines too, yet there are times when the use of the product seems justified.

BASIC RULES FOR APPLYING ANY PESTICIDE

After having purchased the smallest package that will supply sufficient product to do the job, study the label. You men out there—even if you never read instructions as a point of pride—make pesticides your exception. Follow the instructions. If the can says 1 tablespoon per gallon, then do not use 2 tablespoons "just to be sure."

Unnecessary   **Recommended**

We feel that the best sprayer for the treatment of lawns is a compressed-air sprayer. Look for one with an adjustable nozzle, spray extension and positive on-off valve which will help you control the spray. If you use a backpack sprayer, try to find one with a shield on the end of the spray nozzle that keeps drift to a minimum. It is important to target the pesticide accurately to avoid drift onto nearby shrubs and flowers.

Dress properly. You do not have to prepare for walking into a nuclear reactor, but you need to use real common sense when applying pesticides, any pesticides, even the "natural" ones. You want to cover all your bare skin, so don long sleeves and long pants regardless of the temperature. Wear a hat, garden gloves or rubber gloves, safety goggles (even if you wear glasses) and sturdy work shoes with socks.

The only real danger in using any pesticide in small amounts is that you might be allergic to the product unknowingly. While you will not get cancer from one exposure to any pesticide approved for consumers, you might conceivably get ill if it turns out you are very allergic to a particular pesticide product. That is why you dress properly; to protect yourself from spray-back and any contact with the material. If you are applying pesticide in the form of a powder or dust, it is a good idea to wear a mask over your mouth and nose—yes, it looks "funny" but wear it anyway.

When spraying, set the sprayer nozzle to deliver a coarse spray. Apply it at low pressure, holding the wand down low to the ground. Walk back and forth over the target area, moving the sprayer nozzle back and forth in front of you in an even pattern. When spot-treating patches of weeds, spritz the localized area, then turn off the nozzle before moving to the next patch.

After you finish spraying, thoroughly rinse your sprayer with clear, cool water several times. Then partially fill it with rinse water and pressurize it so that you can spray the water through the wand and nozzle to rinse them.

If you have a small property and need only the small quart or 1-gallon sprayers, it's a good idea to have a couple of sprayers and dedicate your sprayer to the general pesticide product that you initially sprayed from it—e.g., herbicides in one and insecticides in another. Once used for herbicide, reserve that sprayer for just herbicide. Use a different one for insecticides and fungicides. This way, any herbicide remaining in the sprayer will not contaminate an insecticide and kill the grass along with the pest bugs.

STORING PESTICIDES

Properly stored, pesticides retain their potency for many years. Proper storage means storing products in their original containers, tightly sealed. Keep them in a cool, dry place where temperatures do not drop below 50° or exceed 85°. Store pesticides away from household products, food and pet supplies, and out of the reach of children. If you have already diluted a pesticide product to make a spray, use it up; do not store it over the winter.

DISPOSING OF PESTICIDES

Across the nation, municipalities and states are becoming much more conscious of the proper disposal of all pesticides. Most labels on pesticide packages ad-

Approximate Pesticide Shelf Life

Insecticides
Diazinon: 5–7 years

Malathion: indefinite

Sevin (carbaryl): 3–5 years

Dipel liquid (Bt): 2 years

Dipel powder (Bt): 3 years

Rotenone: more than 2 years

Pyrethrum: more than 2 years

Insecticidal soap: 3–5 years

Herbicides
Roundup (glyphosate): 4–5 years
SharpShooter: 3–5 years

vise you to simply tighten the cap or lid, wrap the unused portion of the product in newspaper and throw it in the trash. However, in many areas of the country local communities are passing much more stringent requirements. All pesticides, when disposed of in these communities, must be taken to a special facility managed by the experts in the town government responsible for waste disposal. Check with your municipal officials about special rules before just throwing away an old bottle of insecticide that has been sitting in the basement for four years.

FINAL STRATEGY

This chapter has been devoted to the general issue of pest control and pesticide use. As we see it, a two-pronged strategy—identifying and correcting the immediate pest problem, then identifying the underlying environmental factors that may be predisposing the lawn to the stress that made it vulnerable to problems and addressing them—is both practical and effective over the long term. It is, fortunately, also consistent with the goal of a low-maintenance lawn. Take the time and invest the effort in developing a lawn that is vigorous and healthy so it can support its own defense system. Then sit back and let the beneficials take charge.

Now it is time to discuss how to diagnose those occasional immediate problems that inevitably turn up in even the healthiest lawns. How does a yardener figure out the cause of a brown patch of grass in the lawn? Is it insects? Is it a disease? Is it fertilizer burn? Is it dog urine? While we can't provide a foolproof method of diagnosis, we can give you a chart to help start you off. Diagnosing lawn problems is, like so many other things, something of an art as well as a science, and is best mastered by experience.

The chart below groups the most common lawn problem symptoms into general categories to help with the initial analysis. We've tried to list all the possible causes for each type of symptom, e.g., brown patches, dead grass, etc. Please do not use this chart as your only tool in deciding what to do. It may give you a clue, but then you must examine the turf closely. Remember, some problems occur only in certain seasons or only under certain weather conditions.

Consult the chart for a preliminary diagnosis, then follow up by reading a detailed description of the cause in one of the next three chapters to confirm it and learn what the remedies are for that problem.

Signs of Lawn Disease and Distress

Brown Spots or Patches
Billbug larvae: grass pulls up.
White grubs: grass pulls up.
Cutworms: grass pulls up.
Sod webworm: grass pulls up.
Brown patch: grass does not pull up.
Dog urine: grass does not pull up.
Fertilizer spill: grass does not pull up.

Yellow Patches
Chinch bugs: grass disappears.
Fusariuim patch: grass does not pull up.

Dark Green Patches
Fairy ring: grass does not pull up.

Bleached or Gray Spots
Dollar spot: grass does not pull up.
Snow mold: grass does not pull up.

Greasy Look to Lawn
Pythium: grass does not pull up.

Red or Pink Symptoms
Rust: grass does not pull up.
Red thread: grass does not pull up.
Snow mold: grass does not pull up.

Chapter Ten

Controlling Weeds in the Lawn

A vital, healthy low-maintenance lawn will have some weeds. There is simply no way to have a lawn that is absolutely weed free and have it be healthy and low maintenance. This is the essential paradox of modern lawn care.

It is possible to control insects and disease, and even some pest animals, by routinely using proper cultural techniques. It is even possible to control a minor weed problem with cultural techniques. Ten years of experience and effort have persuaded us, however, that when more than 20 or 30 percent of a lawn is weeds, then it is necessary to use herbicides at least once to get initial control.

Yardeners who want to avoid the use of any kind of "chemical" pesticide face yet another paradox. In some situations you have to use pesticides so that you can avoid using pesticides.

Consequently, getting from here to there—from your present lawn situation to a healthy low-maintenance lawn—may involve a few compromises. It is on this premise that we offer the advice below.

Some Weeds Are Inevitable

To achieve weedless perfection, it is necessary to either spend every waking minute of your life out on the lawn hand pulling weeds, or to routinely treat a lawn with preventative herbicides twice annually, year after year. An investment of this kind of time, money and energy eliminates the low-maintenance aspect of lawn care. The application of so many herbicides eliminates the healthy part.

Repeated doses of chemicals inevitably degrade the soil quality and severely stress the grass. While there may be no weeds, there will also be no beneficial insects. Thus, there will surely be chronic insect and disease problems in this type of lawn.

So, a healthy low-maintenance lawn will inevitably have some weeds. There are not likely to be many, and they will be virtually unnoticeable, but they will be there. Yardeners who want low-maintenance lawns realistically accept this fact of life.

Efforts to prevent weeds by building lively soil and then thickly sowing vigorous, high-quality grass seed are very effective against weeds. However, the opportunistic dandelion, ground ivy and plantain are always a threat. The wind blows seeds from the neighbors' or birds drop them as they pass through the yard, so there will always be some new ones.

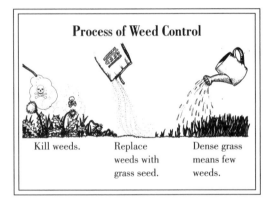

Process of Weed Control

Kill weeds.   Replace weeds with grass seed.   Dense grass means few weeds.

While it may be impossible to keep a low-maintenance lawn totally weed free, it is possible to control most of the weeds most of the time. The first step is to get rid of existing weeds, which is not difficult. The second step, the one seldom taken by yardeners, is to take action to prevent those weeds from coming back.

This second, preventative, step is important to long-range control. You can avoid repeated preemptive spraying of herbicides if you are willing to follow up for a year or two while the new, dense turf gets established.

This strategy requires some hard work in the first couple of years while your brand-new or overseeded lawn grows thickly over the rehabilitated soil. Once it is mature, the turf grasses are so dominant that most weeds are unable to compete. Those few that do are easily handled.

Why Do Lawns Have Weeds?

Rampant weeds in a lawn are a signal that something is very much amiss. The soil may be compacted and infertile, and the grass may be so weak that it is unable to spread and fill in bare spots. Perhaps the grass has been cut too short so weed seeds get the light they need for germination. In a good lawn, healthy soil and proper maintenance keep grass growing vigorously enough to crowd out most of the weeds automatically.

Every lawn has weed seeds. In fact, there are probably thousands of weed seeds lurking in every square foot of your lawn soil at this very moment. While some drift in from elsewhere, most are longtime residents of the soil under your turf. It's not uncommon for weed seeds to germinate after thirty years of sitting in the soil! All they need is light and the right conditions. So, while you may never get rid of weed seeds, you can try to prevent them from ever germinating. This is the all-important second step in weed control.

Meanwhile, there are already mature weed plants established in your lawn. We will discuss below how to get rid of them, the first step in weed control.

Weeds As Problem Indicators

Very often an outbreak of a particular type of weed is indicative of some specific environmental problem in the lawn's ecosystem. For example, prostrate knotweed *(Polygonum aviculare)* indicates compacted, droughty soil, whereas yellow nutsedge *(Cyperus esculentus)* indicates waterlogged soil. If you cut your grass too short, you're likely to see more crabgrass, clover and chickweed. A soil that is too acidic tends to support the sorrels and the docks, common broadleaf weeds.

A higher incidence of all weeds may indicate overfertilization. Too much fertilizer, especially the quick-acting forms, harms the soil, thus weakening the grass which then gives way to weeds more readily.

Identifying Weeds

It isn't at all that necessary for yardeners to be able to identify and name the various lawn weeds in order to fight them. Nor does it matter if they know the difference between an annual, biennial or perennial weed.

The only distinction that is important to be aware of is the difference between broadleaf and the grassy-type weeds. The timing for control of each of these types is somewhat different, and the herbicides that might be used for each group of weeds is also different.

So, although we are not suggesting that you must become a botanist, we will cover a few of the most familiar and common members of the two groups, just to give you some general guidelines to enable you to distinguish between them.

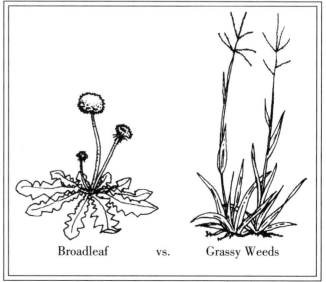

Broadleaf   vs.   Grassy Weeds

COMMON BROADLEAF WEEDS

Broadleaf weeds include such common pests as dandelion, plantain, clover, chickweed, buckthorn, dichondra, ground ivy, oxalis, knotweed, purslane and prostrate spurge.

Dandelion—Dandelions are easily spotted because their circle of deeply notched, lance-shaped leaves lies close on the soil surface, obstructing grass from growing. Everyone recognizes the telltale yellow flower when it blooms at the tip of the tall stem, and then turns into a fuzzy, round seed ball. Dandelions have long, thick taproots, which makes it extremely difficult to eradicate this weed by hand. Dandelions move in when irrigation is inadequate.

Ground Ivy and Lawn Pennywort—Both of these creeping weeds send out stems over and just below the soil surface, rooting as they go. Ground ivy has larger leaves, a mint smell and tiny purple flowers. Both prefer a damp soil surface.

Clover—White clover and burclover are the problem varieties in most lawns. Clover thrives in soil with low fertility. Clover forms thick patches of matted stems, small shamrock-type leaves and tiny white flowers that choke out grass. In some situations clover is an effective ground cover, but it is objectionable in lawns because it mars the smooth look of the turf.

Broadleaf Plantain and Narrowleaf Plantain—Often mistakenly called crabgrass, plantains are obviously broadleaf weeds. Their coarse leaves, shaped like large tablespoons, grow flat on the soil. As they mature they send up seed-bearing spikes. Patches of plantain quickly take over bare spots in lawns.

Cinquefoil—Cinquefoil leaves resemble strawberry leaves. It bears clusters of little yellow flowers from June to August. Its presence indicates acidic, infertile and sandy soil.

Common Chickweed—This weed grows in clumps of delicate stems and tiny leaves which rapidly spread across a lawn. It bears tiny, white flowers from March to December and is notorious for producing zillions of seeds before it dies with the frost. Chickweed prefers cool, moist weather and shade, as well as slightly acidic soils. It grows poorly in summer heat. Fortunately, it is easy to pull by hand before it goes to seed.

Thistle—Thistles are large, obtrusive weeds. They sport sharp spines or prickles all over their tough, fibrous, silvery stems and deeply notched leaves. When mature, they produce soft, silky flowers that are usually purple or pinkish. Like dandelions, they have a stubborn, deep taproot that makes effective hand or mechanical removal impossible.

COMMON GRASSY WEEDS

As the term suggests, grassy weeds are plants that have long, narrow, green foliage similar to that of turf grass. However, because they are a different plant species than bluegrass, tall fescue or perennial rye, they don't blend in with the rest of your lawn. Their foliage is generally coarser, thicker and off-color. Also, some grassy weed plants tend to grow in thick humps and clumps so they mar the smooth appearance of turf.

Grassy weeds include crabgrass, nutgrass, goose grass, dallis grass and annual bluegrass *(Poa annua)*. As these weeds mature, they form a coarse, spreading mat that looks different from your regular grass.

Of all of these grassy weeds, however, crabgrass seems to attract the most attention in the weed control literature. Crabgrass is universally hated by almost everyone who has tried to have a nice lawn.

Crabgrass—This is an annual grassy weed *(Digitaria sanguinalis)* noted for its broad blades and rough texture. The seeds dropped the previous fall sprout to form new plants in late spring to early summer. Suddenly, the tough clumps of coarse foliage become obvious in the lawn in early fall. Germination varies depending on how soon the soil has warmed to the proper temperature, and that depends on what region of the country you live in.

Crabgrass requires high light-intensity, but once established it will tolerate high temperatures, compacted soils and dry soils better than most turf grasses. This explains why it makes itself at home in older, unrenovated lawns so readily.

It has a low-growing, prostrate habit, shallow but strong roots and it can't stand the shade. Again, depending on where you live, sometime between midsummer and early frost each clump of crabgrass develops tough stems on which purplish seed heads form. They often attract attention from seed-eating birds, especially sparrows, who flock to lawns with crabgrass.

In the fall, frost turns the crabgrass clumps brownish red and they die. Invariably, they leave behind thousands of seeds for next year's crop.

Annual Bluegrass—Annual bluegrass is shallow-rooted and sprouts so early that it may already go to seed by late spring. These seeds, in turn, sprout and the new plants seed again in the fall. It likes cool and moist conditions, and will wilt severely in midsummer, opening up space for other weeds to grow in. Just because it has "bluegrass" in its name, do not be misled into thinking this is a desirable grass to have in your lawn.

Goose Grass—This weed is also known as silver crabgrass and is often mistaken for crabgrass. It is a summer annual that germinates four to six weeks later than crabgrass. Goose grass is characterized by fibrous roots and very flattened sheaths having a silvery green color, especially near the center of the plant. It produces fingerlike seed heads on which seeds are arranged like teeth in a zipper on the seed stalk. Goose grass grows well on heavily compacted soils.

How Many Are Too Many?

So, if it is normal and inevitable to have a few weeds in the healthiest of low-maintenance lawns, then how can you tell when a weed problem becomes serious and needs attention? How many are tolerable; how many are too many?

As much as 10 percent—or even 15 percent—weeds is acceptable in an otherwise healthy, dense turf. In this concentration they are virtually invisible, unless you get down on your hands and knees and study each square foot of lawn closely. Our general rule of thumb is that if weeds are clearly visible as you gaze casually over the lawn, then there are too many. It also depends on the weeds, some being far more obvious at a glance than others.

Homeowners generally have a lower tolerance for coarse, broadleaf weeds such as dandelion or plantain, which are impossible to overlook when they send up their flower stems. The grassy weeds or creeping broadleaf weeds, such as ground ivy or chickweed, are less objectionable because they are less obvious.

In either situation, when the weeds exceed your tolerance level, then it is time to pull them or spot-treat them with a spritz of herbicide. Once the dense turf of your renovated lawn is established, you can determine how many weeds you are willing to tolerate before you take action.

Three Approaches to Weed Control

The method for the control of weeds is pretty much a function of how prevalent they are in your lawn. Isolated, individual weeds are easily controlled. The more pervasive they are, the most powerful the remedy must be.

More powerful remedies also have correspondingly more impact on the lawn environment, so it is desirable to address weed problems before they become too entrenched. Three approaches to weed control in the lawn are outlined below.

SPOT TREATMENT

If broadleaf or grassy weeds represent something less than 30 percent of your lawn, they can be fully controlled within a year. Spot-treat each weed chemically with herbicide or pull them individually by hand or with a tool.

Control their spread by raising the lawn mower to 2 or 3 inches so taller grass will shade them out. Time your fertilizing: Feed the grass in the fall or early spring to give it a head start on the weeds. The new, vigorous grass will shade weed seeds and discourage their germination in the spring.

Obviously, conscientious spot treatment early in the season forestalls a more extensive weed problem later. This approach is the least toxic to the lawn ecosystem, because the use of herbicide is minimal and, in many situations, can be avoided altogether.

KILL WEEDS BUT NOT GRASS

If the broadleaf or grassy weeds in your lawn represent something between 30 percent and 60 percent of the area, spot treatment is no longer practical. In this situation it is best to kill all the weeds in the entire lawn at once with a selective herbicide, which is designed to kill weeds but not lawn grass. Hopefully, you will only need to use this kind of product once or, at the most, twice.

There are two times to take chemical action on weeds—the spring and the fall. Do not apply herbicides during the heat of summer. Of course, you can pull weeds by hand or mechanically anytime.

KILL EVERYTHING

If your lawn is more than 60 percent weeds, there is not enough grass worth saving. We recommend that you start over. Kill the whole lawn with a nonselective herbicide, one that kills weeds and grass alike, and take this opportunity to upgrade the soil and plant modern grass seed.

Spot-Treating Weeds

While you can learn to live with a few weeds as the price of a low-maintenance lawn, do not totally ignore them even when they represent less than 30 percent of your lawn. Unless you take action to control both broadleaf weeds and grassy weeds, they will spread. Aggressive action at this stage prevents a future takeover, and eliminating individual weed plants is relatively easy early on.

BROADLEAF WEEDS

Most broadleaf weeds are perennials, so they typically have deep root systems that help them survive winters. Often when the weed is pulled, some root fragments remain in the soil. Each one is capable of producing a new plant. So your choice of individual, spot treatment method must take this into account. Sometimes a combination of methods is most effective.

HAND PULLING

The easiest way to deal with the random, occasional weed is to hand pull it. This method works best when the soil is moist and the weed is young. Grasp the crown of the plant where the stems meet at the soil surface between your thumb and forefinger. Avoid the temptation to yank the weed abruptly, because that usually tears the roots, many of which remain in the soil. Instead, pull slowly but firmly and steadily so that the entire root system emerges from the soil intact. Liz enjoys a pleasant stroll around the yard after dinner early in the season. It is a good time to casually scan the lawn for weeds and pull them then and there. Make every effort to get the entire root system.

MECHANICAL REMOVAL

There are a number of hand tools on the market for removal of broadleaf weeds from turf. Some are "pluckers." They are designed to go down a few inches and pull up a major portion of the roots. Others are "cutters" that essentially cut off the weed from its roots a few inches down into the soil.

The best time to mechanically pull weeds is when they are in flower. At that time they tend to be a little weaker from producing flowers, so when the plant and a goodly portion of the roots are removed, the remaining roots have more trouble producing another plant.

If you get 5 inches or more of the root you have an 80 percent chance of killing the weed on the first try. If you don't catch a weed at the ideal time, then it is likely that you will have to pull it two or three more times over the season before you totally eradicate it. Any perennial weed can be eventually killed by repeated pulling. It all comes down to who is more stubborn and persistent, you or the weed.

BURN THOSE SUCKERS!

Flaming or burning weeds is a common practice in Europe, but has not been widely adopted in this country; yet it is a very easy technique. We are not talking about burning off your lawn. Flaming means using a propane torch, sold in hardware stores for home workshops (used for soldering plumbing joints). The flame produces temperatures of 2,000°F which heat the sap in the cell walls of the plant tissue and cause the cells to expand and rupture. The weed wilts and dies, although it may take up to twenty-four hours before death is obvious.

You do not hold the flame on the target weed until it starts to burn up and sizzle. In fact, if the flamer is held over a weed long enough to blacken it, the result could be to stimulate growth from remaining roots. Think about "searing" the plant rather than "burning" it. The whole point is to heat the cell sap, and you do this by slowly passing the flame over the plant. You may not see any evidence of wilting, let alone plant death, for several hours or even until the next day. Flaming works best with young weeds not more than a few inches tall. This technique is particularly effective against broadleaf weeds.

Hold the torch 3–6 inches above the weed and wave it over the plant just briefly. It takes some experience to master this technique, but it works very well. Once the weeds have wilted and died, you can come back and remove them or simply pass the flaming torch over the dead plant and burn it into ash, which can decompose and provide minerals to your lawn's soil. Obviously, this is not a technique to use on weeds in droughty turf that is dried and brittle from heat and lack of rain. It wouldn't do to start a fire!

Spot Use of Herbicide

There are several reasonably safe herbicides that are very effective against dandelion, plantain, thistle and other pesky broadleaf weeds. Their ready-mixed, spray bottle packaging makes them ideal for spot or individual treatment of each weed to avoid spraying the entire property.

SharpShooter, a soap-based material, kills weeds by dessication. Within hours, sprayed plant tissues dry out and weeds shrivel and turn brown. Roundup, a glyphosate salt, causes weeds to stop producing protein and they starve to death in a week to ten days. Both products are contact killers; they kill by contact with plant tissues, rather than by taking up the poison through the roots.

However, both of these herbicides are nonselective. That means they will kill any plant they touch—including grass—not just specifically weeds. When spraying these products, be sure to shield neighboring plants or healthy grass that is in proximity to the target weeds. Draping newspapers over adjacent plants and on the grass works well.

In difficult situations when weeds crowd other plants, painting the herbicide on the weed foliage with a small artist's paintbrush, rather than spraying it, effectively prevents drift onto neighboring plants. Do not spray on a breezy day. These herbicides are most effective when the air temperature is over 70°F.

GRASSY WEEDS

Since crabgrass is far and away the most common and annoying grassy weed, the discussion below will focus on it. However, many of these techniques are effective with other grassy weeds.

Hand Pulling

Crabgrass tends to grow in dense clumps. If they are not too extensive, they are easily hand-pulled or dug out with a weeding tool. Remember to drop some grass seed in place of each bare spot created in this manner. Unlike the perennial broadleaf weeds, the roots of the crabgrass are not deep and if a few get left in the ground they will not regenerate new plants.

Mechanical Control

Of course, as we mentioned above, mowing techniques help control weeds, even crabgrass. Mowing tall discourages germination of weed seeds, as does catching clippings at certain times of the year.

Later in the season, when the weeds that do appear develop seed heads, mow somewhat lower and more frequently than usual and catch the seed heads and clippings in a bag attachment. This effectively prevents seeds from falling to the soil for next year's weed crop.

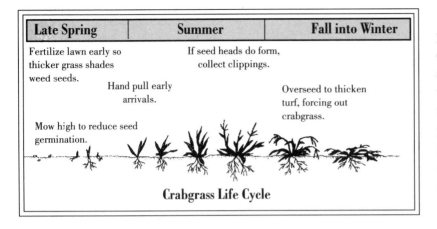

Late Spring	Summer	Fall into Winter

Fertilize lawn early so thicker grass shades weed seeds.

If seed heads do form, collect clippings.

Hand pull early arrivals.

Overseed to thicken turf, forcing out crabgrass.

Mow high to reduce seed germination.

Crabgrass Life Cycle

Normally, grass clippings should go into the compost pile or onto bare soil under shrubs or in the flower garden as a mulch. However, clippings that contain crabgrass seeds are a different matter. Lest they sprout wherever the clippings fall, compost them only if you actively manage your compost pile, turning it frequently so that its internal temperatures exceed 140°. Otherwise, seed-filled clippings must go into the trash.

SOIL MAINTENANCE

Cool-weather fertilization in the fall or early spring gives grass a head start over weeds. In addition, upgrading the health of your soil discourages crabgrass. Crabgrass thrives in infertile, compacted soil. Create a hostile environment for it by aerating and adding humus to your turf as well.

SPOT USE OF HERBICIDE

For large, tough clumps you may wish to use some kind of spot chemical control. Spot-treat clumps of crabgrass with glyphosate (Roundup, Kleenup) or a soap-based herbicide (Safer Superfast). See the section on spot control of broadleaf weeds for tips on using herbicide for spot treatment.

FILLING IN THE BARE SPOTS

Remember, if the dying weeds leave a bare spot on the lawn, it is important to reseed that area. Otherwise, opportunistic new weeds will move in and take over again. We have a box of perennial ryegrass on the shelf for just this purpose. It is the only grass that will germinate and succeed in any season—spring, summer or fall.

Perennial rye also germinates very quickly, making it eminently suitable to quickly cover bare spots before weed seeds can germinate there. Remember to water new seed daily for at least two weeks and then keep the soil moist until seedlings have become established.

Kill the Weeds, Save the Grass

As we noted above, weeds in concentrations representing from 30 percent to 60 percent of your turf need more intensive treatment. They are then so numerous that there is no practical way to hand pull or mechanically pull them. Cultural techniques will have some effect, but it will take years for satisfactory results. In these situations, herbicides are the most practical tool for killing all the weeds while not harming the existing grass.

KILLING BROADLEAF WEEDS

In this situation, a postemergent, selective herbicide is most effective. This type of herbicide kills weeds after their seeds have germinated and the seedlings have emerged and are growing. Also, it kills only the weeds and not the grass. Used just once to solve a major weed problem and then followed up with good cultural practices, this type of chemical herbicide offers good control of significant weed problems. It may never be necessary to use it again over the whole lawn. Occasional spot treatment will maintain control.

Remember, it is not enough to simply kill broadleaf weeds in your lawn and call it a day. Be sure to replace those weeds with new grass (seed or sod) because your existing lawn will not spread quickly enough to fill in the bare spots by itself. Therefore, the timing of this project is important.

USING BROADLEAF HERBICIDES

While most broadleaf herbicide labels permit their use any time during the growing season, we feel that there are only two times when their use is appropriate. The best time is in the late summer or early fall; late spring, after weeds have appeared, is second best.

The issue is not whether the weeds are effectively eradicated by the herbicide. It is how readily new grass can be introduced into the bare spots where weeds have died. Since fall is the best time to plant grass seed, it follows that early fall is a good time to kill weeds, so new replacement grass can be sown at its best time.

Two weeks after using a broadleaf herbicide, overseed the bare spots with a quality grass seed, which will have plenty of time to grow and develop strong roots before winter. By spring the turf should be thick enough to discourage germination of most dormant weed seeds. There will inevitably be some weeds that may need spot treatment. It will take two years to get them truly under control.

If you chose to do this job in the spring, wait until the broadleaf weeds have produced mature foliage so that the herbicide can make good contact with the plants. Plan on planting perennial ryegrass in the bare spots. It has the best chance of withstanding the summer heat. Next fall you can overseed with Kentucky bluegrass or tall fescue if you wish.

Glossary of Terms

Desiccant—Having the quality of drying. An herbicide, such as SharpShooter, kills plants by drying up the moisture in cell membranes. Diatomaceous earth dessicates ants and slugs when they come in contact with it.

Fungicide—A product that kills the fungi that cause various diseases in plants (and people too!).

Glyphosate—The active ingredient in Roundup herbicide. It kills plant tissues by interfering with their metabolism.

Insecticide—A product that kills insects by inhibiting their growth, their ability to eat or their progress into the next life phase. Some insecticides kill by touching the insect, others by entering their system and making them fatally ill. They kill by paralyzing, poisoning, dehydrating or suffocating the insect.

Insecticidal soap—Commercial insecticide compound formulated of fatty acids. When it contacts soft-bodied insects, it paralyzes them, causing them to starve to death.

Biological pesticide—An insect, microorganism or bacteria that kills pest insects. Examples are predatory nematodes or *Bacillus thuringiensis.*

Pesticide—A general term denoting a product that kills plant pests. The pest may be a weed, an insect or a disease.

> **Selective**—Describes a pesticide product that kills a specific class or species of pest only. A selective herbicide will kill broadleaf weeds, but not turf grass.

> **Nonselective**—A pesticide that does not "select" or distinguish its target from other similar plants, insects or disease pathogens.

Herbicide—A product that kills plants. Various formulations kill grassy or broadleaf weeds. Roundup is an example.

> **Preemergent**—Type of herbicide that kills weed seeds before they have a chance to germinate.

> **Postemergent**—Describes an herbicide that kills weeds after they have sprouted from seeds and emerged as seedlings.

Important: Delay planting grass seed for at least two weeks after spraying a selective, postemergent herbicide such as "2,4-D" or a nonselective glyphosate herbicide. Also, do not allow pets or children to walk on the lawn the day that herbicide is sprayed on the grass. Herbicide residues on turf are less likely to rub off onto pets and pedestrians as each day passes. Lawns with thick thatch have longer-lasting residues than lawns with minimal thatch.

CHOOSING A BROADLEAF HERBICIDE

There are a number of herbicides on the market for selectively killing just broadleaf weeds. Regardless of your choice, respect the fact that they are powerful and toxic; otherwise they would not be able to do the job.

Check the label to make sure the product kills broadleaf weeds like dandelion and plantain. The fine print should list either 2,4-D, MCPA, MCPP or Dicamba as the primary ingredient. Follow label instructions for use, storage and disposal carefully.

We should note that there are several preemergent herbicides on the market for preventing broadleaf weeds from growing in the first place (e.g., Isoxaben). Sometimes they are mixed in with fertilizer for spring application. They kill weed seeds before they can sprout. We do not recommend those products, not because they don't work, but simply because we believe a postemergent herbicide, followed up by overseeding, is a more effective method and requires the minimum amount of pesticide to be spread on the lawn.

The preemergent broadleaf herbicides are sold assuming that you will use them every year, year in and year out; we are not persuaded that this practice is at all necessary or desirable for yardeners. It certainly is not consistent with a low-maintenance lawn.

Herbicides for Broadleaf Weeds

Check the active ingredients listed on the herbicide label for one of the following:

- 2, 4-D (Dimethylamine Salt of 2, 4-Dichlorophenoxyacetic acid) is a growth-regulating hormone compound. It is not a persistent pesticide in the soil. In somewhat warm soil its half life is two weeks or less. 2,4-D is not a persistent pesticide in water. There is 90% disappearance in less than two weeks. It decomposes in sunlight.
- Dicamba (Dimethylamine Salt of Dicamba (3,6-dichloro-o-anisic acid) is used in mixtures with other herbicides such as 2,4-D and MCPP. Do not use products containing this ingredient around trees and shrubs, which may absorb it through their roots. It stays active in the soil. Good for most weeds.
- MCPA (2-methyl-4-chlorophenoxyacetic acid).
- MCPP (mecoprop: 2-methyl-4-chlorophenozypropionic acid).

PLANTING GRASS TO REPLACE BROADLEAF WEEDS

After a herbicide has effectively killed the 30–60 percent of your lawn that was weeds, there is going to be that much bare space in the turf. In a race between existing grass spreading and weeds sprouting in bare areas, weeds always win. Besides, the grass that remains in your lawn is already tired from competing with all those former weeds.

Consequently, it is very important to reseed all open areas promptly. In the fall you can plant your choice of grass—bluegrass, tall fescue or perennial rye. It will have plenty of time to germinate, develop strong root systems and grow to 2 inches before the soil warms enough next spring to sprout weed seeds. In the spring, fill bare spots with quick-germinating perennial rye, which will beat the weed seeds to the punch.

Keep the seedbeds and seedlings moist and follow the cultural practices outlined in Chapters Two and Three to assure that the replacement grass is healthy.

KILLING GRASSY WEEDS

If grassy weeds represent more than 20–30 percent of your lawn, attack them more aggressively, because those weeds can spread really quickly in just one year when left to their own devices. You have three choices here, and two of them—the chemical ones—are not our favorites. You can deal with grassy weeds using cultural techniques. We prefer that approach but it takes a few years. The short-term, quick-results approach requires the use of one of two types of herbicide. You can use a preemergent herbicide for this type of weed in the

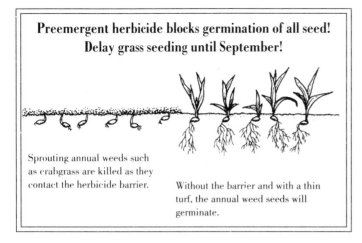

**Preemergent herbicide blocks germination of all seed!
Delay grass seeding until September!**

Sprouting annual weeds such as crabgrass are killed as they contact the herbicide barrier.

Without the barrier and with a thin turf, the annual weed seeds will germinate.

spring to prevent the weed seeds from ever germinating. That may be an effective approach, but it means you can't plant new grass seed for three to four months.

An alternative is to use a postemergent herbicide designed to kill just grassy weeds and not harm the existing lawn grass. This approach is not favored by professional turf managers because it takes more than one application (sometimes three) to be effective. So if professional guys don't like it, neither do we. We give you basic information about the two herbicides on the belief that if you really choose to go that route, you need to understand how to use those tools safely.

THE CULTURAL APPROACH

The cultural approach to grassy weed control takes two or three years. It is not very complicated. You simply raise your lawn mower to 2 or more inches. Then you overseed the lawn each fall for two years. That approach gives you a dense turf that is high enough to keep light away from the seeds waiting to germinate in the spring. In most cases this approach takes care of serious grassy weed problems. You can see why we like that approach; it requires no pesticides.

USING PREEMERGENT HERBICIDE

If you know from past experience that your turf is infested with a grassy weed, take action before it appears again this season. Use preemergent herbicide in the spring to prevent

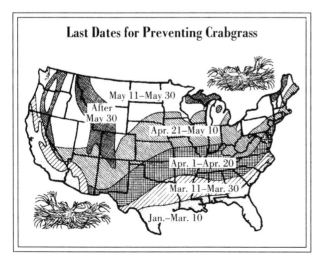

Last Dates for Preventing Crabgrass

May 11–May 30
After May 30
Apr. 21–May 10
Apr. 1–Apr. 20
Mar. 11–Mar. 30
Jan.–Mar. 10

crabgrass or in the fall to prevent annual bluegrass.

Apply preemergent herbicides (usually in granular form) ten to fourteen days before the weed seeds are due to germinate. Because crabgrass begins to germinate when the temperature in the upper inch of soil reaches approximately 58–60°F, try to estimate when that will be and be ready with the herbicide two weeks prior to this time.

For instance, in our Philadelphia area the soil warms to 58° between April 20 and May 1, about the same time as our dogwood blooms. A rule of thumb in the spring is to apply preemergent herbicide before lilacs bloom, during forsythia bloom or when the early blooming magnolia petals fall. Some preemergent herbicides last as long as eight months and can be put on the lawn in the late fall those years when you are not overseeding with new lawn grass.

Don't worry about being too scientific here. Most of the preemergent crabgrass herbicides also kill young crabgrass seedlings, so if you are off by a week or so, no big deal.

If goose grass is the problem, use the preemergent product about three to four weeks after the normal application date for crabgrass. Your local garden center or your county extension agent should know pretty precisely when to apply preemergent herbicide for grassy weeds in your area.

Do not use a fertilizer that contains preemergent herbicide. Use the pesticide by itself. Be sure to read and follow the instructions on the product label.

Important note: When using a preemergent herbicide, do not aerate or de-thatch the lawn while it is being treated to prevent weed seed germination. The chemical works by establishing a film or cover over the seeds and if it is broken, the effectiveness of the preemergent control is greatly reduced.

Preemergent herbicides are very powerful chemicals and, while they have been tested to be safe in the environment, we suggest their use only as a last resort. You can't plant any new grass seed for three to four months after using these chemicals. That means you will have thinned the lawn's turf by preventing the crabgrass from emerging but will be unable to plant new seed until fall. By that time other broadleaf weeds will have appeared.

Using Postemergent Herbicides

Another method in the "kill the weeds/save the grass" approach is to use a postemergent herbicide in the late summer to kill grassy weeds but not the real grass. The problem here is that one application is often not enough to do the job. You may have to repeat the process two, or even three, times to get effective control.

On top of that, these postemergent products tend to cause severe discoloration of your regular grass, especially fine fescue and bentgrasses if you have those types. The grass recovers, but it looks lousy for a week or two. So this approach is definitely not our favorite.

Choosing a Grassy Weed Herbicide

There are a number of herbicides on the market for selectively killing just grassy weeds. Again, we remind you to respect the fact that they are powerful and toxic; otherwise they would not be able to do the job.

Check the label to make sure the product kills grassy weeds like crabgrass or goose grass. Note whether the product is a "preemergent" or "postemergent" product because the timing is very different for the two products. In any case, follow label instructions for use, storage and disposal carefully.

Weed control in shady lawns is a special situation. Crabgrass and many other weeds will not grow in shade, so do not automatically apply herbicide to your shady areas. Those sections of lawn are already in some stress because of reduced light, so applying herbicide unnecessarily just adds to that stress.

KILL THE WHOLE LAWN

Any lawn that is more than 60 percent weeds of any kind begs to be put out of its misery. The grass that persists in weedy turf is typically so stressed and so weak that it is not worth trying to save. This is a good opportunity to upgrade your soil and grass at the same time.

Consult Chapter Eight for instructions on how to renovate a lawn. In this case, you will use a nonselective herbicide such as Roundup to kill both grass and weeds. Choose to reseed either with the dead turf in place or by tilling in or removing the dead turf. Unless there is a compelling reason to disturb the soil, it is easiest to aerate, topdress, fertilize and seed directly over the closely cut dead turf.

Stop New Weeds Fast

Of course, there will always be the occasional weed in your lawn from time to time. That is the way of nature, and part of having a low-maintenance lawn is accepting this.

Weeds are easy to control if you catch them early. Keep an eye out while you are mowing, and pull new arrivals before they mature and multiply. We keep a spray bottle of Roundup on the shelf which we use to paint on broad-leaved weeds that appear. Liz usually pulls the grassy weeds that show up before they even develop into a clump.

Once your lawn has a thick, dense turf, very few weeds will intrude. Any area that does not support dense turf is a potential trouble spot. Typically, areas under trees where there is a chronic lack of sufficient light for grass, are plagued with weeds. So are areas of poor, compacted soil. The grass is always in stress there and weeds have no trouble subduing grass that is under stress.

Consider abandoning efforts to grow grass in these areas. Maybe it's time to think about alternative ground covers such as pachysandra or English ivy.

The bottom line is that weeds are easy to eliminate and easy to keep away if, and only if, you have a healthy, dense turf.

Chapter Eleven

Controlling Insect Pests

Pest insects rarely cause problems in dense, vigorous turf managed by low-maintenance techniques as described in the first four chapters of this book. The best way to prevent damage by pest insects is to take pains to keep your lawn healthy and free of stress.

For instance, troublesome Japanese beetles do not like to lay eggs in turf that is 2 inches or taller. They do like to lay eggs in moist grass. So a properly mowed lawn that is not overwatered discourages the incidence of the grubs that develop from the eggs. Sod webworms prefer lawns with thick thatch. A healthy lawn that has little or no thatch is not attractive to egg-laying sod webworm moths, and they go elsewhere.

A properly maintained lawn that has been spared repeated doses of broad-spectrum insecticides naturally supports significant populations of all kinds of beneficial insects. Under normal conditions, they effectively control most pest insect populations without our even being aware of their activity.

Looking Again at the Good Guys

At the risk of being repetitive, we can't stress enough the critically important role that beneficial insects and songbirds play in lawn pest control. An understanding and appreciation of nature's built-in defense system equips homeowners to manage the occasional pest insect problem in their lawns with a minimum of effort.

GOOD BUGS OUTNUMBER BAD BUGS

They're everywhere. All kinds of insects lurk in every nook and cranny of your property—in grass, shrubs, trees, flowers, under mulch, in the top few inches of the soil and even in any standing water in the yard. Of all the many, many kinds of insects on your property, probably only a few kinds—1 or 2 percent—might cause problems if for some reason their population exploded.

All the rest—98 percent—are either benign or beneficial to the backyard ecosystem because at some stage of their lives they feed on pest insects. The more varied the plantings in your landscape, the more diverse the insect population will be and the more likely there will be many kinds of beneficials on duty.

Homes surrounded by turf alone are much more vulnerable to insect problems than homes that have trees, shrubs, flower beds, and yes, maybe even some weeds along the back fence line. So, obviously, one way to minimize pest insect problems in the lawn, as well as over your entire landscape, is to plant many kinds of plants to attract as many kinds of beneficial insects as possible. Then, let them police the yard.

There are literally dozens and dozens of different kinds of beneficial insects in a healthy landscape. Some of them, such as ants, spiders and ground beetles, are familiar to you, although perhaps not in their role as beneficials. Others, such as parasitic wasps and lacewings, are unfamiliar because they are so tiny you have never noticed them.

While there is no need to discuss all the kinds of beneficial insects here, it is important that you appreciate that they are out there. The next time you are tempted to squash a bug, think twice. Odds are, it's a "friendly."

There is even friendly fungus among us! Research shows that *Beauvaria bassiana* fungus attacks and destroys chinch bugs in large numbers. Once infected, chinch bugs become fuzzy and pale white; then they quickly die. In Maryland, this disease reduced chinch bug populations 40–82 percent within three to four days following several days of cool, wet weather. Interestingly,

---

Most Common Beneficial Insects Found in a Healthy Lawn

Ants

Big-eyed bugs

Braconid wasps

Rove beetles

Earwigs

Firefly larvae

Ground beetles

Mites

Spiders

Spined soldier bugs

Stinkbugs

Tachinid flies

Vespid wasps

Wheel bugs

researchers also noted that frequent fungicide applications decreased the effectiveness of this fungus. No surprise there.

Of course, the bottom line to all of this is that if you spray a broad-spectrum insecticide (which by definition kills insects) over your lawn, you destroy an impressive natural defense system along with the target pests. While there may be situations where pest insect populations have so overwhelmed the beneficials that you have no choice but to spray insecticide, it is worth taking every action possible to avoid this kind of Pyrrhic victory.

Eventually, the insect life in the yard recovers from the holocaust. Both friends and foe rebuild their populations. Experts estimate that most beneficials take from one to four months to reestablish themselves. Unfortunately, in most cases, the pest insects come back sooner and have at your lawn for some days and weeks before the good guys are back on the scene.

Birds Eat Lots of Bugs

Birds are also a natural defense against pest insects. We put out food for them year round to encourage them to include our yard in their territory. Jeff also mounted several birdhouses around the property so they could set up housekeeping and raise their families nearby.

Even seed-eating species, such as sparrows, finches and cardinals, become deadly insect hunters when they have to feed a nest full of babies. These songbirds, both seed eaters and those who eat only insects, such as wrens, constitute our daytime aerial defense patrol against pest insects. By the way, we encourage bats in our yard and they take over the insect control duties at night.

Many birds have a taste for the Japanese beetle grubs that lie just below the soil surface under the lawn. Grackles, meadowlarks, crows, catbirds, cardinals, blackbirds, robins and starlings eat lots of grubs. Starlings, robins, catbirds and cardinals also eat adult Japanese beetles.

Robins and starlings will go after webworm larvae if they are in your lawn. Webworm caterpillars (the larvae) are also favorites of blackbirds, bluejays, brown thrashers, meadowlarks, sparrows, starlings and wrens, as well as other critters such as moles, shrews, snakes and toads. Swallows and bats eat the adult sod webworm moths.

Before getting specific about dealing with various kinds of pest insects that may threaten your lawn, we must urge you to practice prevention by reinforcing the natural defense system that is already in place in your yard.

How? Build and maintain a healthy turf with the techniques we have presented in the first two sections of this book. Attract beneficial insects, birds and other natural predators in any way you can. Avoid using broad-spectrum insecticides. In short, do everything you can to keep your grass free of stress and protected by an army of good guys.

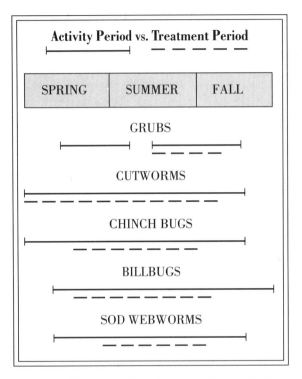

Activity Period vs. Treatment Period

Dealing with Pest Insects

Of course, there are invariably environmental stresses on lawns that a homeowner cannot prevent. Extremes of weather, damage from heavy equipment used for home renovation, street or utility repair, visits from wild and domestic animals or spills of toxic substances will occur occasionally. The stress that they promote in the turf may trigger pest infestation no matter how healthy your lawn is. To help you deal with those situations, we have provided specific information on how to diagnose and treat pest insect problems in your turf.

The key to effective control of a pest insect is correctly identifying the culprit. This is not as difficult as it would seem, even for yarderers who have no experience with insects. It is fairly easy to narrow down the possibilities once you notice symptoms of a problem in the lawn.

First, consider the time of year. Different insects cause problems in different seasons. You can rule out Japanese beetles as the cause of holes chewed in the blades of grass in the spring, because they are still under the soil in their grub stage.

Next, consider the region of the country you live in. All pest insects are not found in all parts of the United States. Japanese beetles do not exist in Oregon; they have a different kind of grub in lawns there. Furthermore, many of the most common insects are more prevalent in certain areas even though they might be found from time to time in others.

A knowledgeable neighbor, a local county extension agent, a master gardener or a staff horticulturist at your local garden center will help you identify your pest insect. He or she will know what is most common in your neck of the woods at that time of year.

THE BIG FOUR

Whole books have been written about pest insects in the lawn, so the discussion that follows is not comprehensive by any means. We have selected four of the "baddest" bad guys according to experts in the lawn care industry. They are the pests you are most likely to encounter at some point.

Detailed information on the control of grubs, sod webworms, chinch bugs and cutworms follows. More general information on other turf nuisances such as billbugs, armyworms, ants and deer ticks rounds out the discussion of identifying and dealing with pest insects.

Grubs

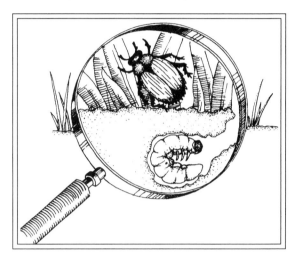

Grubs are the larval stage of the many kinds of beetles found throughout the country. Typically, adult beetles lay their eggs in lawn and other grassy sod in midsummer. These eggs hatch into grubs which winter down in the soil, eventually emerging as May beetles, June bugs, Japanese beetles, masked chafers or Asiatic brown beetles.

In the northeastern United States, grubs of Japanese beetles are the most common grubs found in residential lawns. Masked chafer grubs are found more in middle America and June beetle grubs are more common in the West.

DESCRIPTION

White grubs look as unattractive as their name suggests. They are plump, whitish worms with brown heads. From 3/4 to 1 1/2 inches long at maturity, they rest in a characteristic C-shaped curl just under the surface of turf soil. As they grow, they feed on grass roots, stressing the plants.

MOST OBVIOUS GRUB SYMPTOMS

Sometimes increased activity by birds and animals in the yard signals a white grub problem long before the grass shows damage. The presence of an unusual number of grazing blackbirds, starlings or other birds on the lawn, or signs that moles, skunks or raccoons are digging up the turf, indicate a grub infestation. These natural predators are feeding on them.

Eventually, grub damage to lawns shows up as irregular brown patches of grass. This can happen in late spring when the mature grubs are moving to the surface, or in September and October when the newly hatched grubs have been working for awhile. Affected sections of the lawn appear to be scorched. The sod lifts up easily in these spots because the roots have been destroyed by grub activity. Peel up a portion of damaged sod and check for grubs in the soil just beneath it. They do the most damage in late spring or early fall.

The best way to determine if a lawn is infested with grubs before actual damage is evident is to look for them. In late May to mid-June, and a little later in the Far North, examine several areas of the lawn. Cut three sides of a 1-square-foot piece of sod to a depth of 4–5 inches, and carefully peel it away from the soil. Gently scrape the dirt from the roots and look for the white, curled larvae. After inspecting the roots, lay the grass back in place, tamp it and water it in.

How Many to Worry About?—A vigorous, well-established lawn can withstand the damage from as many as twenty to forty grubs per square foot in the spring because at that stage they are not eating very much. However, in the fall even a healthy lawn suffers when the population of grubs exceeds ten to fifteen per square foot, because this is their big binge-eating time. If your lawn is not in good condition, more than ten grubs per square foot will do considerable damage. Lawns with fifty or more grubs per square foot will likely be destroyed by season's end without treatment.

BEST GRUB CONTROLS

SPIKING GRUBS

White grubs migrate toward the soil's surface in late spring as they prepare to turn into beetles. Again in August and September, grubs newly hatched from recently laid eggs linger in this same area among grass roots prior to burrowing deep into the soil when cold weather arrives. During these times they are vulnerable to some kind of spiking tool.

Sharp spikes that penetrate at least 2 inches into the soil impale and kill grubs. While golf shoes do not do the job, special shoes with spikes attached to the bottom for this purpose are now available. So is a hand-spiking tool that does a good job.

Spiking also contributes to lawn health, as many golf course managers know. While it is not as effective as core aerating, it does fight soil compaction.

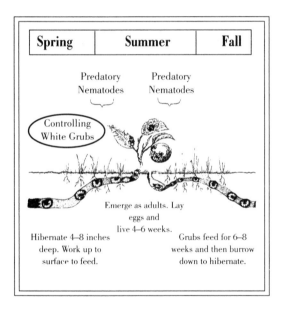

Turf that is spiked frequently gets more oxygen down near grass roots. With stronger root systems it can better resist drought, as well as insects.

PREDATORY NEMATODES

Beneficial or predatory nematodes are microscopic organisms that feed on grubs. Products like this composed of naturally occurring bacteria, microbes, insects and other living organisms to fight pest insects are called biological insecticides. They are gradually replacing the traditional petroleum-based products that came into common use after World War II. They are safer because they are very specific, harming only the type of pest that they normally victimize in nature.

Predatory nematodes are packaged as a powder to be mixed with water. Spray the resulting slurry on the lawn and the newly activated nematodes will get busy. They enter the soil in the moisture and do what comes naturally—seek out grubs to parasitize. As they attack, nematodes introduce a bacteria into the grubs which kills them in a few days. Then the nematode feeds on the dead grub and reproduces in abundance. After about ten days or more, the new generation of nematodes seeks out more grubs to feed on. We feel this will become the pest control method of choice in many situations in the home landscape in the future. Check the end of this chapter for details about how to use this product.

BROAD-SPECTRUM INSECTICIDES

Biological controls are not instantaneous. If a white grub infestation has gotten out of hand and the damage to the lawn is so far advanced that it may be destroyed, it may be necessary to resort to a faster-acting chemical insecticide. Consult the end of this chapter for a discussion about the various broad-spectrum insecticides available to yardeners.

BEST LONG-TERM PREVENTION

There is another biological product that offers long-term control of grubs in lawns, but due to difficulty in manufacturing it in large quantities it is not generally available in stores. Called Milky Spore disease, it is a bacteria *(Bacillus popilliae)* that, when sprayed on the lawn, enters the soil and fatally sickens white grubs. Over a period of three to five years the bacteria multiplies and eventually can wipe out virtually all the grubs in a lawn. It lingers for decades, coming alive when grubs appear and dispatching them. We describe it here because, if they can solve the problem of keeping the bacteria viable while producing it in large quantities, it will be available in the future.

MOW LAWN PROPERLY

Beetles prefer to lay their eggs in short, stubby turf. They do not like grass that is taller than 2 inches. Discourage egg-laying beetles at the same time you discourage weeds and encourage healthy grass roots by maintaining your lawn at a height of 2–3 inches.

COLLECT ADULT BEETLES

The best way to prevent white grubs is to eradicate adult beetles before they lay eggs in the soil. That is the principle behind the popular Japanese beetle traps. By means of sex and floral-scented lures, they attract beetles to a hanging bag into which they fall in a dither of excitement.

We do not recommend these traps because they are too effective. They attract beetles from as far away as 500 yards, almost a quarter of a mile! They actually encourage beetles to visit your yard. If you have bolstered the natural defense system of beneficial creatures in your yard as described above, depend on it for basic control of beetles and back it up with your own efforts.

While it is not exactly low maintenance, knocking Japanese beetles from your plants into a jar of soapy water is the simplest, most direct way to cut down their population. It's a simple matter to pick the offending pests from roses, hollyhocks, zinnias, elms and linden trees, grapes, raspberries and other favorite plants where they predictably congregate in large numbers. Take a jar of soapy water along as you tour your property once or twice a day in midsummer when adult beetles first appear and drop them in to drown. Every dead beetle is one that will not be laying eggs in your lawn. A few weeks of this will definitely reduce next year's grub population.

Sod Webworms

Sod webworms *(Crambus* species) are the larval, or caterpillar, stage of a moth. The worms grow from 3/4 to 1 inch long at maturity. They have dark, shiny, brown heads, but the color of their bodies varies from greenish to beige, brown or gray, depending on the species. They have four parallel rows of distinctive dark spots along their length from which protrude long, stiff hairs.

The adult moths are buff-colored with a wingspan of about an inch. They fly in the early morning or late evening in a jerky zigzag pattern, just a few feet above the lawn. Mowing the lawn or disturbing shrubs will flush these moths from their hiding places. They are readily attracted to lights at night.

The moths themselves do not damage lawns. However, they drop eggs into the grass that, upon hatching six to ten days later, develop into voracious caterpillars. They immediately begin feeding on grass blades (always at night) and building silk-lined tunnels in the thatch near the soil surface.

Sod webworms are found throughout the United States and in southern Canada. They particularly like Kentucky bluegrass, bentgrass, tall and fine fescues and zoysia grass. In the warmer areas of the country, webworms may produce up to three generations a year. In western and southern states, webworm generations may overlap, with all life stages—eggs, caterpillars and moths—occurring simultaneously.

Most Obvious Webworm Symptoms

In late spring, the appearance of small brown patches in the lawn signal a sod webworm problem. By midsummer these small 1–2 inch spots become large dead patches. Infested lawns look their worst by July and August.

Sod webworms cut grass blades off just above the thatch line, and drag them into their silken tunnels to eat them. The grass in the damaged spots isn't actually dead, it's just been chewed off at ground level.

Look for sod webworms in the thatch in the damaged areas of the lawn. Carefully break apart the thatch and search for their silken tubes. You also may find greenish tan pellets about the size of a pinhead; they are the excrement of the caterpillars. The sudden presence of lots of birds, and even moles, feeding on the lawn often indicates a burgeoning population of webworms.

Typically, webworm control efforts are too late, because by the time real damage is evident, the caterpillars are about finished feeding and are ready for their next life stage. They eat about 70 percent of their total food supply in the last ten days of their development. This is why severe damage occurs so suddenly.

Early detection is essential for successful control. Keep a lookout for the buff-colored moths starting in midspring. They are visible in the early morning or late evening flying in their characteristic jerky, zigzag pattern just a few feet above the lawn.

Once you see moths, then expect a caterpillar problem in a few weeks. Prepare to address it then and not delay until flocks of robins or other birds signal a problem already nearly out of control.

To determine if a webworm population is large enough to require your intervention, in the early summer mark off two sections of lawn measuring 2 feet by 2 feet. Locate one in a damaged area and one in an undamaged area.

Then mix 2 tablespoons of liquid household detergent into 1 gallon of water and, using a sprinkling can, saturate each lawn area evenly. Sections with thick thatch may require several gallons of soapy water. Because the soap irritates webworms lurking in the turf, they will be visible crawling to the surface within five to ten minutes. If no webworms appear, lawn damage is probably due to disease or some other insect.

How to Find Those Webworms

How Many to Worry About?— If you count more than ten webworms per square foot of healthy turf, some control steps are necessary. An infestation of even a few caterpillars per square foot of lawn already stressed from compacted soil, lack of water or lack of food must be treated.

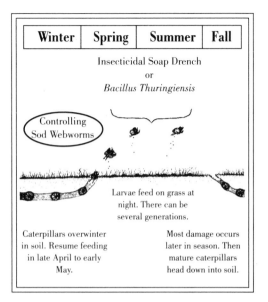

BEST WEBWORM CONTROLS

INSECTICIDAL SOAP DRENCH

This type of soap is formulated specifically for pest insect control. It is easily and safely sprayed on infested lawns and plants. We discuss this technique in detail at the end of this chapter.

BACILLUS THURINGIENSIS (BT)

This is a bacteria which preys exclusively on caterpillars. When they eat it, they sicken and die within a day or two. Using Bt requires some special information. We provide all the details at the end of this chapter.

PREDATORY NEMATODES

Beneficial or predatory nematodes are biological controls. These tiny organisms feed on caterpillars and grubs. A relatively new pest control technique, spraying nematodes in a water solution on the grass so they can enter the thatch and seek out webworms is simple and safe. We feel this will become the pest control method of choice in many situations in the home landscape in the future. Check the end of this chapter for details about how to use this product.

BROAD-SPECTRUM INSECTICIDES

If a webworm infestation gets out of hand, it may be necessary to resort to an insecticide to save the lawn. Consult the end of this chapter for a discussion about the various broad-spectrum insecticides available to yardeners. Use these as a last resort, because they will kill all the insects in your lawn, including the beneficial ones.

BEST LONG-TERM PREVENTION

There are a number of steps you can take to reduce the chances of a recurrence of a webworm problem next year.

GET RID OF THATCH!

A healthy lawn has little or no thatch, therefore it will not support major infestations of sod webworms. To keep grass healthy and prevent thatch, aerate your lawn at least once a year initially. After a few years, when the soil and grass are improved, move to a three-year aeration schedule.

Also every three years, topdress the lawn with a 1/4-inch layer of organic material such as peat moss, composted municipal sludge, topsoil or sifted compost. This will virtually eliminate the buildup of thatch that serves as home for webworms.

KEEP LAWN COOL

Because webworms prefer turf that is dry and warm, do not allow your lawn to get too dry in the hot summer months. Water it deeply every week or ten days (depending on the vigor of the grass) when rainfall is sparse. Watering in the late morning provides moisture to the grass and also keeps the soil surface cooler, making the area less attractive to webworms. Cut the grass no shorter than 2 inches. Longer grass blades shade the soil and keep it cool.

Chinch Bugs

Chinch bugs *(Blissus* species), called hairy chinch bugs in the North, are so small and inconspicuous that they can destroy a lawn right under your eyes without your being aware they are there. During every stage of development, from nymph to mature adult, they damage turf grass.

Adult bugs are only about 1/5 inch long, about the size of a ladybug. They have black bodies marked by a black, triangular pad which separates white, folded wings. Immature bugs are reddish colored. Chinch bugs cluster down among grass blades and suck their juices, sometimes causing them to appear red-stained.

These bugs thrive in hot, dry weather, becoming active when temperatures are in the high 70s. Chinch bugs occur throughout most of the country, but are worst in the Midwest, East and South. In the Northeast, they favor Kentucky bluegrass and red fescue.

MOST OBVIOUS CHINCH BUG SYMPTOMS

Chinch bugs do their worst damage in the heat of the summer—in August and early September. Suspect chinch bugs when you see large, distinct, circular patches, primarily in the sunny areas of your lawn, that turn yellow, then brown and then die.

The afflicted patches often first appear near sidewalks and streets, where heat is reflected onto the lawn. They eventually spread outward

Finding Chinch Bugs

into the rest of the lawn. The yellowish spots show the greatest damage at their centers. This is where the chinch bugs congregate.

Why Do You Have Chinch Bugs?

Chinch bug infestations are fostered in lawns by conditions of excess thatch, too little water and too much or too little nitrogen; however, excessive thatch is the most common attraction for chinch bugs.

Water Trap Diagnosis—Where chinch bugs are suspected, cut the bottom from a can and push it a few inches into the soil where the grass is beginning to turn yellow. Then fill it with warm water. If they are present, chinch bugs will float to the surface within a few minutes.

How Many to Worry About?—If your lawn is in good condition, ten to fifteen chinch bugs per square foot probably will not cause a problem. They will be kept in check by naturally occuring predators. However, if the lawn is stressed by compacted soil, drought or heavy thatch, even a few chinch bugs will do damage.

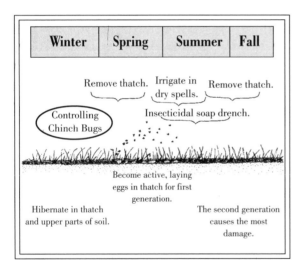

Best Chinch Bug Controls

Remove Thatch Layer

Conscientiously removing thatch buildup that is more than 1/4 inch thick goes a long way toward reducing chinch bug problems since it denies them shelter in the turf. Removing the thatch exposes the lurking bugs to their bird and insect predators.

Insecticidal Soap

This soap solution is especially formulated for pest control. Look for techniques on how to use insecticidal soap at the end of this chapter.

Broad-Spectrum Insecticides

If a chinch bug infestation gets out of hand, it may be necessary to resort to an insecticide to save the lawn. Consult the end of this chapter for a discussion about the various broad-spectrum insecticides available to yardeners.

Best Long-Term Prevention

There are several steps you can take to minimize problems with chinch bugs.

Maintain Healthy Lawn

A healthy lawn has little or no thatch, therefore it will not foster major infestations of chinch bugs. It can withstand minor incursions of this pest. To keep grass healthy and prevent thatch, aerate your lawn at least once a year initially. After a few years, when the soil and grass are improved, move to a three-year aeration schedule.

Also every three years, topdress the lawn with a 1/4-inch layer of organic material such as peat moss, composted municipal sludge, topsoil or sifted compost. This will virtually eliminate the buildup of thatch that serves as home for chinch bugs.

Cool Lawn in Hot, Dry Weather

Because chinch bugs prefer turf that is dry and warm, do not allow your lawn to get too dry in the hot summer months. Water it well when rainfall is sparse. Watering in the late morning provides moisture to the grass and also keeps the soil surface cooler, making the area less attractive to chinch bugs. Cut the grass no shorter than 2 inches. Longer grass blades shade the soil and keep it cool.

Cutworms

"Cutworm" is an umbrella term that covers the larvae, or caterpillar stage, of more than two hundred species of moths. Some kinds of these larvae are significant pests in every part of the country. Indiscriminate eaters, they attack all kinds of plants, including food crops.

Cutworms may be either gray, brown, bronze, black, greenish-white or red, but all are fat and soft, with coarse bristles sparsely covering their bodies. They come in different sizes as well, but most are from 1 to 2 inches long when they become avidly interested in your plants.

If touched, cutworms quickly roll up into a ball. You probably won't see them since they feed at night and hide in the soil during the day.

While more than one cutworm species attack turf grasses, the most common is the variegated cutworm. Variegated cutworm larvae live on the soil surface. They feed above ground, commonly crawling up and chewing the upper leaves of plants. They chew grass blades near the surface of the soil.

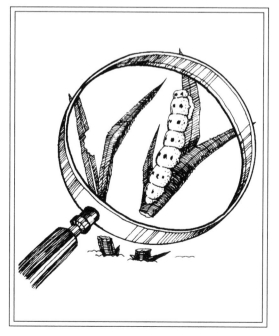

Mature variegated cutworms are gray, mottled with dark brown markings and distinguishable by a row of four to six small, white-to-yellow spots down the middle of the back.

Most Obvious Cutworm Symptoms

Cutworms injure turf by chewing grass blades off at or near the soil surface. They also eat tender grass roots, causing dead brown spots to form in the lawn in both round and irregular patches of 1 or 2 inches in diameter. Because these pests chew blades of grass below the mowing level, look for patches of closely cut grass stubble. Most cutworm damage occurs during warm weather, especially in May or June when there are lots of tender new blades of grass to eat. They feed mostly at night and bury themselves in the soil during the day.

Drench an area of the lawn where you suspect cutworm activity with water laced with insecticidal soap early on a spring evening. Return after dark to see if there are cutworms on the surface of the turf. This will enable you to diagnose the cause of suspicious spots in the turf.

Bear in mind that spilled gas or too much fertilizer in an area of the lawn causes damage similar to that done by cutworms.

How Many Are Too Many?—One corn hill can harbor as many as sixty cutworms. There can be one hundred around a single peach tree. In a garden filled with seedlings, one cutworm is too many. In a lawn, you begin to see damage when you have more than five cutworms per square foot.

BEST CUTWORM CONTROLS

Controls for cutworms are similar to those for the other members of the Big Four bad guys. You have several choices.

BENEFICIAL NEMATODES

Beneficial or predatory nematodes are tiny organisms that feed on cutworms. A relatively new pest control technique, spraying nematodes in a water solution on the lawn where they can penetrate turf and thatch and seek out cutworms is simple and safe. We feel this will become the pest control method of choice in many situations in the home landscape in the future. Check the end of this chapter for details about how to use this product.

BACILLUS THURINGIENSIS (BT)

This is a bacteria which preys exclusively on caterpillars of various kinds. When they eat it, they sicken and die within a day or two. Using Bt requires some special information. We provide all the details at the end of this chapter.

Other Occasional Lawn Pest Insects

There are, of course, lots and lots of other pest insects that might find their way into your yard. Here is a quick sampling of some of the more notorious ones.

Billbugs

Billbugs are particular problems for Kentucky bluegrass lawns. Members of the weevil family, the adults have long snouts. Adult billbugs are 1/4–1/2 inch long and brown or gray. They live in the thatch layer just above soil level. They feast on both stems and grass blades. Billbug larvae are small, legless, white grublike creatures with yellow-brown heads, resembling grains of puffed rice. They feed on stem tissue, causing infested shoots to turn brown and die.

Most Obvious Billbug Symptoms

Billbug damage typically appears from mid-June through July. Affected areas in the lawn appear brownish. Small circular patterns that turn yellowish and brown may develop. Dead sections of grass lift away easily from the soil. Mature turf stands are more likely to sustain damage than grass that is less than three years old.

You may spot adult billbugs on sidewalks and driveways in May and June. To confirm suspicions that they are in the lawn, cut the bottom from a can and push it a few inches into the soil where the grass is beginning to turn brown. Fill the can with warm water mixed with liquid detergent (about 2 tablespoons per gallon). If billbugs are lurking, they will stagger into view on the thatch surface within a few minutes.

How Many Are Too Many?—It does not take many billbugs to cause trouble. As few as one adult or ten larvae per square foot of lawn requires some control measures.

Best Billbug Controls

Remove Thatch Layer

Routinely removing thatch that accumulates to more than 1/4 inch thick will go a long way to reducing billbug problems, since they live in thick thatch. Removing the thatch exposes the bugs to their bird and insect predators.

Insecticidal Soap

This soap solution is especially formulated for pest control. Look for techniques on how to use insecticidal soap at the end of this chapter.

Broad-Spectrum Insecticide

If a billbug infestation gets out of hand, it may be necessary to resort to a chemical insecticide to save the lawn because they work quickly. Consult the end of this chapter for a discussion about the various broad-spectrum insecticides available to yardeners.

Best Long-Term Prevention

To reduce the chances of a recurrence of a billbug problem next year maintain a healthy lawn. A young, healthy lawn can withstand minor infestations of billbugs. Aerate at least once a year. Topdress it with a 1/4-inch layer of organic material such as peat moss, composted municipal sludge or sifted compost each year to control the buildup of thatch which shelters and protects billbug populations. If thatch does accumulate, remove it when it exceeds 1/4 inch thick. Use only slow-release nitrogen fertilizer on the lawn.

Armyworms

Irregular bare patches in the lawn may be a sign of armyworms *(Pseudaletia unipuncta)*. The damage they cause looks very similar to that caused by sod webworms. If armyworms have infected your lawn, symptoms usually appear in late summer or fall. These pests feed at night and rest under brown or dead sod during the day. In significant numbers, they will chew the grass down to the soil level.

Armyworms are easy to identify. They are about 1 1/2 inches long with brown, somewhat hairy bodies and black heads with prominent white V or Y marks. Three distinctive yellowish white lines run down their backs from head to tail. Each flank sports a dark stripe with a yellow wavy line splotched with red beneath it.

Adult armyworm moths fly at night and are attracted to light. Females begin depositing eggs on grass in May. Upon hatching, larvae immediately start to feed, migrating as a group as they graze on the lawn.

To control these voracious worms, spray Bt *(Bacillus thuringiensis)* on the area of the lawn where they are feeding. Thoroughly cover the grass blades so that the worms will ingest the bacteria when they eat. They'll sicken and die within days.

If you use Bt in liquid form, spray the lawn every ten to fourteen days until the pest is gone. Reapply Bt after it rains. Beneficial nematodes that are specifically used to control armyworms are now available commercially. Milky Spore disease *(Bacillus popilliae)* is another bacteria that controls armyworms, but it takes three to five years to be completely effective. It is not readily available at garden centers due to production difficulties.

Ants

In light of all the bad press that ants get, we may be the first to suggest that they are generally "good guys" in your lawn. As we've indicated in numerous places in this book, ants are one of the most effective predators of pest insects in a lawn. Their appetite for pest insect eggs is a boon to yardeners.

So what about the mounds ants build in the middle of my lawn, you ask? Well, we concede that while they do not eat grass, their nests may smother areas of turf or their tunnels may cause grass root zones to dry out, harming the lawn. Certainly, the mounded nests disrupt the uniformity of the turf. In these instances, we agree that ants would qualify as pests and need to be dealt with.

One technique for eliminating ant colonies in the lawn is to pour boiling water onto the anthill. It may take two or three drenchings over a few days to wipe them out. If they persist, move to plan B, which is using a product such as Insectigone by Chemfree containing diatomaceous earth and specially formulated baits that attract ants. Sprinkle the white powder on and around the anthills according to instructions on the package label. When the ants come in contact with the powder, or eat the bait, they literally dry up. Most die within forty-eight hours.

Now, the reason ants are colonizing the lawn is probably that your soil has problems. As in the other pest situations, it is important to follow up anti-ant measures with soil rehabilitation measures to assure that the ants do not come back. Chances are that the soil under your turf that is hosting ants is compacted and deficient in organic matter. Correct these conditions for long-term control of ants.

Deer Ticks

The incidence of Lyme disease is increasing nationwide. In the eastern United States, Lyme disease is caused by a spirochete bacteria that is transmitted to humans by the bite of a deer tick *(Ixodes dammini)*. Because deer ticks typically spend an interval between animal hosts in tall grasses and weeds, many people have concluded that they are common in lawn grass.

We mention deer ticks here to refute this assumption. While they may be a problem in certain local areas, they are not likely to infest a regularly mown residential lawn.

Only if *all three* of the following conditions prevail need you be concerned about deer ticks and Lyme disease:

1. You live in either of the two regions where deer ticks are prevalent (see map), *and*
2. There are white-tailed deer common within a mile of your home, or if you visit areas such as woods, parks or meadows, commonly frequented by white-tailed deer, *and*
3. If it is the right time of year for most deer tick contacts, which is April through August.

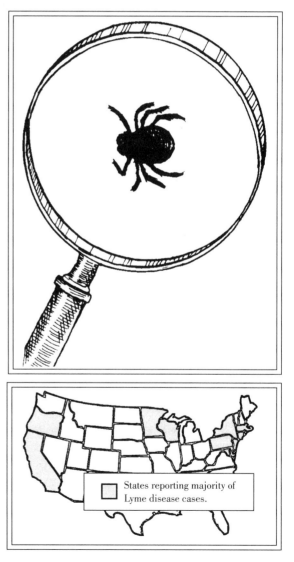

States reporting majority of Lyme disease cases.

No Deer/No Deer Ticks—If there are no deer populations within a mile or two of your home and you are confident there have been no deer on your property for the past few years, it is very unlikely that you will have any problems with deer ticks on your property. The closer you live to areas frequented by deer, the more alert you should be for possible contact with deer ticks during peak months. Even then, not every deer tick carries the bacteria for Lyme disease.

Because deer ticks usually rest in weeds and brush between 2 inches and 20 inches high, they are uncommon in mowed residential lawns and fields. Any deer ticks in your area are likely to be concentrated in brush along the margins linking forests and fields, in fence rows, in brush piles, on stone walls, in flower gardens and in vegetable gardens.

Think about areas where mice might be happy to live, and that is where deer ticks will also prefer, because mice are alternate hosts to deer ticks. So, incidentally, are dogs and cats, so don't allow pets to run freely in overgrown brushy areas. If they do, groom them regularly and check their favorite indoor sleeping spots for ticks.

WHAT DEER TICKS LOOK LIKE

Unfortunately, deer ticks are so tiny that they are difficult to spot. They are much smaller than the common dog tick. In their nymph stage, when they are most problematic, they are the size of this period (.) or a poppy seed. Gray-brown and translucent, they most resemble a crawling freckle. After feeding on a host's blood, nymphs appear darker brown and round, about the size of a regular pinhead.

Adult deer ticks are a bit bigger—about the size of this letter (o), or a sesame seed. Red-brown before they feed, when engorged they turn gray-brown and swell as large as a sunflower seed.

Adults should check for them on their shoes, socks and pants cuffs. Ticks can be anyplace on children. Pay special attention to the groin, back, armpits, behind the knees, head and hair.

If you believe deer ticks are a problem in your community, your local health department will have literature about how to deal with them locally. In any case, we strongly recommend that you do not spray your entire yard with any broad-spectrum insecticide every month, as is suggested by several insecticide companies for controlling deer ticks.

Tools for Controlling Insects

If you've taken a minute to scan the solutions recommended for each of the pests covered in this chapter, you'll notice that there are not all that many different products available to address the various pest problems in lawns. Fortunately, many of them are effective against several kinds of pest insects.

Here, finally, in this last section of the chapter are the promised details about the pesticide products. Since a product is most safe and effective if it is used correctly, it is important to take a minute to learn about the nature of the product and how to use it.

Insecticidal Soap

Insecticidal soap is commonly used to treat pest problems on plants in gardens, green-houses and in homes. It is also a useful tool in dealing with certain lawn pests. A contact pesticide, it must touch the insect to kill it.

Insecticidal soap is commonly mixed with water and poured on the lawn where pest problems are suspected. Such a drench, or soaking, irritates any pest insects lurking near the surface of the soil, driving them upwards into the grass blades to escape the moisture and dry off.

Here they are vulnerable to attacks by predator birds or a yardener with a rake. In some cases, especially with soft-bodied insects, insecticidal soap actually kills the pest.

The primary ingredients in commercial insecticidal soap products are fatty-acid salts. Because these salts are relatively nontoxic, they are safe for use on lawns.

Soap Drench

Prepare a soap drench by thoroughly mixing about 2 tablespoons of insecticidal soap concentrate into 1 gallon of water. With a sprinkling can, pour it onto affected areas of turf until the grass is soaked.

For Monitoring Pests—As we described in the discussions of individual pests, an insecticidal soap drench is useful for confirming the presence of pest insects. Water the soap/water mixture into a small area of sod, or sink a coffee can with both ends cut out down about 4 inches into the soil and then fill it with the soap/water mixture. Any pests present will float into view where they can be identified.

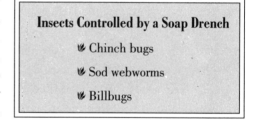

Insects Controlled by a Soap Drench

🌿 Chinch bugs

🌿 Sod webworms

🌿 Billbugs

For Controlling Pests—To control pest insects with an insecticidal soap drench, soak the whole area of affected turf and its thatch thoroughly with the soap/water mixture. Then, after about ten minutes, rake up the thatch, irritated insects and all. Either put the soapy, soggy thatch in a compost pile (the insects will not move back into the lawn) or discard it in the trash. It costs about $5 to treat 1,000 square feet of lawn with an insecticidal soap drench.

Bacillus thuringiensis (Bт)

Bacillus thuringiensis, usually referred to as "Bt," is a naturally occurring bacterium that is lethal to most leaf-eating caterpillars, including sod webworms and cutworms. It is harmless to all other insects, animals and humans.

Bt is sold as a dry powder for use as a dust, or, diluted with water, for use as a spray. It is also available in liquid form ready for spraying on the lawn where caterpillars are feeding. This "foliar" spray, which coats the blades of grass where the caterpillars are eating, is the most effective way to use Bt.

As they feed, the voracious pest caterpillars ingest the bacteria. The Bt paralyzes their digestive tracts, causing them to stop eating within two hours. In a day or two, certainly no longer than seventy-two hours, the caterpillars die. Bt does not work on moths, the adult stage of caterpillars.

Because death by Bt is delayed, caterpillars are still visible for awhile even when it has taken effect. However, if there are no more noticeable holes in plant foliage, the spray has done its job. Properly applied, Bt will kill from 70 percent to 90 percent of the pests. Any survivors will be handled by birds and other natural predators.

Once it is sprayed on grass, Bt in liquid form is potent for only twenty-four hours. Wait three to five days to spray again if new evidence of caterpillar feeding appears. Some common trade names for Bt products are: Caterpillar Killer, Dipel, Thuricide and Worm Attack. It costs about $1 to treat 1,000 square feet of turf with Bt.

How to Use Bt

For best results, mow the lawn before spraying it with Bt. To help the Bt stick to the grass, mix a surfactant or "spreader sticker" in the sprayer with the Bt. A surfactant also helps the Bt penetrate the layer of thatch. These products are found in the better garden centers or in some mail-order catalogs.

Coat each grass blade thoroughly with Bt solution, since it works only if sod webworms, cutworms and other caterpillars actually eat it as they chew blades of grass. It is most effective on newly hatched caterpillars, so if you are aware of when these unwelcome visitors arrive in your yard each year, be ready for them.

Typically, insects have predictable schedules, so their larvae will emerge on almost the same day every year, plus or minus a day or two. Bt is most effective in the spring and again in the late summer, when caterpillar feeding activity is greatest.

Spray Bt on the grass two weeks after seeing the sod webworm moth in your yard. That is about the time their eggs will hatch and young worms emerge. Spray it on the lawn as soon as you spot cutworms.

Bt breaks down in sunlight, so spray in the late afternoon or on cloudy (but not rainy) days to prolong the effectiveness of this insecticide. Also, do not use hard water in diluting Bt for spraying. Because alkaline, or hard, water can reduce its effectiveness, use water with a pH of 7.0 or lower.

Shelf Life

Bt spray that has been mixed from either a powder or a liquid concentrate is viable for only about twelve hours. Dispose of leftover spray by pouring it into the soil. It will not harm the soil or its denizens. It can be poured down the sink since it will not harm aquatic life.

If stored in a dark room no cooler than 35°F or warmer than 90°F, the liquid concentrate or the powdered form of Bt will last for at least two years. Actually the powder will last longer, but because it is difficult to maintain ideal storage conditions it is recommended that the product be replaced at least every three years.

Predatory Nematodes

Predatory, or beneficial, nematodes commercially packaged as a biological insecticide are a safe and effective weapon against many lawn pests. Unlike the harmful root-knot nematodes which attack plants, beneficial nematodes only attack soil-dwelling insects, such as white grubs, cutworms and billbug larvae.

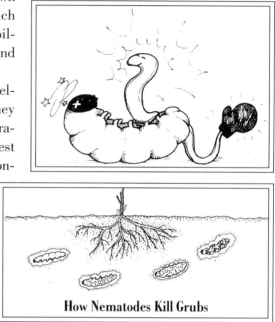

Nematodes are microscopic, nonsegmented, eel-like worms measuring .1–.125 inch long. While they occur naturally in soil, they are rarely in concentrations sufficient to control a major outbreak of a pest infestation. Commercial packages of nematodes contain billions of these good guys plus some inert ingredients to assure their well-being on the garden center shelf.

When you introduce millions of beneficial nematodes at a time into an area of the lawn infested with grubs, you unleash a powerful weapon. Carried into the soil by moisture, the tiny worms seek out the grubs and other pest insect larvae and kill them.

How Nematodes Kill Grubs

Beneficial nematodes are attracted to the heat and carbon dioxide emitted by the larvae. They enter the host through natural body openings and release a toxin that is fatal only to the grub within twenty-four to forty-eight hours. The nematode then reproduces, and when the eggs hatch its many progeny leave the host's body and begin searching actively for other susceptible insect pest larvae.

Beneficial or predatory nematodes can live in the soil and kill insects for many weeks, depending on the soil's moisture and temperature. The soil should be moist and the best results occur when the temperature of the soil is above 75°.

There are at least two strains or varieties of beneficial nematodes on the market—*Heterorhabditis heliothidis* (Hh) and *Neoaplectana carpocapsae* (Nc). Both are effective grub controls.

EFFECTIVENESS

Properly applied, predatory nematode products should achieve 60–80 percent control within two weeks. As with all pesticides, the concentration of predatory nematodes in a spray solution is very important to its effectiveness. Consequently, if you are using a concentrated form that requires that you dilute it with water, read the instructions on the package label carefully for the proportions. After about two weeks, lift up a piece of turf carefully to check the status of your grubs.

Pests Controlled by Predatory Nematodes

- Armyworms
- Asiatic garden beetle larvae
- Billbug larvae
- Japanese beetle larvae
- June beetle larvae
- Leather jackets/crane flies
- Oriental beetle larvae
- Sod webworms
- White grubs
- Wireworms

LAWN INSECTS CONTROLLED

Predatory nematodes will control the following lawn pest insects:

To target most lawn grubs, especially the Japanese beetle grub, introduce nematodes into the lawn in either late summer or midspring, when the grubs are likely to be most active. It costs roughly $10 to treat 1,000 square feet of lawn with predatory nematodes.

HOW TO USE PREDATORY NEMATODES

Use predatory nematodes only when you have positively identified grubs as the cause of your turf problem. For best results, spray them in the late afternoon or early evening. After a light rain is an ideal time. Otherwise, water the lawn until the soil is moist.

To assure maximum effectiveness, use all of the nematode mixture within three hours of preparation. Using a pressure sprayer, spray the liquid slurry of nematodes diluted in water onto the damp lawn. Plan to water the area again lightly immediately after application. If it does not rain over the next few days, water the treated area periodically to keep the soil moist.

If you happen to have a soil thermometer in the utility room, the best soil temperature for best results is a range between 55°F and 85°F. Under optimum moisture and temperature conditions, predatory nematodes should remain effective for six to eight weeks.

WHAT NOT TO DO

Do not mix predatory nematode products with fertilizers or chemicals. In fact, allow a week between application of fertilizers or other chemicals to the lawn and the introduction of predatory nematodes. It does not matter which you use first, just be sure to allow the intervening week.

Do not use diatomaceous earth on the same site as you use predatory nematodes. D.E. will harm predatory nematodes.

SHELF LIFE

Most products containing predatory nematodes require refrigeration between 43°F and 47°F. While it is best to use the product as soon as possible, nematodes will survive for six months under those circumstances. Do not freeze them. They will keep up to three months at room temperature if properly packaged.

Broad-Spectrum Insecticides

We have made every effort to offer realistic solutions to all lawn insect problems that do not require the use of any broad-spectrum insecticide. The reason is simple. Such insecticides kill indiscriminately. Beneficial insects die along with the pest insects.

We are persuaded that beneficials really do make a difference and their continued presence in your lawn is very important. Nevertheless, we know there are readers who still prefer to rely on what we call the "big bangers" to get the job done quickly and effectively. So here are the choices.

Dursban—Dursban is one of the most commonly used lawn insecticides. It will control any lawn insect you are likely to encounter. Dursban kills insects by entering their bodies and disrupting their nervous systems. While it has the advantage of almost instant control, it does not kill selectively. It harms almost any insect it comes in contact with, friend and foe alike. It is best used, therefore, only if a pest infestation is so severe that extreme measures are required to control it.

Spread the granular powder on the mowed infested areas of the lawn according to the directions on the package label. Then water it into the soil with repeated heavy waterings. In a lawn with heavy thatch, it is best to rake away the thatch first, so that the insecticide can soak into the soil thoroughly.

Use Dursban in granular form by itself. Do *not* use it in combination with fertilizer products. Plants under stress, as grass is when it is attacked by insects, should not be fertilized. It costs roughly $2 to spread Dursban over 1,000 square feet of turf.

Other insecticides—There are a number of other broad-spectrum insecticides that control the major lawn insect pests, but we recommend them only as a last resort. For the organic homeowner, pyrethrum is an appropriate control. For others, carbaryl (Sevin) is an effective product. Remember, it takes two to four months for a population of beneficials to regenerate in a lawn sprayed with a general-purpose, broad-spectrum insecticide.

Avoid Diazinon—Avoid using any insecticide containing granular diazinon. While this product is effective in killing grubs and other pest insects, it is known to kill songbirds and has been banned from use on public golf courses for that reason.

The Best Defense Is a Good Offense

On those occasions when even the healthiest lawn becomes stressed and pest problems develop, early control is important. The sooner you spot an incipient problem and address it, the less time, effort and money is involved. Also, a less-toxic remedy is likely to be most effective on insects or disease organisms in the early stages of infestation.

For this reason, one of the best pest control measures is careful observation. Develop the habit of examining your turf closely every few weeks, in addition to the cursory once-over you give it while you are mowing.

Pest Control Do's

1. Observe lawn regularlyi to catch damage early.

2. Examine damage closely to determine correct cause.

3. Identify pest insect before choosing a control method.

4. Choose a control method appropriate for the insect and the stage it is in.

5. Select the least toxic control method whenever possible.

6. Consider weather conditions before using a pesticide.

7. Follow instructions on product label.

8. Limit pesticide treatment to the specific afflicted area.

The bottom line is that the best defense is a good offense. An emphasis on wellness and long-term prevention of pest problems makes good sense. Your efforts to develop and maintain a dense, vigorous turf yield not only a lovely landscape but a healthy ecosystem.

By protecting and encouraging the natural system of beneficial microlife in the soil and friendly insects and birds above ground, you are establishing a sturdy defense against opportunistic disease organisms and pest insects. By respecting that natural system with your choice of pesticides when the occasional pest problem develops, you are sustaining and reinforcing the health of your lawn.

Chapter Twelve

Solving Other Lawn Problems

Problems in lawns are not limited to the occasional invasion of pests or weeds. Unfortunately, there are assorted other conditions that develop from time to time. In this last chapter, we review some of these other difficulties and discuss how to handle them in a low-maintenance lawn. The good news is that all of the problems discussed below are solvable and there are steps to take to assure that they rarely recur.

Grass and Trees

One reality that homeowners who are lucky enough to have lovely trees and shrubs in their yards face is that trees and lawn grass are not very compatible. In fact, grass and trees are constantly engaged in a fierce competition for available light, nutrients and water.

While trees always win by virtue of their size and extensive root systems, they pay a price. They are stressed. Locked in the struggle with competitive trees, adjacent lawns are also stressed. The grass struggles to survive literally in the shadow of trees and large shrubs. As we have pointed out in previous chapters, stress saps the vigor of plants over time, making them vulnerable to secondary disease and pest problems. Let's deal with some of the problems resulting from this common but unhappy combination of trees and turf.

SHADE

A major source of stress for grass growing near trees is that it does not get enough light (see p. 95). Grass needs lots of sun to be healthy and even moderate shade induces enough stress in a lawn that it is frequently plagued with some other problem such as moss, weeds, insects or disease.

Unless you are prepared to cut down offending trees and shrubs or tear down walls and buildings that shade areas of turf, the only way to solve chronic grass problems in these areas is to eliminate it altogether. As we emphasized in Chapter Seven, no lawn grass grows well in deep shade.

The solution to the shade "problem" is to replace the grass with a ground cover which will handle the reduced light situation and will not compete with the tree roots for water and nutrients so aggressively. Review the discussion in Chapter Eight on how to determine which areas are appropriate for growing grass and which should be devoted to attractive and easy-to-care-for ground cover.

SURFACE TREE ROOTS

Then there are surface tree roots. As we pointed out in Chapter One, they are there because the soil is compacted. They migrate to the surface in search of air. The roots of any turf in this area are similarly deprived of sufficient oxygen, so it is also chronically in dire straits.

If you aerate the soil and topdress it with some organic material every few years, the compaction problem should go away. Unfortunately, those tree roots already on the surface will not go away. Their presence makes establishing turf there virtually impossible. Here's another situation where some other ground cover is more appropriate. Certainly an attractive mulch or patch of pachysandra is better for the tree. Check Chapter One for a description of how to deal with existing surface roots.

TREES HATE GRASS

Most yardeners don't realize that tree roots that access soil nutrients are shallow. Unlike its deeply probing support and water-seeking roots, a tree's feeder roots snake through the top 4–6 inches of the soil. They fan out from the trunk in search of food one to two times the distance of the drip line.

Grass roots and tree roots both depend on the same top 4–6 inches of the soil for pretty much the same nutrients—nitrogen, phosphorus, potassium and lots of micronutrients. Grass plants, being heavy feeders, are likely to monopolize available food, leaving inadequate amounts for the tree. Consequently, the reality is that trees living in turf never get sufficient nutrients. They are in varying degrees of stress at all times and will never live a full, healthy life. Their life expectancy may be reduced by as much as half.

Also, research indicates that turf grass is actually "allelopathic" to young tree saplings. That means grass roots stimulate a harmful chemical reaction in tree roots that drains a young tree's vigor. For this reason, any young tree planted in turf should be surrounded by mulch out at least 2 feet from its trunk. This will protect it from the toxic effect of grass roots and thus reduce its stress.

Another way to reduce the conflict between grass and trees is, as we suggested above, to replace any turf directly under the tree with a ground cover. This puts the marginal grass out of its misery while simultaneously improving the tree's situation. Ground covers are not as heavy feeders as turf grasses. They will also cool the soil around the tree and reduce compaction. Not only are they attractive, but they offer the bonus of reducing your lawn size, making it even lower maintenance—a win-win situation for you and your landscape plants.

Thatch

A little bit of thatch is natural and acceptable in any lawn. A thatch layer 1/4 inch thick or less poses no threat. Typically, though, residential lawns don't have just a "little bit." They develop excessive thatch and that is harmful to the grass.

WHAT IS THATCH?

While thatch appears to be wads of grass clippings, they do not cause thatch, as is commonly assumed. Thatch is actually a ruglike mat of dead grass rhizomes, crowns and stems that accumulates on the soil surface among live grass blades.

Constituted of tough substances such as cellulose, hemicellulose and lignin—all of which are difficult for soil microbes to break down—this mat does not decompose readily. Clippings fall down onto it and are temporarily trapped there. However, because they are 85–90 percent water, they break down easily. Meanwhile, the thatch persists and gradually builds up.

You may become aware of excessive thatch when it becomes really difficult to push the lawn mower over the lawn or if you can rake through the turf with your fingers and pull up handfuls of brown, dead material. When thatch is really thick you might find yourself inadvertently scalping

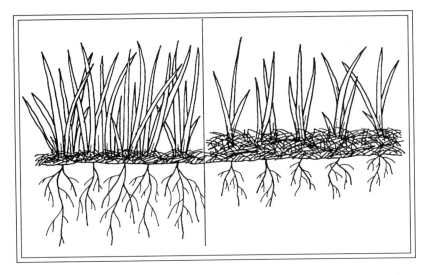

areas of the lawn where the mower exposes it as it cuts back the grass blades.

When thatch gets too thick it absorbs moisture itself, but obstructs most rainwater from reaching the soil. Therefore, water does not get down into the soil uniformly. Its impenetrability promotes runoff during rains or watering, again depriving the turf's soil of moisture.

Thatch also prevents healthy air circulation near the soil, providing an ideal habitat for various harmful bacteria and pest insects. It generates high humidity in the turf, which fosters disease. Ultimately, excessive thatch inhibits grass root development.

In other words, too much thatch is injurious to lawns. Do not allow it to build up to more than 1/4 inch—ever. This thin layer is considered acceptable because it cushions the turf against wear and insulates the soil somewhat against temperature extremes.

Check Thatch Thickness—It is easy to determine whether the thatch in your lawn is too thick. Take a pencil and carefully poke it down into the thatch layer until it strikes the soil (it takes a gentle touch). Mark the top of the thatch with your thumb. Then pull up the pencil and measure the space from its tip to your thumb. If the space exceeds 1/4–1/2 inch, plan to take some remedial action in the spring or fall, whichever comes next.

WHAT CAUSES THATCH?

Thatch may be present in lawns with both lousy and healthy soil. Thatch in lousy soil is more of a problem.

THATCH IN POOR SOIL

There are two common causes of thatch. Unfortunately, one or both of these situations can be found in over half the lawns in America.

1. Compacted soil—When soil is compacted, grass roots are unable to penetrate the soil so they migrate to the surface where they crowd into a thick mat. As they subsequently die, they create thatch.
2. Too much quick-acting nitrogen fertilizer—Quick-acting fertilizers tend to make soil more acidic. Acidic soil repels earthworms (kings of the decomposers) and re-

duces the microbial population, so there are fewer decomposing-type bacteria to process thatch. Simultaneously, the fertilizer stimulates grass growth, creating a greater volume of clippings to process.

Most lawns that have been on intensive chemical fertilizing programs eventually develop a thick layer of thatch. The soil-dwelling creatures in charge of the decomposing organic waste just are not there to do the job.

Thatch in Healthy Soil

Unfortunately, thatch may also develop in a perfectly healthy turf thriving in wonderful, aerated soil. Ironically, that very dense turf that is the keystone of a low-maintenance lawn also fosters thatch buildup.

Remember, grass plants constantly renew themselves over the growing season; some die and new ones emerge to take their place. The dead plants will decompose naturally; however, they may be so numerous (as may be the case in a lawn densely planted with grass) that the volume of dead organic material exceeds the healthy population of decomposing microbes in the soil. The existing microbes have difficulty keeping up with the job, so a thatch will slowly develop. It might take two or three years for a layer thicker than 1/2 inch to accumulate.

HOW TO HANDLE THATCH

This first section addresses thatch problems in poor soil. A top priority in this situation is fixing the soil as part of dealing with your thatch problem. The idea is to get rid of existing thatch first, then upgrade the soil and change your lawn care practices to minimize the problem in the future.

Mechanical Removal of Thatch

A thatch layer that is more than 1/4 inch thick must be removed. There are hand tools designed for removing thatch, but our experience has been that they are not all that effective and they represent an enormous amount of very hard work.

A thatch problem usually does not develop again for three to four years, so we believe that it makes sense to rent a thatch-removing machine from your local tool rental agency. It will do a more thorough job, and do it more quickly. De-thatching machines can be rented for about $50 a day. Most rental agencies will deliver and pick up for a small extra fee. Some residential size Rototillers have de-thatching attachments as well. Perhaps a gardening neighbor has one you can borrow.

Power de-thatching tools are designed to rake up the dead thatch material while doing the least amount of harm to the live grass. They will generate many bags of dead thatch, even from a modest-sized lawn. This is organic material, so dispose of it in your compost pile, if you have one.

Do not de-thatch the lawn in the middle of the summer when the turf is already stressed from heat and low-moisture conditions. Early fall is the best time for bluegrass, fescue and ryegrass lawns. Late spring is the second-best time.

Many homeowners prefer to combine de-thatching with other fall lawn jobs and get it all over with at once. They de-thatch, aerate, overseed and then lightly topdress. The payoff comes the following spring when the revitalized lawn is gorgeous. Proper maintenance over time will assure that thatch is only a modest and occasional problem in the future.

BIOLOGICAL REMOVAL OF THATCH

A number of biological products for treating thatch are now available in garden centers and hardware stores. Lawn Rx by Ringer and D-Thatch by Sudbury are two examples of this type of product that come in powdered form. They contain microorganisms and enzymes that decompose thatch which are activated when you add water and spray them on the lawn. While these products are effective, they do take several months to break down the thatch. They are certainly easier to use than a power de-thatching machine.

LAWN AERATION AND THATCH

The only effective way to reduce the soil compaction which promotes thatch is to core aerate the lawn with an aerating tool or machine. Aeration introduces air (oxygen) down into the soil where it stimulates an explosion of microbial activity for more efficient decomposition of dying turf. This slows thatch buildup.

Meanwhile, the cores, or plugs, of soil that fall on top of the turf in the aerating process break down in the rain, depositing decomposing microbes onto the thatch layer from above. These microbes promptly set about the job of breaking down the existing thatch. In this manner, aerating helps control thatch buildup.

OTHER THATCH CONTROLS

Topdressing a lawn with topsoil or a compost also helps eliminate thatch. A 1/4-inch topdressing of good topsoil, composted sludge or regular compost spread on a lawn helps to correct soil problems that cause thatch buildup. At the same time, the topdressing material, just like the soil cores from aerating, introduces decomposing microbes into the thatch to help break down what is already there.

Spreading lime on the lawn will also encourage thatch decay. It corrects excessive soil acidity. As it raises the soil pH, the natural microbial population of the soil increases, thereby increasing the decomposing power in the surface of your lawn.

Some yardeners have found that spraying stale beer on a thatchy lawn (1 pint per 500 square feet diluted from thorough watering) encourages the decomposers to get busy working on that thatch more quickly. Seems like a waste of good beer to Jeff.

CHANGE YOUR WAYS

After de-thatching by whatever means you choose, shift to using a slow-release nitrogen fertilizer on the lawn. If you have not yet aerated and topdressed the lawn, do so. Plan to aerate and topdress every three or four years from now on to discourage thatch from building up excessively in the future.

Consider the implications of the previous sentence: Even if you do all the right things this year to create a healthy, low-maintenance lawn (e.g., aerate, overseed and topdress), you cannot rest on your laurels and assume your thatch problem is over. You will have to do these jobs again.

In three or four years that thatch will be back, even though you used slow-release fertilizer. There is no escaping the fact that soil needs aerating and topdressing every three to five years to stay healthy and to avoid the buildup of more than 1/4 inch or so of thatch.

Moss in Bare Spots

Moss grows in lawns whose soil is sick—conditions in the soil favor the growth of moss and discourage grass. Typical soil problems are shade, excess acidity and poor drainage. A very cool, wet spring may cause moss even in sunny areas of a poor lawn.

In most cases, moss signals seriously compacted soil. If you just kill the moss and don't improve the soil, moss will return. You must change the fundamental conditions in the soil to eliminate moss from your lawn for good.

KILLING MOSS

Kill moss either mechanically by raking it up or chemically by spraying it. A spray of copper sulfate (3–5 ounces per 5 gallons of water per 1,000 square feet) or iron sulfate (3 ounces per 5 gallons of water per 10,000 square feet) will kill moss. A soap (fatty acid) spray called "De-Moss" will also kill moss. However, killing it is only the first step.

Preventing the return of the moss is the next step. Abandon efforts to grow grass in shady areas where patches of moss thrive instead of the grass. Shift to ground covers instead, which will eventually overwhelm the moss.

If you feel you must have grass in a shady spot which has historically produced more moss than turf, get to work. Aerate the soil and topdress it with compost or topsoil. Then overseed with a grass seed labeled for shade (a fine fescue mixture). This may well permanently discourage the moss. The aeration is probably the most important step in the process.

Mushrooms in Lawn

A crop of mushrooms in a lawn signals that something is decaying under the lawn's surface. An old stump or scrap wood from construction, for example, can be the source of decaying material for many years. If wood chips are incorporated into your topdressing material, you'll have mushrooms for awhile.

There is no way to cure or eliminate mushrooms in turf. They do not damage grass, and they are easy to remove by simply knocking them down or mowing over them. Eventually, the woody material will decompose completely and the mushrooms disappear.

Any mushrooms growing in your lawn are not edible mushrooms, so don't be tempted to drop them into a salad!

Dealing with Disease

We don't devote much space in this book to a discussion of lawn disease problems for a number of reasons. Most diseases are caused by unusual weather conditions and there is nothing you can do about that. Furthermore, it is very difficult for untrained yardeners to properly diagnose a lawn disease. Finally, it is often the case that once disease symptoms are visible, it is too late to treat it. Most chemical products must be applied *before* the disease emerges.

Our view is that if indications of a disease appear in a healthy lawn, then chances are that when the weather changes the disease will go away. Also, we feel that while treatment is problematical, prevention is the key to dealing with lawn disease problems.

Virtually all diseases can be prevented by changing cultural practices. For example, we have been recommending in many of the chapters in this book that a topdressing of some kind of composted organic material will do wonderful things to the lawn and its soil. Add preventing disease to that list, because research has shown that any kind of composted material has fungicidal properties that routinely discourage fungal diseases such as dollar spot, brown patch and Pythium blight from getting out of hand.

Healthy lawns can handle minor outbreaks of almost any disease that might develop because of weird weather. For this reason, the use of fungicides is not necessary in a low-maintenance lawn.

This next section essentially summarizes information that might be helpful when disease is a problem in the lawn. Knowing a bit more about specific situations may be helpful, although it is likely that your healthy, low-stress lawn will successfully fight off most disease problems all by itself.

What Disease?

While there are some bacteria and viruses that cause turf disease, most diseases of turf grass are caused by fungi. Fungal spores inhabit the turf grass's foliar canopy, thatch layer and the upper levels of topsoil. These pathogens are there all the time, generally in balance with other microbes that eat or kill the pathogens.

Problems occur when the lawn grass becomes stressed—usually due to a sudden change in its environment. Often, extreme moisture and/or heat triggers the explosive growth of a particular pathogen. Overwhelming its natural predators, it will show as a patch of grass coated gray or as spots of brown or yellow grass in the lawn.

To determine whether the problem is a disease, try to pull up the damaged grass plants. Unlike insect-damaged lawns, grass that has died from disease remains firmly attached to the ground. The exception is root-and-crown rot, which softens the grass so that it pulls up easily. If the damaged grass does not pull up easily, it probably has a disease.

Disease from Weather

Most diseases develop because of atypical predominant weather affecting your neighborhood for a prolonged period of time. There is nothing you can do about the weather, but knowing that disease is so often weather-related, you might recall the prevailing weather over the month prior to the appearance of a problem. Noting previous unusual weather conditions may help confirm that disease is its cause.

As the sidebar chart indicates, certain diseases favor certain weather. Knowing this, you may even be able to narrow down the cause of the problem to a few possibilities. Of course, there is always red thread disease that seems to accommodate extreme weather of any kind.

Disease by Type of Grass

Various diseases tend to more commonly attack certain kinds or varieties of grass. This is partly a function of the vulnerability of the particular species of grass and partly of the location where that grass is planted. The important point here is that sometimes a certain variety of grass is simply vulnerable to a certain disease in your yard, no matter how much you try to create perfect conditions for a healthy turf.

Weather Conditions vs. Diseases

Cool weather (below 60°F)
Fusarium patch
Powdery mildew
Red thread
Slime mold
Smut

Warm weather (60°–80°F)
Dollar spot
Necrotic ring spot
Red thread

Hot weather (above 80°F)
Brown patch
Fusarium blight
Pythium
Rusts

Dry weather
Dollar spot
Red thread
Rusts

Wet weather
Brown patch (hot and humid)
Fairy ring
Leaf spot
Melting out (cool and wet)
Pythium
Red thread
Slime mold

Most Common Diseases Associated with Grasses

❧ Kentucky blue: dollar spot (some resistant varieties available), fusarium blight, fusarium patch, leaf rust, necrotic ring spot, powdery mildew, pythium, red thread, smuts, summer patch.

❧ Perennial rye: crown rust, fusarium patch, red thread, smuts, brown patch, pythium.

❧ Tall fescue: crown rust, dollar spot, fusarium patch, pythium, brown patch.

❧ Zoysia: dollar spot, leaf rust.

Stresses That Lead to Disease

Too much fertilizer: brown patch, fusarium blight, fusarium patch, powdery mildew, pythium.

Too little fertilizer: brown patch, dollar spot, melting out, red thread, rusts.

Too acid a soil: dollar spot, stripe smut.

Too much shade: powdery mildew, pythium.

Too low a clipping height: fusarium blight, necrotic ring spot.

Too much thatch: fusarium blight, fusarium patch, leaf spot, slime mold, stripe smut.

If your lawn experiences problems with the same disease two or more years in a row, and quirky weather can be discounted, consider changing the type of grass in your lawn. Your particular grass just may be especially vulnerable; it's therefore easier to change grass than to keep fighting the disease.

Disease by Type of Stress

After the weather, the condition of the lawn is the next most important variable in determining whether a disease will become a problem or not. It is safe to say that if you have a healthy turf living in a healthy soil, disease is seldom a problem in your lawn.

If, on the other hand, the lawn develops a disease problem, you can be pretty certain it is experiencing some sort of stress. Many diseases seem to thrive under certain stressful conditions in turf. Eliminate the source of stress and you virtually eliminate the chance of that disease returning next year.

Most Common Diseases

Here is a brief discussion of some of the more common diseases found in northern lawns where conditions meet their preferences. The information is organized to help you compare the symptoms you see in your lawn with the most common symptoms of each of these diseases.

The addition of favored weather conditions of each disease may help with the diagnosis, as will information on the stress points to look for. Finally, we offer some suggestions for dealing with the immediate problem.

Dollar Spot

Symptoms of dollar spot are similar to those of Fusarium blight. This disease gets its name because it appears as tan or straw-colored spots in the lawn the size of silver dollars. This fungus *(Sclerotinia homeocarpa)* thrives on dry, undernourished lawns. Infected lawns show small, white, cobwebby spots in the morning that turn brown later in the day. Infected areas may increase in number but they rarely grow together.

Weather to Watch For—Dollar spot is more likely to occur in moderate temperatures (60-85°F) in areas with excessive moisture and heavy thatch. Underfertilized lawns are prone to attack. High humidity within the turf activates the fungus.

Remove Lawn Stresses—Acid soil and low levels of nitrogen in the soil make grasses more prone to infection from this disease. Apply flowable sulfur fungicide to the infected areas every three to five days until the symptoms disappear.

Here is one time when quick-acting liquid lawn fertilizer might be helpful. Spray the fertilizer twice, about two weeks apart, to boost nitrogen levels and help the grass fight off the dollar spot. Since dollar spot fungi prefer dry conditions, water the lawn deeply every week during dry spells.

Also, recent studies have shown that spraying diluted seaweed extract on the grass regularly every month or so helps control this fungus. When you mow grass infected with dollar spot, collect the clippings and dispose of them in the trash to avoid spreading the infection. Remember to add lime in the fall if soil pH is low to help avoid the problem next year.

BROWN PATCH

Brown patch, also called summer patch *(Rhizoctonia solani)*, kills oval to circular areas of grass up to 2 feet in diameter. The infected areas change color and resemble a frog's eyes— a circular green spot surrounded by a discolored ring of grass. (The circles also look a little like brown smoke rings.) Grass in these patches will probably be thin.

Weather to Watch For—This disease hits hard during hot (75–95°F), humid weather.

Remove Lawn Stresses—Brown patch infects turf areas with poor air circulation and prolonged periods of high humidity. This fungus flourishes in the warm temperatures and damp conditions typical in thatch, and excessive nitrogen fertilization and/or poor drainage encourages it to spread.

For immediate treatment, spray flowable sulfur fungicide on grass foliage in infected areas every three to five days until symptoms disappear. A more important long-term treatment, though, is to remove thatch with a rake or de-thatcher and dispose of it in the trash. Avoid overdosing your lawn with nitrogen fertilizer, especially in the summer.

If drainage needs improving, aerate the soil and topdress the lawn with organic matter. Avoid

Disease Pattern Shapes

Circle: brown patch, snow mold.

Irregular: pythium, slime mold.

Patch: red thread.

Ring: fairy ring.

Spot: dollar spot, fusarium blight, necrotic ring spot, stripe smut.

Unpatterned: powdery mildew and rusts.

late afternoon watering during hot weather. To improve poor air circulation thin out nearby trees or shrubs by selective pruning of branches.

PYTHIUM BLIGHT

Pythium blight is also known as cottony blight or grease spot. Caused by Pythium fungi, it will kill spots or streaks of grass if it infects a newly established lawn. The first sign of its presence is the appearance of blackened, water-soaked patches of grass in the lawn. During humid weather, a cottony growth on the grass may be visible.

Pythium blight may affect an area as small as a few inches or as large as several feet in diameter; however, it typically makes spots about 2 inches across. Infected grass lies flat on the ground. The fungus is often spread by water, so infected areas often occur in streaks that reflect the direction and pattern of surface water runoff flows. Do not step on infected turf and walk around, as you may spread it by tracking the spores on damp shoes.

Weather to Watch For—Pythium can infect lawns pretty fast in hot, humid weather. Dry weather stops this disease.

Remove Lawn Stresses—This blight frequently develops on closely cut lawns, on lawns with poor drainage and on lawns with a thatch problem. It will infect northern lawns when they have been watered in the evenings during hot, humid weather. This disease is virtually impossible to stop once it has infected your lawn. Try to prevent it by following proper watering, fertilizing and mowing practices.

FUSARIUM BLIGHT

Reddish brown spots 2–6 inches in diameter are the telltale symptom of Fusarium blight (*Fusarium tricinctum*). Eventually, the spots turn tan and, finally, yellow. Circular, light tan areas appear on the lawn and increase in size until they grow together. Healthy turf may remain in the center of each infected circle.

If you suspect Fusarium blight, confirm the diagnosis by examining the roots and crowns of the grass blades closely. If this disease is the culprit, they will show rot and may be covered with pink fungal threads.

Weather to Watch For—Fusarium thrives in heat and humidity and can ruin an entire lawn under such conditions. Look for Fusarium blight as temperatures approach 90°F. The disease occurs only in sunny areas, often near a walkway or driveway. If the weather remains unusually warm and dry, Fusarium blight may persist through the summer.

Remove Lawn Stresses—Fusarium blight is common in lawns with a thatch problem. Improper watering and improper fertilizing may also stress a lawn enough to invite this disease.

To control it, mow the grass high and bag and discard the clippings in the trash. Remove thatch and refrain from fertilizing the lawn in late spring or early summer. Because drought conditions encourage Fusarium, proper deep watering will help. Eventually, lower temperatures and increased precipitation deactivate the disease, so infected lawns usually recover from Fusarium blight in the fall. At that time you may have to overseed a severely damaged lawn. Look for a seed variety that has resistance to Fusarium blight.

RED THREAD OR PINK PATCH

If circular patches of scorched grass appear in your lawn, get down on your hands and knees and look more closely. Fine red or rusty threads on the grass blades means that red thread *(Laetisaria fuciforme)* has infected the lawn. Pink, gelatinous masses indicate pink patch *(Limonomyces roseipellis)* is present. These fungi are related and occur most often in the Northeast and the Pacific Northwest.

Weather to Watch For—Both red thread and pink patch thrive under cool, damp conditions with moderate temperatures and high humidity.

Remove Lawn Stresses—Turf that is nitrogen deficient is often predisposed to infection by red thread. Spray the grass with liquid, quick-acting nitrogen fertilizer to stimulate its growth so it can battle this disease. Mowing cuts off the infected blade tips but be sure to dispose of the clippings in the trash.

SNOW MOLD

Snow mold is a collective term for fungal diseases that may occur under the cover of snow. Two different fungi are responsible for the problem. Typhula blight *(Typhula* spp.), or gray snow mold, is most common on lawns that have been covered by heavy snow throughout the winter. When the snow finally melts in spring, patches up to 2 feet in diameter covered with white or gray fungus become visible.

Another culprit, Fusarium patch *(Fusarium)* produces similar symptoms. In spring, melting snow reveals white or pink dead patches of matted grass 1 foot or larger. Fusarium patch may occur even if it doesn't snow. In this case, the spots will be smaller, only 1–2 inches in diameter. They change from purple to tan to white, and may develop pink mold.

Weather to Watch For—Both of these diseases are fostered by cool to cold, wet weather. Often they occur where snow is packed close to the ground under foot traffic.

Remove Lawn Stresses—Spray flowable sulfur fungicide on the infected areas every three to five days until the symptoms disappear. Aerate the soil and improve its drainage. Avoid excessive nitrogen fertilizing in the fall, and remove thatch if you have more than 1/4 inch. Enforce the "no walking on the lawn" rule during the winter too, especially if there is snow cover.

FAIRY RING

If it appears as if bright green, circular areas in the lawn are growing more rapidly than the rest of the turf, the grass is probably infected with the fairy ring fungus *(Marasmius oreades)*. This disease might have an enchanting name, but you won't find it charming at all.

A ring of grass around these bright green spots turns brown, and eventually the overgrown patches of grass decline too. Often a circle of mushrooms develops around the edge of the infected area. This disease typically occurs where turf has been planted over the site of an old tree and the trunk and some roots are still just below the surface.

Weather to Watch For—Fairy ring often develops in the wake of an extended rainy period when moisture builds up on the lawn. It is usually only a problem in the Pacific Northwest.

Remove Lawn Stresses—Sometimes fairy rings appear after a sprinkler system has been installed in the yard. Use these systems judiciously.

Try liming the entire lawn with dolomitic limestone, followed by closer than normal mowing for a few times (1 1/2 inches or so), saving and disposing of the clippings. Apply copper sulfate or iron sulfate drenches to the ringed areas to kill the fungus. These are the same products used to kill moss.

A more radical and difficult method for removing the fungus is to dig out the infected areas of the lawn to a depth of 2 feet and extending 1 foot beyond the diseased patches in all directions. Then fill in and replant those places.

LEAF SMUT

An overall pale green appearance and stunted growth of grass blades are signs of leaf smut *(Ustilago* spp. and *Urocystis* spp.). On individual blades, black stripes develop, which rupture and expose masses of spores. The blades curl, tear easily and look shredded. Leaf smuts are active in spring and fall.

Weather to Watch For—Leaf smuts thrive under cool, moderate to moist conditions.

Remove Lawn Stresses—Do not allow the thatch layer to get thicker than 1/4 inch. Leaf smut can be controlled by mowing the lawn frequently to cut off the infected grass tips and removing the clippings from the lawn.

LEAF SPOT

Leaf spot symptoms occur during early spring and late fall when the fungus produces long, purplish black lesions on the leaf. Reddish brown to purplish black spots on grass are caused by leaf spot fungi *(Helminthosporium* spp.). Eventually, the blades shrivel, crowns and roots rot and die and then irregular patches of thin grass develop over the lawn.

Weather to Watch For—Leaf spot occurs most often when weather is cool and moist.

Remove Lawn Stresses—Spray affected areas of the lawn with flowable sulfur fungicide every three to five days until symptoms disappear.

NECROTIC RING SPOT

Necrotic ring spot *(Leptosphaeria korrae)* causes grass to look tattered. Brown rings develop over the lawn. They usually appear suddenly in grass that very recently seemed perfectly healthy.

Remove Lawn Stresses—This problem is promoted by thatch buildup and poor air circulation near the soil. To control ring spot, remove thatch, mow the grass high and adopt proper watering and feeding practices to reduce stress to the grass.

POWDERY MILDEW

A thin white or grayish powdery coating on grass blades is a sure sign of powdery mildew *(Erysiphe graminis)*. It often appears in shaded areas when nights are cool, especially on Kentucky bluegrass. Severe infection causes grass to turn yellow and die.

Weather to Watch For—Cool and humid.

Remove Lawn Stresses—Spray the affected spots and the area immediately adjacent to them with flowable sulfur fungicide every three to five days until symptoms disappear. If you have an inappropriate grass for a shady area, overseeding or complete renovation might be needed if this mildew problem recurs two years in a row.

RUST

If the turf, or sections of it, develop an overall rust-colored hue, examine the grass closely. Evidence of yellow-orange or red-brown powdery pustules on the blades indicates the presence of rust *(Puccinia* spp.). It can be especially damaging to 'Merion K' bluegrass.

Weather to Watch For—Rust occurs usually in late summer and in the fall during warm, dry weather with moderate temperatures and moderate moisture levels.

Remove Lawn Stresses—Nitrogen deficiency predisposes the grass to rust infection. Spray affected areas of the lawn with flowable sulfur fungicide every three to five days until symptoms disappear. Fertilize by spraying turf with quick-acting nitrogen and mow more frequently, catching and discarding the clippings.

FUNGICIDES FOR DISEASE CONTROL

The significant issue in using fungicides is that by the time the disease is recognized and the pathogen identified, the infection has usually already run its course. The damage is done and no amount of fungicide can bring back the dead tissue. At best, a fungicide applied at that time may reduce the spread of the disease, but then again it may not.

In the discussion of grass diseases above we have recommended the use of flowable sulfur fungicide to try to slow the spread of lawn fungal diseases. While, it will not "cure" an infection, it just might slow its spread.

It is our conviction that the cultural changes you make (remove thatch, fertilize, water properly, mow higher) more effectively address the current and potential disease problems in most situations. While there are many more powerful chemical fungicides on the market, we believe that taking the cultural approach to disease control has better long-term returns and therefore have not recommended those more powerful products.

Remember, compost has fungicidal properties. By periodically topdressing your turf with some kind of composted material, such as homemade or commercial compost, composted municipal sludge or mushroom soil, you are introducing fungus-fighting microbes into the lawn. They are very effective in controlling most of the more common lawn diseases such as dollar spot, brown patch and Pythium blight.

This approach is consistent with our bias that it is best to support and depend on the natural defense system that is already in place in a healthy lawn to maintain lawns and solve their problems. It is cheaper, less disruptive of the environment and more consistent with the goal of low maintenance. Remember that modern grasses have enhanced disease resistance bred into them. Overseeding with new grass helps forestall disease problems.

Dealing with Animal Pests

Animals represent a major lawn care nuisance. We suppose we must include small children in this group. While most of us easily overlook the damage to our lawn caused by small children as long it is our lawn and our children, other animals present major challenges. Space does not permit a full discussion of deer, gophers, raccoons and other wildlife that visit residential landscapes from nearby forests or wooded areas. However, it is important to discuss two major animal problems—moles and dogs.

Moles

Moles visit lawns for only one reason. They are searching for food. Their main diet is earthworms, but white grubs make up a favorite side dish. While some references suggest that getting rid of white grubs rids your lawn of moles, we are not so sure.

Unfortunately, in their perfectly legitimate search for food, moles make an extensive network of tunnels, some of which are used only once. These tunnels, if close to the surface, can push up the soil under the turf, disturbing grass roots and marring the appearance of the lawn. Moles use their tunnels to catch passing earthworms and grubs that inadvertently fall into those spaces in their travels. Moles are solitary animals, so it is likely that only one or two moles are responsible for the damage to a particular lawn.

While it may sound like a broken record, we are convinced from our own experience that the best solution to a mole problem is a dense, healthy lawn with a very extensive and deep root system. As we mentioned earlier, a single grass plant generates miles and miles of roots, if the soil is in good condition. Imagine the density of roots in the top 3–5 inches of soil if there are 9 or 10 grass plants per square inch, the density of good sod. When we had a poor, thin lawn, we had moles.

When we built our healthy, low-maintenance lawn we discovered that we had no mole problems. Conclusion? We don't know for sure but we suspect we still have moles, but they are working down at a level where their tunnels cause no problem to our turf. Moles are active all year long and will tunnel as deep as they need to to keep up with the earthworms and the grubs as those creatures work down deeply to avoid the frozen soil. We believe that building a healthy, deep-rooted lawn will usually eliminate any mole problems. Here are some short-term controls.

Traps can be effective, but they require vigilance, persistence and the will to violently kill the animal. Trapping is best done early in the spring when the first mole ridges appear in the lawn. Identify the active "travel lanes" by stepping lightly on a small section of several tunnels. Disturb but don't completely collapse them. Then mark these sections with stones or garden stakes.

Within two days some tunnels will be raised again. They indicate active runs which are good locations for setting a trap. Both choker traps and harpoon traps are effective for trapping moles. Install them according to the instructions that come with the devices. Restore the turf over unused tunnels with a lawn roller or by treading on them.

Another alternative is to dig out moles. Since moles may be active at any time of the day, it is often possible to spot the soil ridging up as the mole moves along. Insert a shovel into the soil right behind the mole, and flip him out into a bucket. Dispatch the culprit in whichever manner is acceptable to you. Liz has no heart for this type of thing, so we go after the grubs in the lawn and tolerate the occasional mole.

There are lots of home remedies for dealing with moles, such as dropping mothballs or Juicy Fruit gum down into the tunnels. The only one we might recommend, though we have not tested this ourselves, is to use diatomaceous earth, now readily available in most garden centers. This pesticide is composed of the microscopic shards of prehistoric seashells which are razor sharp.

Place 2 or 3 tablespoons of this white powder into each mole tunnel in your turf. Then push the soil down so the tunnels are blocked. It must irritate the nose or the paws of the mole, because reports are that a mole will not reuse a D.E.-doctored tunnel and will eventually decide to move over to a neighbor's yard.

Dogs

You may love dogs, but dog urine kills grass, especially female dog urine. A lawn frequented by a female pooch will develop dead spots that are likely to be surrounded by a ring of very green grass, which distinguishes this problem from disease or some other cause.

While you may feel a bit foolish, you can ease the problem by following your pet around and soaking the spots with clear water after they have been "sprinkled." This dilutes the urine and encourages it to soak down deeply into the soil away from the grass plants. If treated shortly after the dog's visit, the grass should escape harm and will continue to grow. Spots that have gone untreated and turn yellowish can often be restored by a similar drenching with clear water. If the grass does not revive, reseed the spots promptly to prevent weeds from taking over. Another solution is to limit the dog to its own area of the yard, plant ground cover along the edges and spread wood chips in the center where the pet is most active.

In the final analysis, choosing to have a lawn is similar to choosing to have children. You know that there is work involved, but the delights are perceived as well worth the effort. As we never truly escape our role of parent while our children are alive, we also are never able to once and for all accomplish a wonderful, no-care lawn as long as we choose to have one.

In the spirit of that understanding, we posit an approach to lawn care that recognizes the reasonable limits of human energy, financial resources and time, while respecting the natural ecosystem. Through that respect for our own little ecosystem we call our yard, we learn to work within its wonderful and marvelous systems for keeping things balanced. We try to work with nature rather than trying to overcome it. It seems altogether reasonable to us to expect that homeowners can enjoy attractive lawns and still honor the ecosystem that is their yard.

We had fun writing this book and we really hope that its success will allow us to update it in a few years with a second edition. As our comments indicated throughout, new research is yielding new and better products for lawns at a great rate. So we welcome your comments, your questions and your criticisms. There are probably some errors in this book, though Lord knows we've worked hard to make it very accurate. So we are giving you our address; at least a post office box number. We will try to answer your questions (time and postage costs permitting) and we will definitely appreciate ideas, suggestions and corrections.

$\mathcal{I}$ndex